GLOVEBOX ATLAS

EUROPE

3rd edition 2001

2nd edition 1999

1st edition 1997

© Automobile Association Developments Limited, for UK edition.

Produced by the Istituto Geografico De Agostini © 2001

Published by AA Publishing (a trading name of The Automobile Association Developments Limited, whose registered office is Norfolk House, Priestley Road, Basingstoke, Hampshire RG24 9NY. Registered number 1878835)

ISBN 0 7495 3083 9

A CIP catalogue record for this book is available from The British Library.

Printed in Italy by Officine Grafiche De Agostini, Novara.

CONTENTS
SOMMARIO
SOMMAIRE
INHALTSVERZEICHNIS
SUMARIO

4-83 **Tavole cartografiche** 1:2 500 000
Quadro d'unione, segni convenzionali

Maps 1:2 500 000
Map pages, map symbols

Cartes 1:2 500 000
Tableau d'assemblage, signes conventionnels

Karten 1:2 500 000
Kartenübersicht, Zeichenerklärung

Mapas 1:2 500 000
Mapa índice, signos convencionales

84-85 Distanze chilometriche
Distance chart
Distances kilométriques
Kilometrische Entfernungen
Distancias kilométricas

86 Targhe automobilistiche internazionali
International registration letters
Plaques automobiles internationales
Internationale Kraftfahrzeugkennzeichen
Placas automovilísticas internacionales

87-112 **Indice dei nomi**
Avvertenze per la ricerca

Place name index
How to use the index

Index des noms
Notices pour la recherche

Namenverzeichnis
Erläuterungen des Suchsystems

Indice de nombres
Instrucciones para la consulta

Map pages • Quadro d'unione
Tableau d'assemblage • Kartenübersicht
Mapa índice

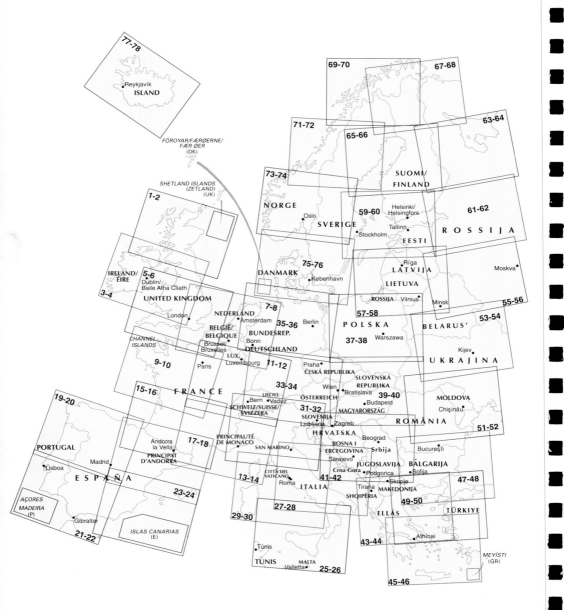

Map symbols • Segni convenzionali
Signes conventionnels • Zeichenerklärung
Signos convencionales

Autostrade • Motorways • Autoroutes
Autobahnen • Autopistas

Strade di grande comunicazione
Principal trunk roads
Routes de grande communication
Fernverkehrsstraßen
Carreteras de gran comunicación

Strade importanti • Important roads
Routes importantes • Wichtige Straßen
Carreteras importantes

Altre strade • Other roads • Autres routes
Sonstige Straßen • Otras carreteras

Carrarecce (Islanda)
Cart-roads (Iceland)
Chemins charretiers (Islande)
Karrenwege (Island)
Caminos carreteros (Islandia)

50
20 30
Distanze in chilometri *
Distances in kilometres *
Distances en kilomètres *
Entfernungsangaben in Kilometern *
Distancias en kilómetros *

Tunnel, traforo • Tunnel
Tunnel • Tunnel • Túnel

A1
Numeri di autostrade
Motorway numbers
Numéros des autoroutes
Autobahnnummern
Números de autopistas

E 35
Numeri di strade europee
European road numbers
Numéros des routes européennes
Europastraßennummern
Números de carreteras europeas

Göteborg
Traghetto • Ferry • Bac
Fähre • Transbordador

Simplon Pass
)(2005
Passo, quota in metri
Pass with height in metres
Col, altitude en mètres
Paß, Höhenangabe in Metern
Paso de montaña, altura en metros

FL
Targa automobilistica internazionale
International registration letter
Plaque automobile internationale
Internationales Kraftfahrzeugkennzeichen
Placa automovilística internacional

Confine di Stato • National boundary
Frontière d'État • Staatsgrenze
Frontera nacional

Punto di frontiera con dogana
Frontier check point with customs
Point frontière avec douane
Grenzübergangsstelle mit Zollamt
Paso fronterizo con aduana

Aeroporto internazionale
International airport
Aéroport international
Internationaler Flughafen
Aeropuerto internacional

WIEN
Città di grande interesse turistico
Town of tourist interest
Ville de grand intérêt touristique
Ortschaft von großem touristischen Belang
Ciudad de gran interés turístico

Lindhos
Altre città interessanti
Other notable towns
Autres villes intéressantes
Andere bemerkenswerte Ortschaften
Otras ciudades interesantes

Chiesa, monastero
Church, monastery
Église, monastère
Kirche, Kloster
Iglesia, monasterio

Castello • Castle • Château
Schloß • Castillo

Rovine • Ruins • Ruines
Ruinen • Ruinas

Grotta • Cave • Grotte
Höhle • Cueva

DOÑANA
Parchi • Parks • Parcs
Parks • Parques

Curiosità naturali
Interesting natural features
Curiosités naturelles
Natursehenswürdigkeiten
Curiosidades naturales

Metri
2000
200
0
Tinte altimetriche
Heights
Échelle des teintes hypsométriques
Farbskala der Höhenstufen
Escala de tintas altimétricas

* Nel Regno Unito e in Irlanda le distanze sono espresse in miglia

* Distances in Great Britain and Ireland are in miles

* Les distances en Grande-Bretagne et Irlande sont exprimées en miles

* Entfernungsangaben in Großbritannien und Irland
sind in Meilen wiedergegeben

* Las distancias en Gran Bretaña e Irlanda son expresadas en millas

La grandezza dei nomi è proporzionata all'importanza dei centri abitati

Size of place name is proportionate to importance and size of town

La dimension des noms est proportionnée
à l'importance des centres habités

Die Namengröße ist der Bedeutung der Ortschaften angepaßt

La dimensión de los nombres es proporcionada
a l'importancia de las localidades

I nomi delle località compaiono sulla carta nella loro forma locale.
Nell'indice sono riportate le traduzioni in italiano.

Places-names appearing on the map are in their local form.
In the index the Italian translations are also given.

Les toponymes figurant sur la carte sont en forme locale.
Dans l'index sont indiquées les traductions italiennes.

Die in der Karte enthaltenen Ortsnames sind in Lokalform.
In den Index sind die italienischen Übersetzungen aufgenommen.

Los nombres de localidades figuran en el mapa en su forma local.
En el índice figuran las traducciones italianas.

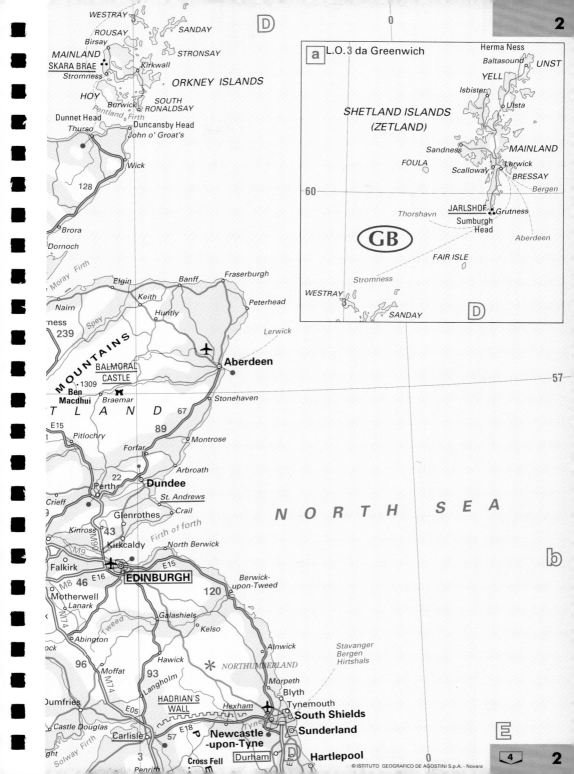

WESTRAY
ROUSAY
SANDAY
Birsay
MAINLAND
STRONSAY
SKARA BRAE
Kirkwall
Stromness
ORKNEY ISLANDS
HOY
SOUTH
Burwick
RONALDSAY
Dunnet Head
Duncansby Head
Thurso
John o' Groat's
128
Wick

Brora
Dornoch
Moray Firth
Elgin
Banff
Fraserburgh
Nairn
Keith
Peterhead
Spey
Huntly
ness
239
Lerwick
MOUNTAINS
BALMORAL
Aberdeen
CASTLE
1309
Ben
Braemar
Stonehaven
Macdhui
57
TLAND
67
E15
89
Pitlochry
Forfar
Montrose
22
Arbroath
Perth
Dundee
Crieff
St. Andrews
Glenrothes
Crail
Kinross
43
Firth of forth
Kirkcaldy
North Berwick
Falkirk
M9
E15
M8
46 E16
EDINBURGH
Berwick-
Motherwell
120
upon-Tweed
Lanark
Tweed
Galashiels
Abington
Kelso
ck
Alnwick
Hawick
NORTHUMBERLAND
96
Moffat
93
Dumfries
Langholm
Morpeth
HADRIAN'S
Blyth
WALL
Hexham
Tynemouth
Castle Douglas
South Shields
Carlisle
57
Newcastle
Sunderland
Solway Firth
ght
-upon-Tyne
Penrim
Cross Fell
Durham
Hartlepool

NORTH SEA

Stavanger
Bergen
Hirtshals

0

L.O.3 da Greenwich

Herma Ness
Baltasound
UNST
YELL
Isbister
Ulsta
SHETLAND ISLANDS
(ZETLAND)
Sandness
MAINLAND
FOULA
Lerwick
Scalloway
BRESSAY
60
Bergen
JARLSHOF
Grutness
Thorshavn
Sumburgh
Head
Aberdeen
GB

FAIR ISLE

Stromness
WESTRAY
SANDAY

b

E

© ISTITUTO GEOGRAFICO DE AGOSTINI S.p.A. - Novara

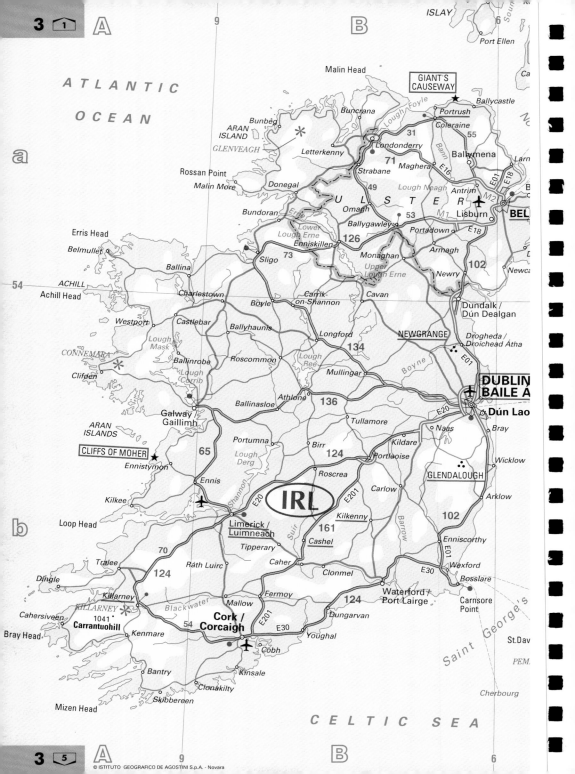

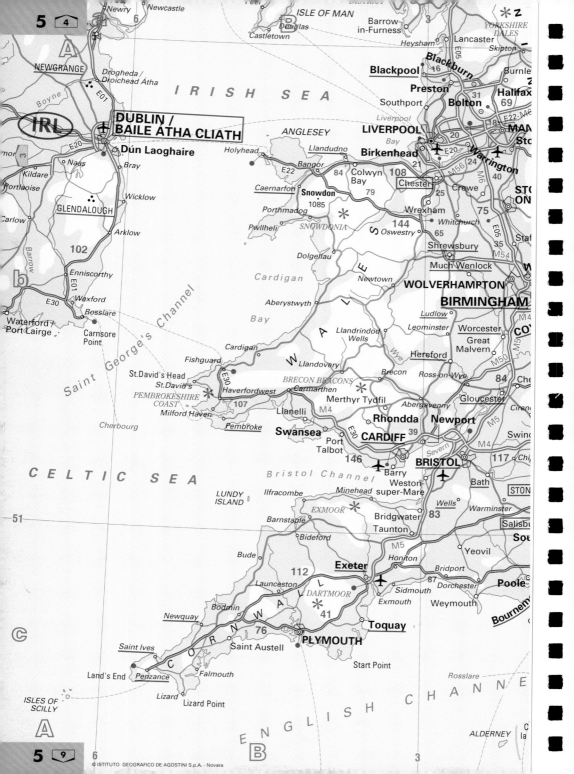

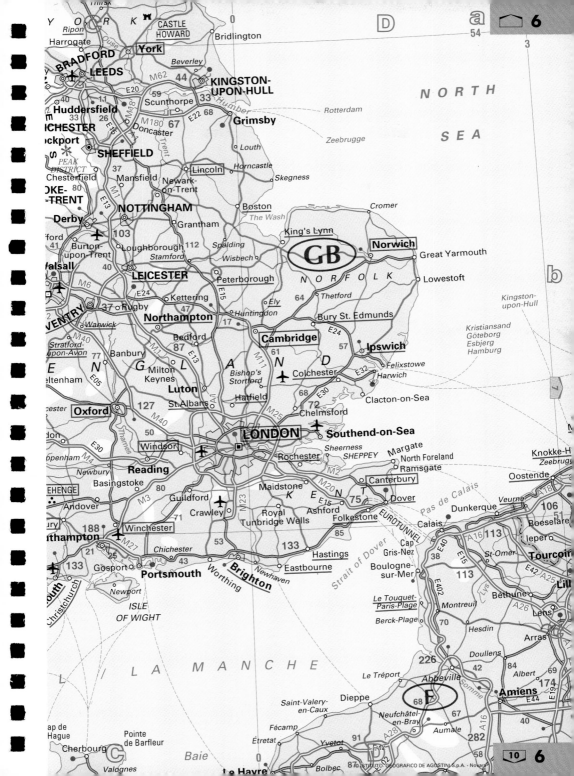

ENGLISH CHANNEL

ALDERNEY

Cap de la Hague

Pointe de Barfleur

Cherbourg

Valognes

120

St. Peter Port

GUERNSEY

SARK

Barneville-Carteret

Carentan

172

Bayeu

CHANNEL ISLANDS (U.K.)

Saint Helier

JERSEY

Coutances

Saint-L

Golfe

Villedieu-les-Poêles

Granville

Perros-Guirec

Tréguier

de St-Malo

Le Mont-St-Michel

231

Roscoff

Lannion

Paimpol

St-Malo

Avranches

ILE D'OUESSANT

St-Pol-de-Léon

Morlaix

142

Guingamp

Dinard

16

31

9

13

Brest

Landerneau

St-Brieuc

Lamballe

Dinan

Dol-de-Bretagne

Fougère

Pointe de St-Mathieu

E50

E60

Pleyben

Cérhaix-Plouguer

75

53

58

Ma

Iroise

Morgat

B

R

E

T

A

G

95

E50

Douarnenez

75

Loudéac

Montauban

Vitré

48

Pointe du Raz

Audierne

Pontivy

Rennes

Laval

Quimper

296

Quimperlé

Locminé

Ploërmel

N

Bain-de-Bretagne

Pont-l'Abbé

Concarneau

Hennebont

E

Segré

Pointe de Penmarch

Lorient

Vannes

Redon

107

Châteaubriant

ILE DE GROIX

Carnac

221

E60

Nozay

A11

89

Quiberon

Pontchâteau

Le Palais

Le Croisic

St-Nazaire

E3

BELLE-ILE

La Baule-Escoublac

NANTES

Loire

Pornic

ILE DE NOIRMOUTIER

Beauvoir-sur-Mer

137

E62

Challans

A83

Chant

ILE D'YEU

St-Jean-de-Monts

La Roche-sur-Yon

O C É A N

Les Sables-d'Olonne

Luçon

319

E3

ILE DE RÉ

E601

La Rochelle

A6

A T L A N T I Q U E

Rochefort

ILE D'OLÉRON

E60

Royan

Le Verdon-sur-Mer

Gir

Soulac-sur-Mer

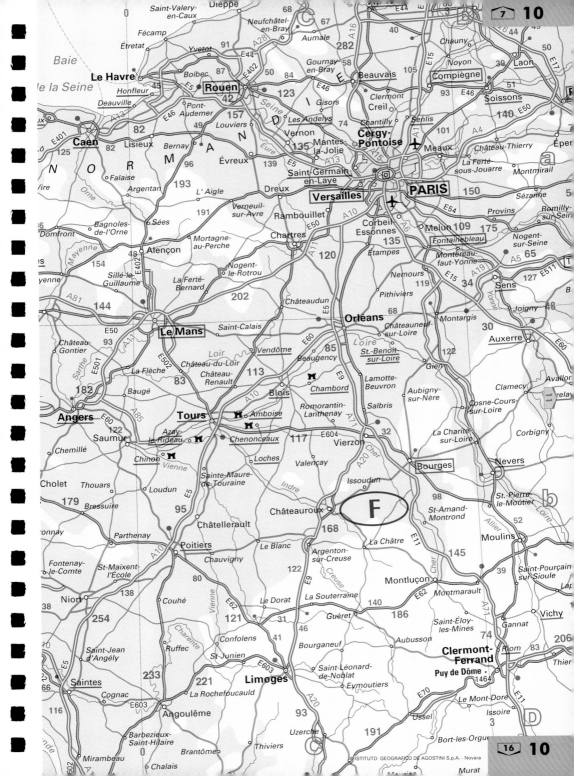

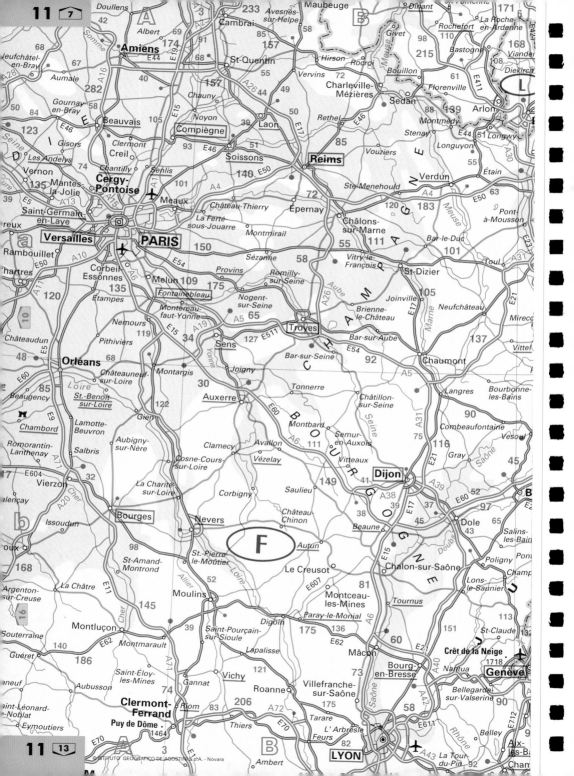

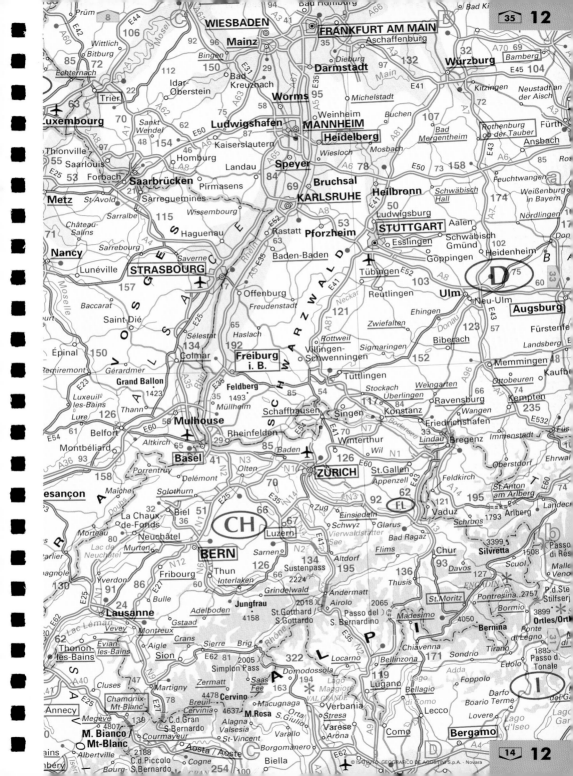

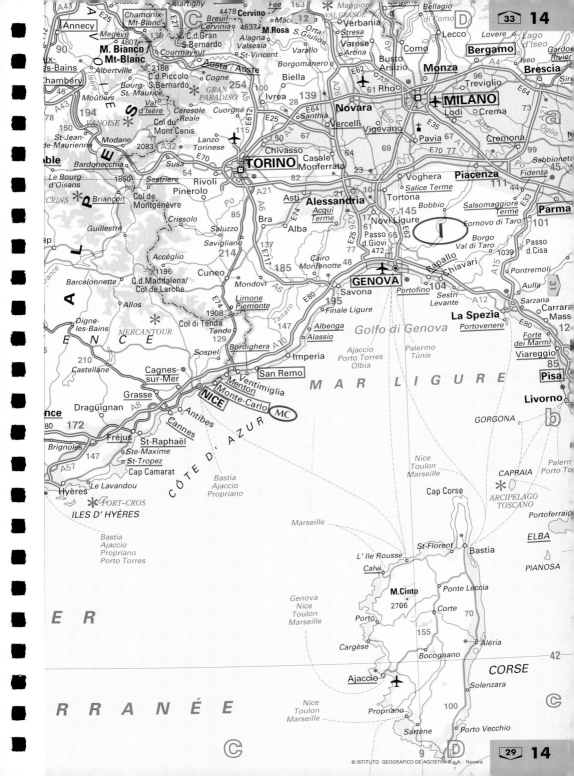

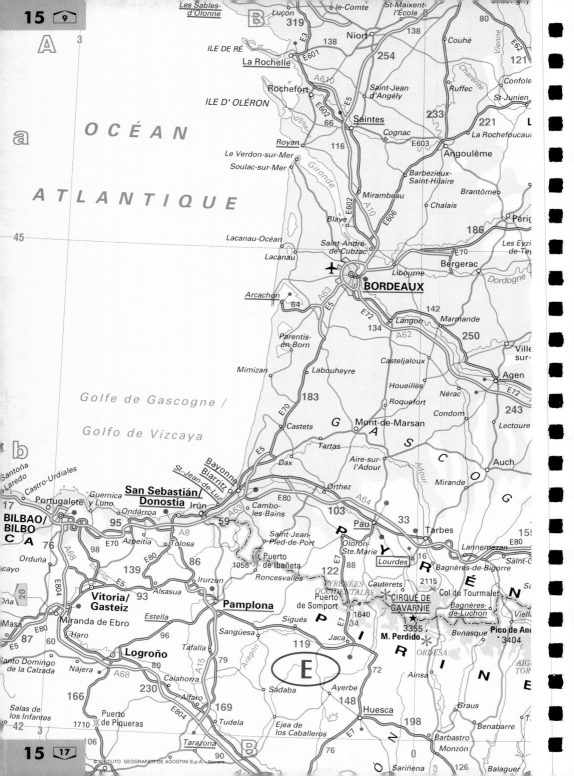

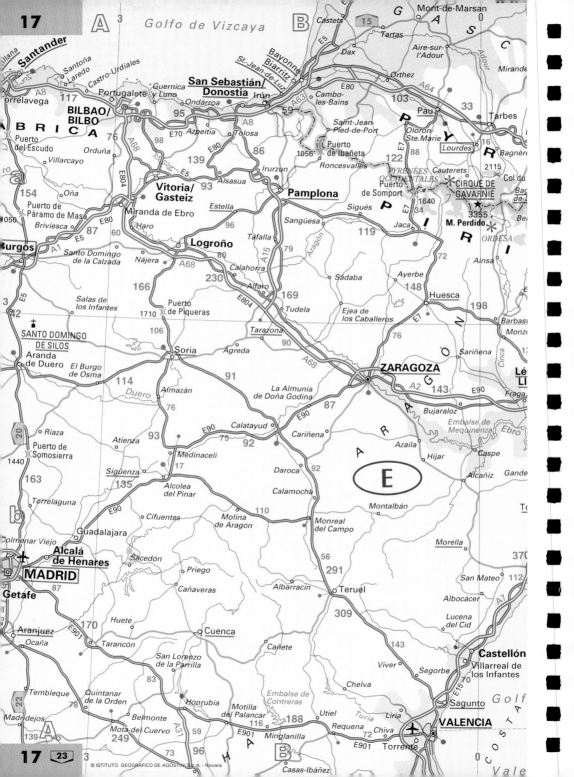

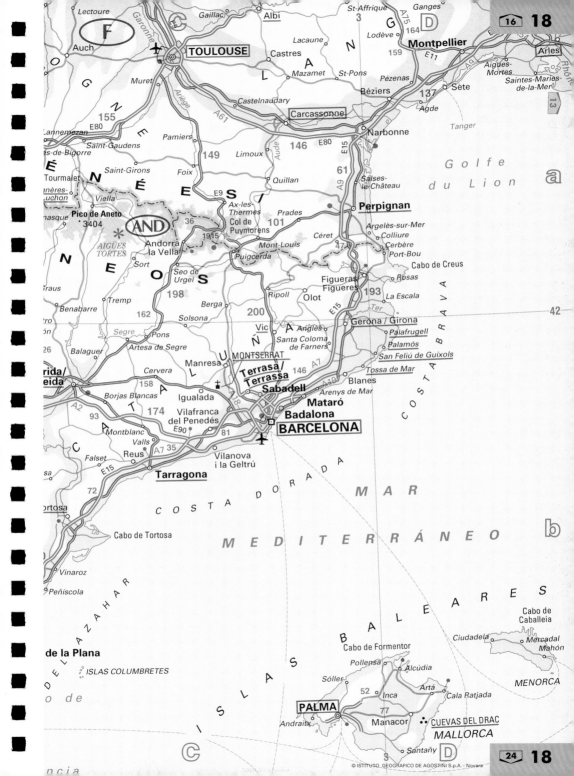

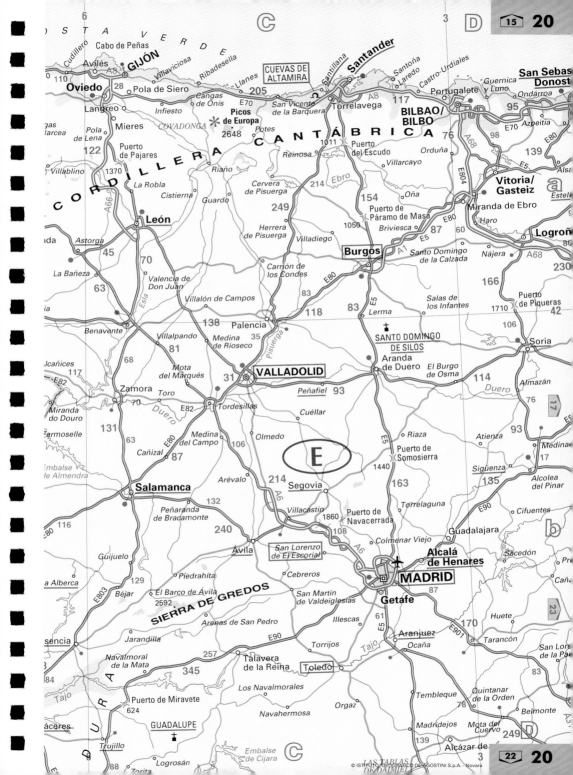

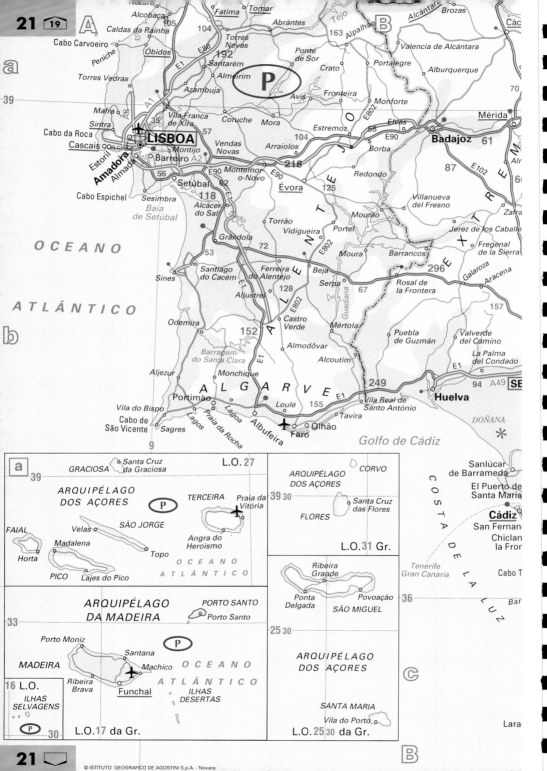

OCEANO

ATLÂNTICO

ALENTEJO

ESTREMADURA

ALGARVE

Tejo

Cabo Carvoeiro
Peniche
Torres Vedras
Mafra
Sintra
Cabo da Roca
Cascais
Estoril
Amadora
Almada
Cabo Espichel
Sesimbra
Baía de Setúbal

Alcobaça
Caldas da Rainha
Óbidos
Santarém
Almeirim
Azambuja
Vila Franca de Xira
Coruche
LISBOA
Montijo
Barreiro
Setúbal
Vendas Novas
Montemor-o-Novo
Alcácer do Sal

Fátima
Tomar
Abrántes
Torres Novas
Ponte de Sor
Crato
Mora
Arraiolos
Évora
Redondo
Torrão
Vidigueira
Portel
Mourão

Alpalhão
Valencia de Alcántara
Portalegre
Alburquerque
Fronteira
Monforte
Estremoz
Elvas
Borba
Villanueva del Fresno
Zafra
Jerez de los Caballe
Fregenal de la Sierra
Galaroza
Aracena

Brozas
Các
Mérida
Badajoz
Alr
Moura
Barrancos
Rosal de la Frontera
Serpa
Beja
Ferreira do Alentejo
Santiago do Cacém
Sines
Grândola
Aljustrel
Castro Verde
Odemira
Mértola
Almodôvar
Alcoutim
Puebla de Guzmán
Valverde del Camino
La Palma del Condado
Monchique
Aljezur
Barragem do Santa Clara
Portimão
Lagos
Praia da Rocha
Lagoa
Albufeira
Loulé
Faro
Olhão
Tavira
Vila Real de Santo António
Huelva
Golfo de Cádiz
DOÑANA
SE
Vila do Bispo
Cabo de São Vicente
Sagres

105 104 E90 E1 192 163 A1 70 57 35 56 62 218 104 58 E90 87 E102 60 61 E802 125 118 53 72 296 67 157 128 152 249 155 94 A49 9 39 218

Avis

COSTA DE LA LUZ

Inset maps:

Ⓐ 39
GRACIOSA — Santa Cruz da Graciosa
L.O. 27
ARQUIPÉLAGO DOS AÇORES
TERCEIRA — Praia da Vitória
Angra do Heroísmo
FAIAL — Horta
Madalena
Velas
SÃO JORGE
Topo
PICO — Lajes do Pico
OCEANO ATLÂNTICO

ARQUIPÉLAGO DOS AÇORES
CORVO
Santa Cruz das Flores
FLORES
39 30
L.O. 31 Gr.

Ribeira Grande
Ponta Delgada
Povoação
SÃO MIGUEL
36
25 30

33
ARQUIPÉLAGO DA MADEIRA
PORTO SANTO
Porto Santo
Porto Moniz
Santana
Machico
MADEIRA
Ribeira Brava
Funchal
ILHAS DESERTAS
OCEANO ATLÂNTICO

16 L.O.
ILHAS SELVAGENS
L.O. 17 da Gr.
30

ARQUIPÉLAGO DOS AÇORES
SANTA MARIA
Vila do Porto
L.O. 25 30 da Gr.

Sanlúcar de Barrameda
El Puerto de Santa María
Cádiz
San Fernan
Chiclan
la Fror
Tenerife
Gran Canaria
Cabo T
Bar
Lara

Albocácer

Lucena
del Cid

0

Huete

Cuenca

Cañete

143

Castellón de

Villarreal de
los Infantes

B

309

Ocaña A

Tarancón

San Lorenzo
de la Parrilla

Viver

Chelva

Segorbe

DEL

3

-901

20

Tembleque

78

83

Honrubia

Motilla
del Palancar

Embalse de
Contreras

188

Utiel

Turia

Liria

Sagunto

Golfo

VALENCIA

a

Quintanar
de la Orden

Madridejos

116

E901

Minglanilla

Requena

72

Chiva

COSTA

139

Belmonte

Mota del Cuervo

249

A31

59

Torrente

E901

Valenc

294

Alcázar de San Juan

73

96

M
A
N
C
H
A

La Roda

Casas-Ibáñez

Júcar

111

Cullera

E5

Tomelloso

37

Albacete

Ayora

Alcira

Játiva

Gandía

Manzanares

30

Munera

73

184

Almansa

Denia

Valdepeñas

79

170

208

Alcoy

178

Villanueva de
los Infantes

60

Yecla

Villena

97

Jijona

A

Albaida

Calpe

Almuradiel

245

Alcaraz

Elche de
la Sierra

Hellín

Jumilla

Elda

E15

Benidorm

94

22

125

Yeste

145

Pinoso

Villajoyosa

E

85

Cieza

ALICANTE

Elche

82

Santa Pola

Villacarrillo

Caravaca

Mula

Orihuela

Úbeda

Puebla de
Don Fabrique

E15

MURCIA

Torrevieja

Quesada

Huéscar

Totana

Segura

55

Santiago de la Ribera

uelma

Vélez Rubio

85

Lorca

La Unión

Cabo de Palos

b

91

Baza

Huércal-
Overa

Puerto
de Mazarrón

Cartagena

B

188

Águilas

97

Guadix

Purchena

128

Véra

COSTA

18

Gérgal

Sorbas

E15

LA PALMA

Barlovento

ISLA

Mulhacén

8.

ERRA NEVADA

243

CALDERA DE
TABURIENTE

*

Santa Cruz
de la Palma

115

E15

Almería

Los Llanos
de Aridane

il

Adra

Cabo de Gata

Puerto de la C

S
O
L

Icod de los Viños

L

Vallehrmoso

Guía de
Isora

Gra
de

GARAJONAY

*

36

ISLA DE ALBORÁN
(ESP.)

36

28

GOMERA

San Sébastián
de la Gomera

Los
Cristianos

c

3

Frontera

Puerto de
la Estaca

18

HIERRO

B

alcón

OUAHRAN

80

72

Reliza

A

12

B

a

29

39

MAR

TIRRENO

USTICA

Napoli
Livorno
Genova

Tūnis
Cagliari
Napoli

Cagliari

Capo San Vito

Punta
Raisi

PALERMO

A26

Bagheria
Termini
Imerese

ISOLE EGADI

Trapani

Erice

107

MARETTIMO

E933

Monreale

A19

47

FAVIGNANA

Alcamo

SEGESTA

106

Corleone

Marsala

73

E90

Mazara
del Vallo

42

A29

Castelvetrano

Lercara
Friddi

SELINUNTE

E391

126

Caltaniss

Sciacca

94

Marseille
Cagliari
Genova

Trapani
Napoli

Agrigento

C

Porto
Empedocle

VALLE DE

Ra's aṭ Ṭīb

Licata

Khalīj Tūnis

Al Marsá

Qulaybīyah

Pantelleria

SICIL

CARTHAGO

TŪNIS

Hammām al Anf

Manzil Tamīm

PANTELLERIA
(It.)

TN

MAR

Zaghwān

Ra's al Ma'murah
Nābul
Ḥammāmāt

DI
SICILIA

Khalīj

An Nafīḍah

Ḥammāmāt

36

143

LINOSA

Sūsah

C

Masākin

Al Munastīr

ISOLE PELAGIE
(It.)

Al Qayrawān

Al Muknīn

A

Al Mahdīyah

12

LAMPIONE

B

LAMPEDUSA

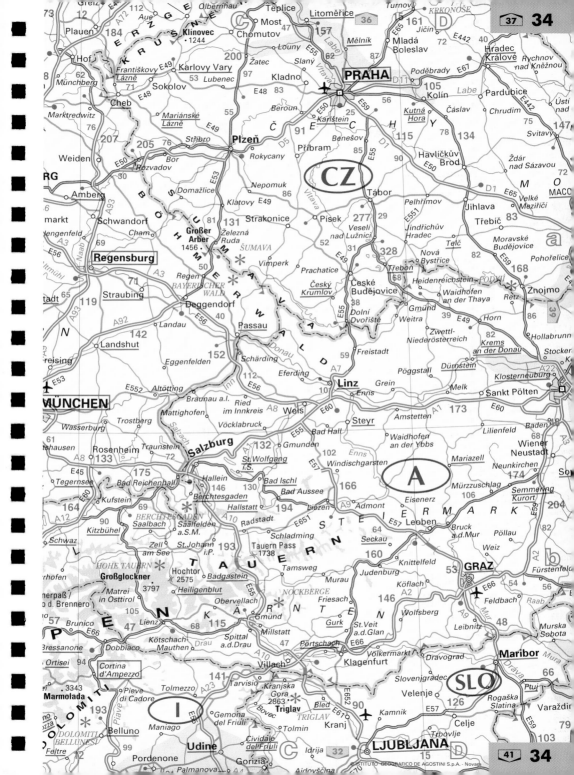

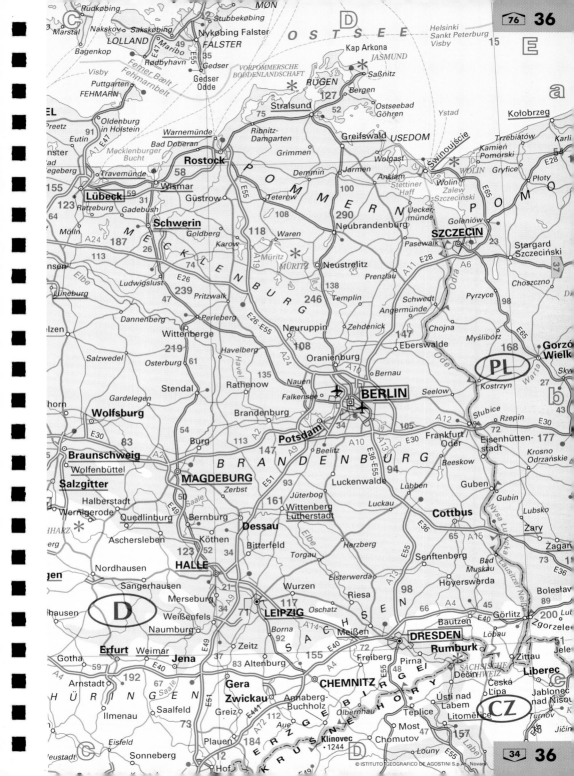

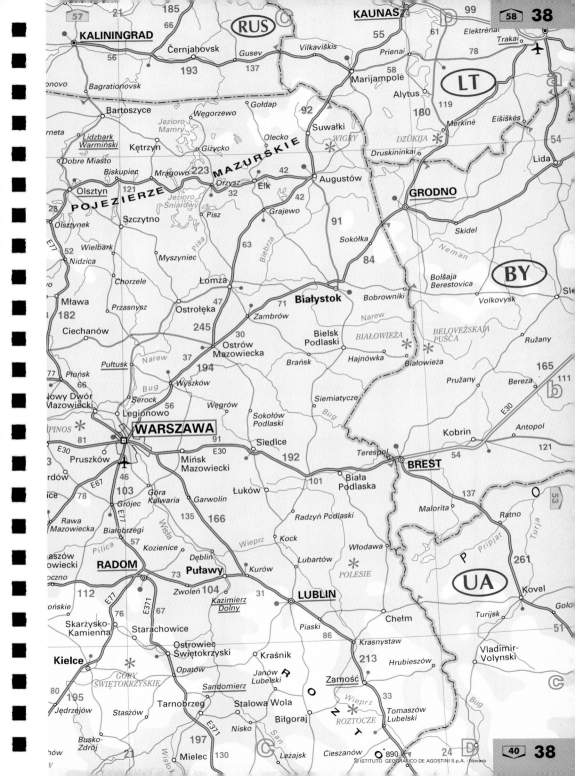

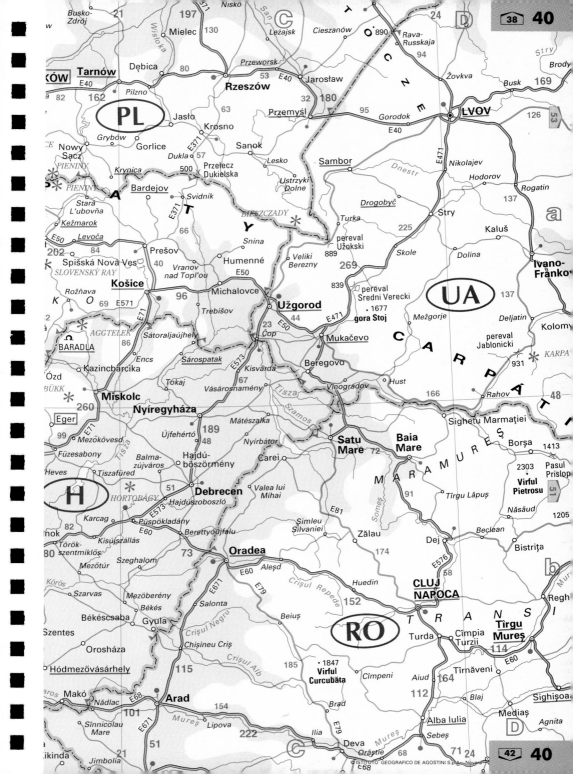

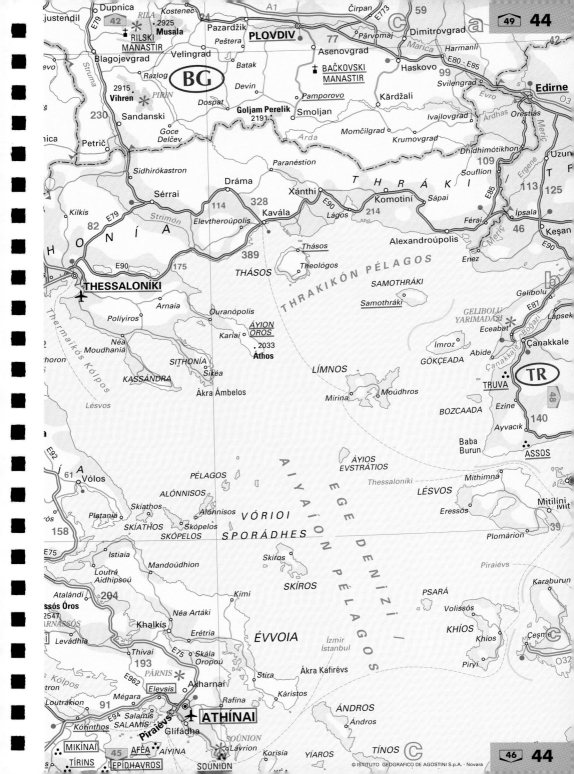

Dupnica
Kostenec
A1
Čirpan
59
E773
ujustendil
E79
42
RILA
·2925
Pazardžik
Dimitrovgrad
a
Musala
Pěrvomaj
77
RILSKI
PLOVDIV
MANASTIR
Peštera
Marica
42
Velingrad
Asenovgrad
Blagojevgrad
E80 · E85
Harmanli
Batak
Haskovo
99
BG
BAČKOVSKI
Razlog
Devin
MANASTIR
Svilengrad
Edirne
2915
PIRIN
Vihren
Dospat
Pamporovo
Kărdžali
Evro
O3
230
Goljam Perelik
Ivajlovgrad
Sandanski
2191
Smoljan
Ardhas
Orestiás
Goce
Meriç
Delčev
Momčilgrad
Krumovgrad
Uzun
Petrič
Arda
Dhidhimótikhon
109
Paranéstion
Souflíon
Ergene
Sidhirókastron
T H R Á K I
E85
113 125
Dráma
Xánthi
Komotiní
Sápai
Sérrai
114
328
Ípsala
Kilkís
E79
Kavála
214
Férai
46
Keşan
82
Strimón
Elevtheroúpolis
Lágos
Meriç
O N Í A
E90
Alexandroúpolis
E90
175
Thásos
Enez
389
THÁSOS
Theológos
THESSALONÍKI
SAMOTHRÁKI
T H R A K I K Ó N   P É L A G O S
Gelibolu
b
Arnaía
Ouranópolis
Samothráki
GELIBOLU
YARIMADASI
E87
Lápsek
Políyiros
ÁYION
Kariaí
ÓROS
Eceabat
Çanakkale
Néa
·2033
Ímroz
Abide
Moudhaniá
SITHONÍA
Áthos
GÖKÇEADA
Çanakkale-Boğazı
TR
choron
Sikéa
LÍMNOS
TRUVA
48
KASSÁNDRA
Ákra Ámbelos
Mírina
Moúdhros
BOZCAADA
Ezine
140
Lésvos
BOZCAADA
Ayvacık
Thermaïkós Kólpos
Baba
Burun
ASSOS
ÁYIOS
EVSTRÁTIOS
PÉLAGOS
Thessaloníki
Míthimna
E92
A I Y A Í O N
Mitilíni
61
Vólos
ALÓNNISOS
LÉSVOS
Skíathos
Alónnisos
VÓRIOI
Eressós
E G E
Plataniá
Skópelos
158
SKÍATHOS
SPORÁDHES
Plomárion
39
E75
SKÓPELOS
D E N İ Z İ
Istiaia
Skíros
Piraiévs
Mandoúdhion
P É L A G O S
PSARÁ
Karaburun
Loutrá
SKÍROS
Volissós
Aidhipsoú
Ataláridi
204
Kími
İzmir
KHÍOS
Çeşme
ssós Óros
Néa Artáki
İstanbul
Khíos
·2547
Khalkís
Erétria
Piryí
ARNASSÓS
ÉVVOIA
O32
Levádhia
E75
Skála
Ákra Kafirévs
Thívai
Oropoú
193
PÁRNIS
Stíra
Káristos
Kólpos
E962
Elevsís
Akharnaí
Ákra Kafirévs
stron
Mégara
Rafína
ÁNDROS
Loutrákion
91
E94
Salamís
ATHÍNAI
Kórinthos
SALAMÍS
Ándros
MIKÍNAI
45
AFÉA
ÁIYINA
Piraiévs
Glifádha
SOÚNION
46 44
TÍRINS
EPÍDHAVROS
SOÚNION
Lávrion
Korisía
YÍAROS
TÍNOS

© ISTITUTO GEOGRAFICO DE AGOSTINI S.p.A. - Novara

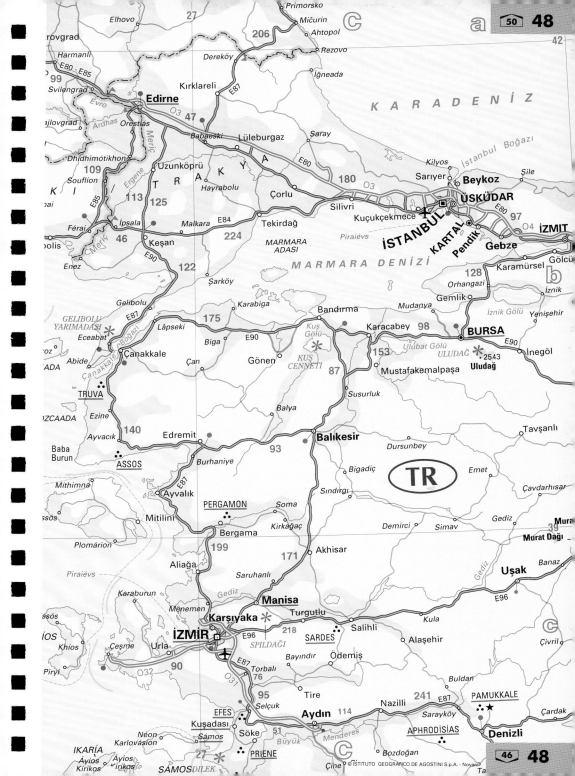

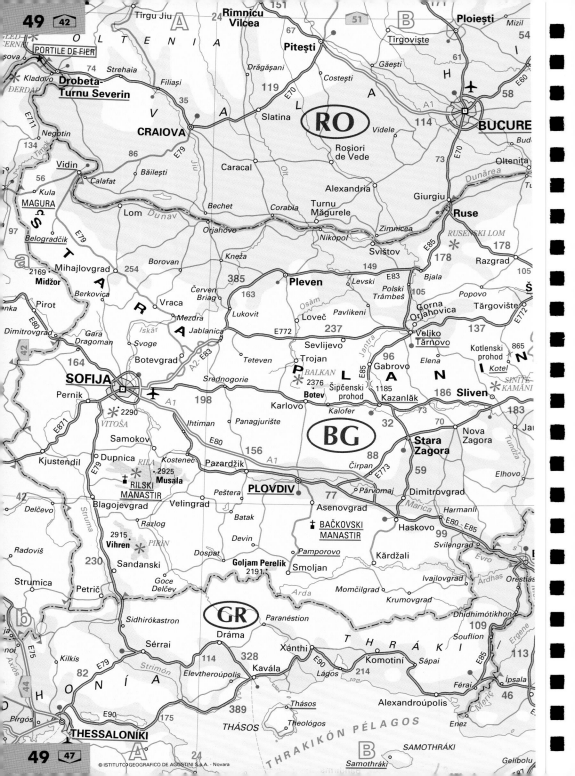

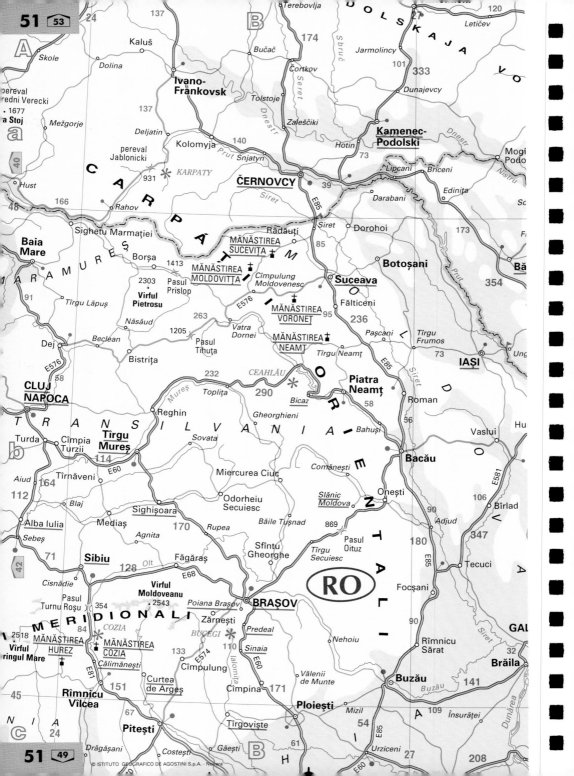

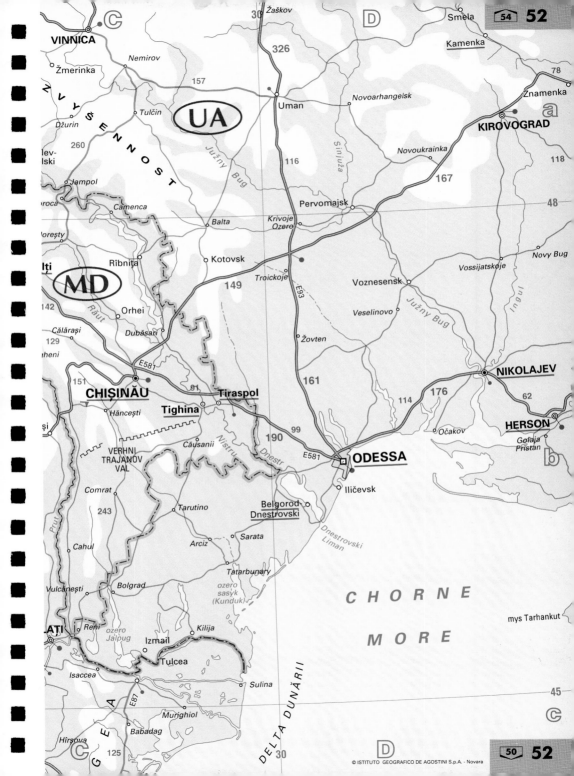

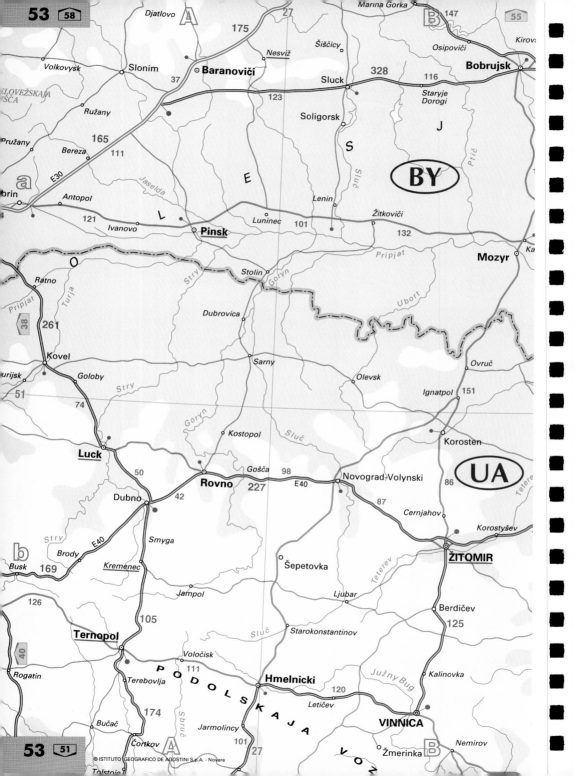

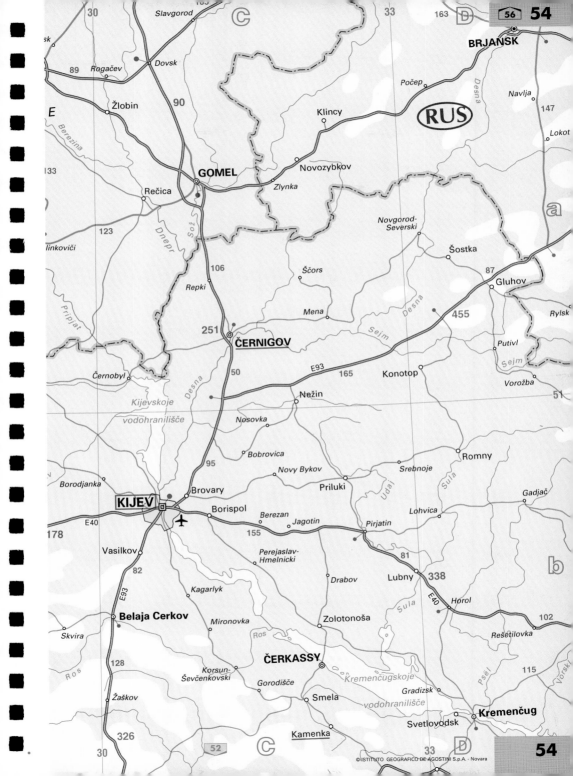

30 Slavgorod C 33 163 D

BRJANSK

89 Rogačev Dovsk Počep Navlja

Žlobin 90 Klincy 147

E Berezina RUS Lokot

133 GOMEL Novozybkov

Rečica Zlynka

Dnepr Soz Novgorod-Severski

123 Šostka

106 Ščors 87 Gluhov

Repki Mena Desna Rylsk

Pripjat 251 ČERNIGOV 455 Sejm Putivl

Černobyl 50 E93 165 Konotop Vorožba Sejm

Kijevskoje Nežin 51

vodohranilišče Nosovka

Bobrovica Romny

Borodjanka 95 Novy Bykov Priluki Srebnoje Sula Gadjač

KIJEV Brovary Lohvica

E40 Borispol Berezan Jagotin Pirjatin

178 155 81

Vasilkov Lubny 338

82 Perejaslav-Hmelnicki Drabov Horol Sula E40

Kagarlyk Zolotonoša 102

E93 Belaja Cerkov Mironovka Rešetilovka

Skvira Ros ČERKASSY Psёl Vorskla

128 Korsun-Ševčenkovski Kremenčugskoje 115

Žaškov Gorodišče vodohranilišče Gradizsk

Smela Svetlovodsk Kremenčug

326 Kamenka

30 52 C 33 D

©ISTITUTO GEOGRAFICO DE AGOSTINI S.p.A. - Novara

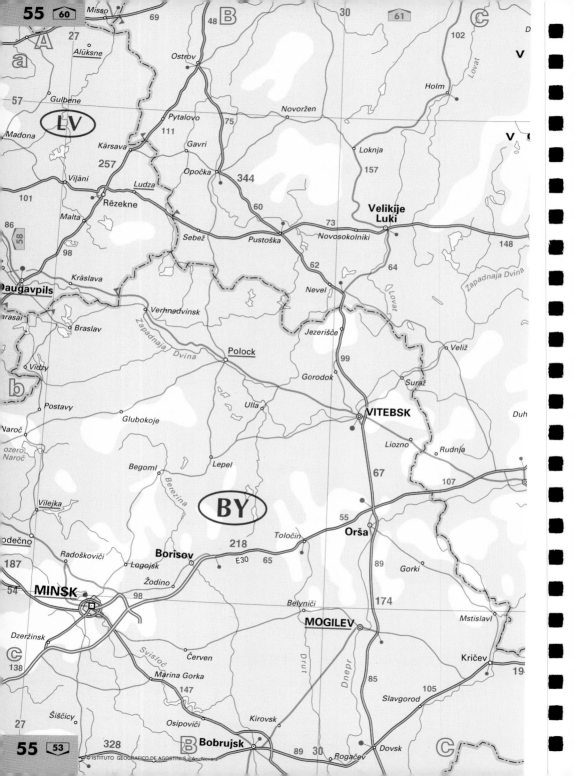

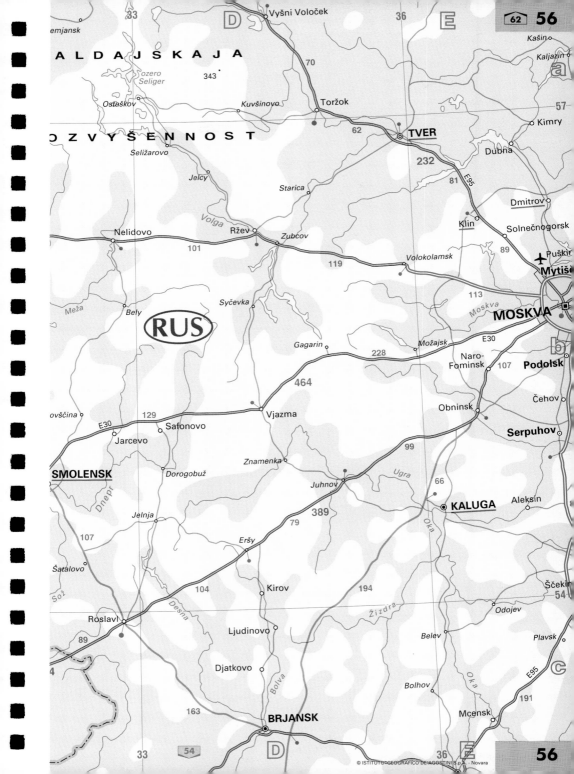

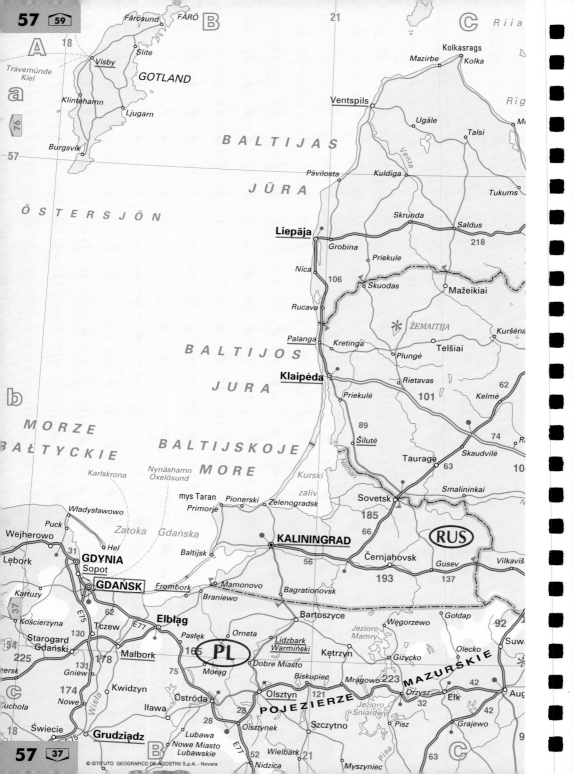

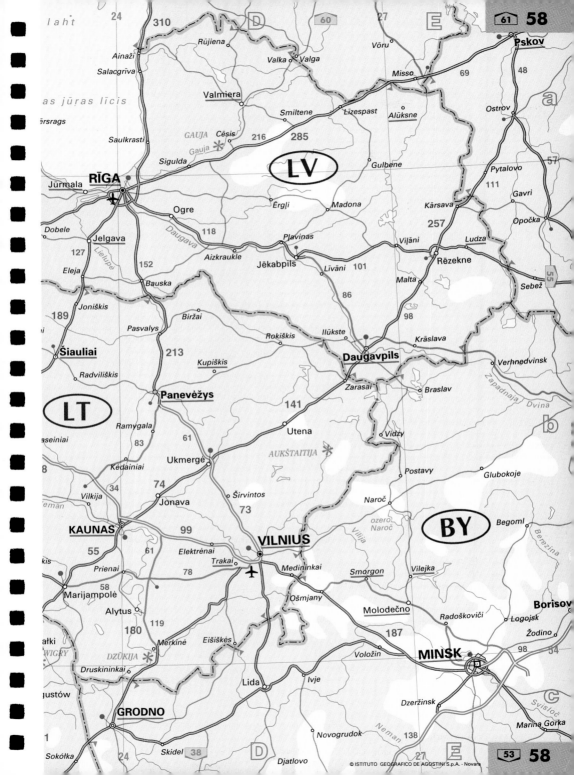

Hassela

A Gnarp 18 B 65 21 LAUH

81 192

Ljusdal

Merikarvia Ka

Delsbo 56 Hudiksvall

Pori
Björneborg

208

Edsbyn

Söderhamn

Rauma

Bollnäs

Pyhäj
Laitila

163

a Bergby

Ockelbo Uusikaupunki 141

Gävle

AHVENANMAA /
ÅLAND

111 Naantali
AL

Hofors Sandviken Älvkarleby

GRÄSÖ Storby
ECKERÖ Lumparland

Korppoo

S Avesta

Dalälven 102 Östhammar

Maarianhamina /
Mariehamn

mora

KÖKAR SAARISTOME

60 L A N D

Sala 174 Hallstavik

215 Uppsala Visby ITÄMERI

Västeras Norrtälje

197 72 Kapellskär

Köping Enköping Sigtuna 94

98 99 E18

Arboga 197 E18-E20 Tallin
Helsinki
Sankt Peterburg

Eskilstuna Strängnäs

Märiefred STOCKHOLM

Flen Södertälje

Katrineholm 57 BALTI

b 113

174 HIIU

61 Nynäshamn

13 Oxelösund Helsinki
Visby
Gdańsk MERI

Norrköping

E4 Helsinki
Gdańsk

E22 GOTSKA SANDÖN

76 GOTSKA SANDÖN

tvidaberg Valdemarsvik Kihelkonna

115

ÖSTERSJÖN

Nynäshamn FÅRÖ
Maarianhamina Fårösund

Västervik Slite

Oskarshamn Maz

Visby
A Travemünde
Kiel 18 GOTLAND B 21

© ISTITUTO GEOGRAFICO DE AGOSTINI S.p.A. - Novara

HELVETINJÄRVI

C Parkano Mänttä D E75 Kangasniemi 27 E

ANVYORI Ruovesi Jämsä 174

SEITSEMISEN 151 Joutsa Puulavesi 40

Ikaalinen Näsijärvi ISOJÄRVI E63 Mikkeli

kaanpää 83 E12 Orivesi Kuhmoinen Hartola Saimaa

Tampere/ 278 FIN 129 Savitaipale

Nokia Tammerfors Heinola

Harjavalta Vammala Valkeakoski

Lempäälä 126 Asikkala Lahti Kuusankoski 146 SALPA Taavetti Lappe

Eura Huittinen 72 78 174 Hämeenlinna 446 a

106 Kouvola 12

Oripää E63 Loimaa Forssa Riihimäki 104 Anjalankoski 409

TORRONSUO LIESJÄRVI 96 Hyvinkää Mäntsälä 213 Hamina

Mynämäki 85 Koski Somero 137 Karkkila Järvenpää E18 Kotka

Salo 165 Kerava Porvoo 129 Loviisa ITÄISEN SUOMENLAHTI

ku/ E18 Lohja HELSINKI/ OSTROV 60

o Parainen Espoo/ HELSINGFORS Suomenlahti GOGLAND OSTROV MOŚCNY

Kimito Esbo Sankt-Peterburg Finski zaliv

KIMITO Karjaa Stockholm

Hanko Ekenäs Nynäshamn Soome laht / Finski

Oxelösund Travemünde Rønne

TAMMISAAREN Narvski zaliv /

SAARISTO Narva laht 91

Stockholm TALLINN LAHEMAA Kohtla- Narva

Paldiski E20 203 Järve

Tapa Rakvere 346

Risti 185

Kärdla Lohusuu b

Haapsalu 129 Märjamaa Paide Mustvee Gdov

IMAA EST Jõgeva Peipsi / Čudskoj

Emmaste Lihula Pärnu- Põltsamaa järv ozero

Orissaare Jaagupi

Kulvastu Virtsu Vändra Viljandi

SAAREMAA Pärnu Vörts järv Tartu

Kuressaare Uulu Elva Pihkva järv

Kilingi-Nõmme 104

Riia laht 310 Rūjiena Võru

Kolkasrags Ainaži Valka Valga 27

irbe Kolka Salacgriva LV E

C 24 Valmiera D

© ISTITUTO GEOGRAFICO DE AGOSTINI S.p.A. - Novara

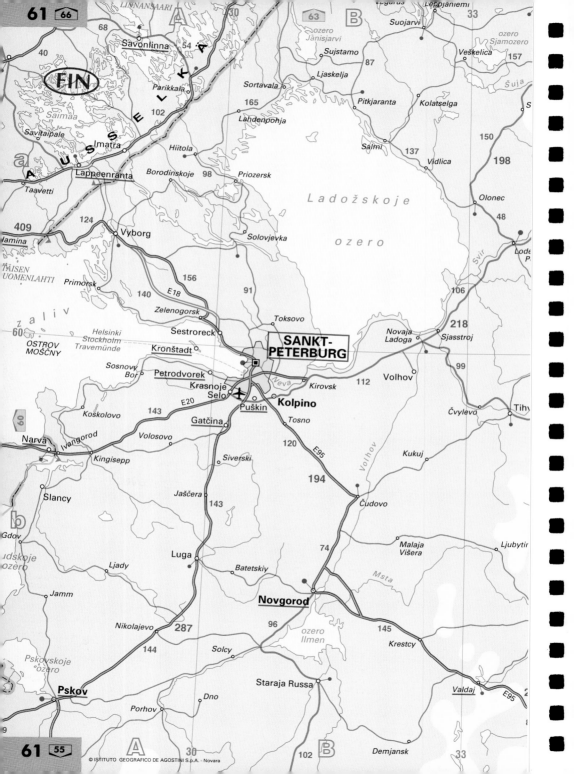

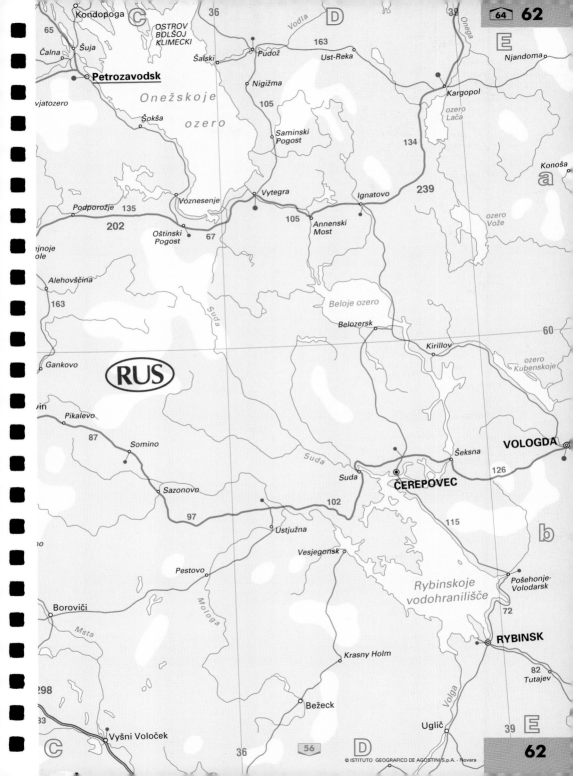

Kondopoga

OSTROV
BOLŠOJ
KLIMECKI

36

D

Vodla

39

Onega

E

65

Čalna   Šuja

Šalski

Pudož   163   Ust-Reka

Njandoma

Petrozavodsk

Nigižma

Kargopol

vjatozero

O n e ž s k o j e

105

*ozero
Laća*

Šokša

o z e r o

Saminski
Pogost

134

239

Konoša

a

Voznesenje

Vytegra

Ignatovo

*ozero
Vože*

Podporožje   135

202

Oštinski
Pogost   67

105   Annenski
Most

60

ejnoje
ole

Alehovščina

Suda

Beloje ozero

163

Belozersk

Kirillov

*ozero
Kubenskoje*

Gankovo

RUS

vin

Pikalevo

87   Somino

Suda

Šeksna

VOLOGDA

Sazonovo

Suda   Suda

ČEREPOVEC

126

97

102

115

b

Ustjužna

Vesjegonsk

Pošehonje-
Volodarsk

Pestovo

Mologa

*Rybinskoje
vodohranilišče*

72

Borovići

Msta

RYBINSK

82
Tutajev

Krasny Holm

Volga

298

Bežeck

33

C   Vyšni Voloček

36

56

D

Uglič

39   E

62

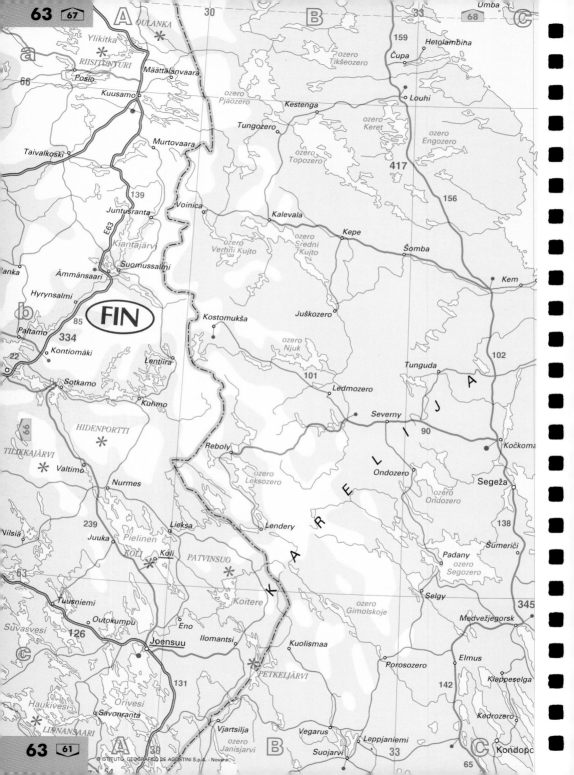

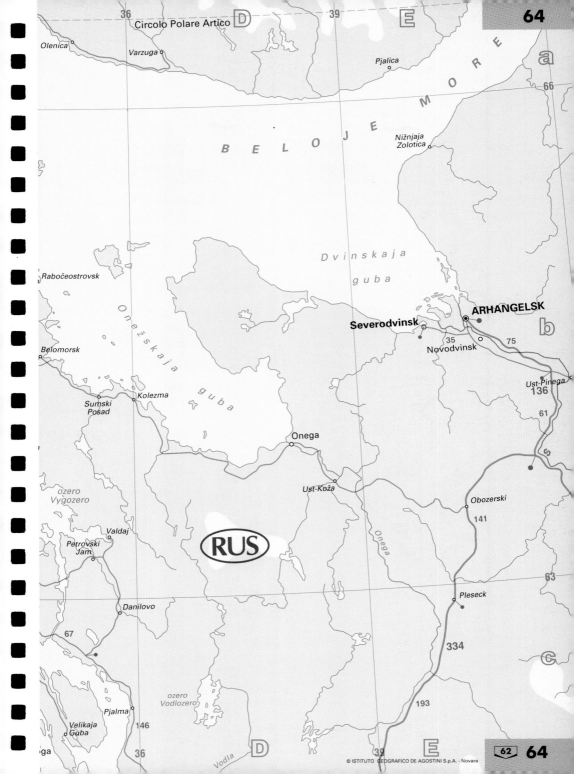

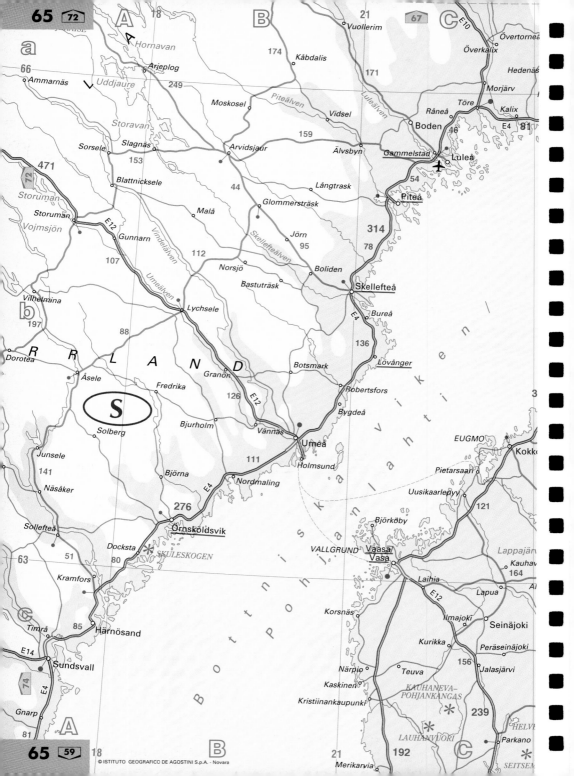

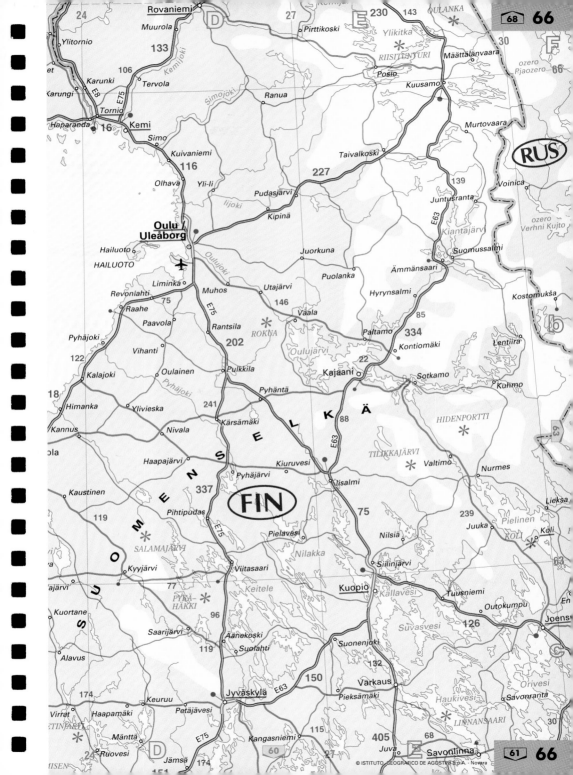

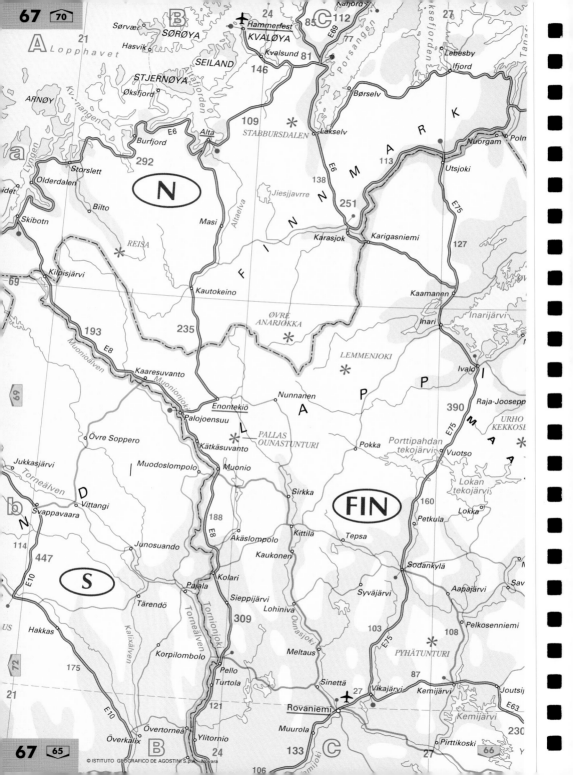

A 21 Lopphavet

Sørvær
SØRØYA
B
24
Hammerfest
KVALØYA
85 C 112
E69
77
Karfjord
27

Hasvik
SEILAND

Kvalsund 81

STJERNØYA
146

Lebesby
Ifjord

Øksfjord

Børselv

ARNØY

Burfjord
E6
Alta
109
STABBURSDALEN
Lakselv
Nuorgam
Poln

a
Storslett
292

138
E6
113
Utsjoki

idet
Olderdalen
Bilto

251

E75

Skibotn
Masi
Altaelva
Jiesjjavrre

REISA

Karasjok
Karigasniemi
127

Kilpisjärvi
Kautokeino

Kaamanen

69

193
E8
235
ØVRE
ANARJOKKA

Inarijärvi

LEMMENJOKI

Inari

69

Kaaresuvanto
Muonionjoki

Nunnanen

P
P

Ivalo
I

390
Raja-Joosepp

Enontekiö
Palojoensuu

L
PALLAS
OUNASTUNTURI

A

Pokka

Porttipahdan
tekojärvi
Vuotso
M

URHO
KEKKOSE

Övre Soppero

Kätkäsuvanto

Jukkasjärvi
Torneälven
I
Muodoslompolo
Muonio

Sirkka

FIN

160

Lokan
tekojärvi
Lokka

b
N
Svappavaara
Vittangi
D

188

Kittilä
Tepsa

Petkula

114
447

E8
Åkäslompolo

Junosuando
Kaukonen

Sodankylä

S
Kolari
Pajala

Syväjärvi
Aapajärvi
Sav

US
Hakkas
Tärendö
Sieppijärvi
309
Lohiniva

103
E75

108
Pelkosenniemi

72
175
Korpilombolo
Tornionjoki
Torneälven
Kalixälven

Meltaus

PYHÄTUNTURI

Pello
Turtola
Sinettä
27
Vikajärvi
Kemijärvi
Joutsi

21
121
Rovaniemi
87
E63
Kemijärvi

Muurola

Övertorneå
Överkalix
B
24
106
133
C
27
66
Y
230

Pirttikoski

© ISTITUTO GEOGRAFICO DE AGOSTINI S.p.A. - Novara

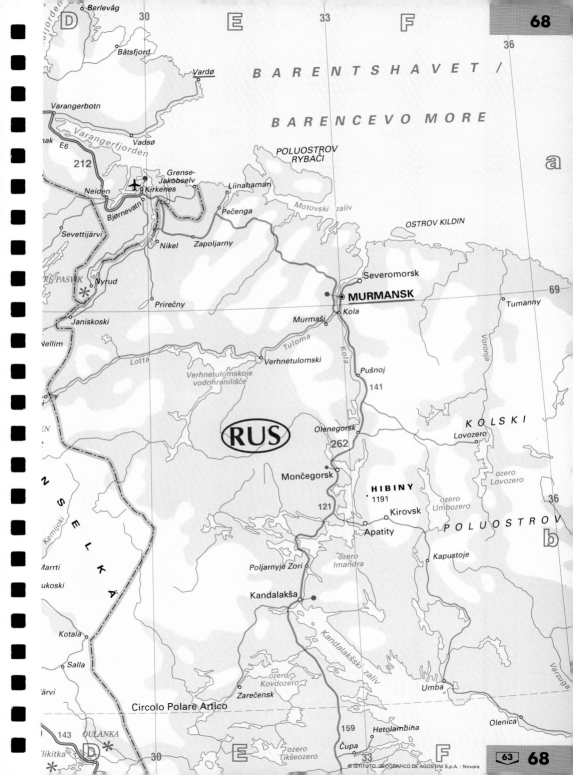

A 15 B 18 C

12

a

NORDKVALØY

VANNA A

N O R S K E H A V E T

RINGVASSØY

Ullsfjorden

KVALØY ● Breivikeidet

Tromsø ✈ Svensby

Lyngseidet

E8

118

VESTERÅLEN

Andenes Torsken SENJA Finnsnes

235

69 ANDØYA Sørreisa Nordkjosbotr

Risøyhamn E6

Myre Andfjorden Andselv

LANGØYA Setermoen 207

Bø Harstad ØVRE

Sortland Lavangen DIVIDAL

HINNØYA

Melbu E10

AUSTVÅGØYA Fiskebøl 210 Bjerkvik VADVETJÅKKA

L 32 Lødingen

O 133 Ballagen Narvik Riksgränsen

F E10 Svolvær Bognes 83 E6 18 Abisko

O VESTVÅGØYA Skarberget ABISKO E10 Torneträs

T Vestfjorden

E Skutvik 158

N Innhavet Kebnekaise

MOSKENESØY 268 ● 2111 Nikkaluokta Kiruna

Sørvågen Nordfold

b Bonnåsjøen 167 STORA

MOSKENESØY Røsvik Akkajaure SJÖFALLET S

63 Vietas

Bodø RAGO Virihaure Stora

Fauske PADJELANTA Saltoluokta Lulevatten A

Rognan Maln

Beiarn 70 E6 SAREK

Ørnes Pieskehaure Kvikkjokk G

A 15 B 18 C Porjus 102

© ISTITUTO GEOGRAFICO DE AGOSTINI S.p.A. - Novara

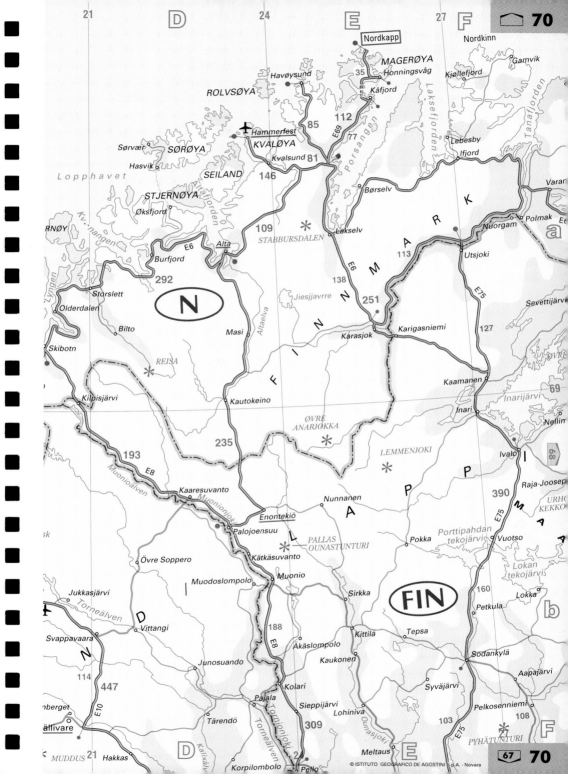

21 · D · **24** · E · Nordkapp · **27** · F · 70

Nordkinn

MAGERØYA · Nordkinn

Gamvik

Havøysund · 35 · Honningsvåg · Kjøllefjord

ROLVSØYA · Kåfjord

112 · Lebesby

85 · 77 · Ifjord

Hammerfest · E69 · Børselv

Sørvær · SØRØYA · KVALØYA

Hasvik · Kvalsund · 81 · Porsangen

Lopphavet · SEILAND · 146

STJERNØYA · Børselv · Varan

Øksfjord · Laksefjorden · Tanafjorden

RNØY · 109 · Lakselv · K

Kv.-nangen · STABBURSDALEN · Nuorgam · Polmak · E

E6 · Alta · 113 · a

Burfjord · M · Utsjoki

292 · 138 · A · E75

Lyngen · Storslett · Jiesjjavrre · 251 · R · Sevettijärvi

Olderdalen · N · K

Bilto · REISA · Masi · N · Karasjok · Karigasniemi · 127

Skibotn · Altaelva · ØVRE

Kilpisjärvi · Kautokeino · Kaamanen · 69

F · Inarijärvi

ØVRE · Inari · Nelli

193 · ANARJOKKA · Ivalo · I

Muonioälven · 235 · LEMMENJOKI · 390 · Raja-Joose

E8 · Kaaresuvanto · Nunnanen · P · URH

Muonionjoki · Enontekiö · A · E75 · KEKK

sk · Palojoensuu · L · Pokka · Porttipahdan · Vuotso · A

Övre Soppero · Kätkäsuvanto · PALLAS · tekojärvi · Lokan

Muodoslompolo · Muonio · OUNASTUNTURI · tekojärvi

Jukkasjärvi · Sirkka · FIN · 160 · Lokka · b

Torneälven · D · Petkula

Vittangi · 188 · Kittilä · Tepsa

Svappavaara · E8 · Äkäslompolo · Sodankylä

N · Junosuando · Kaukonen · Aapajärvi

114 · 447 · Kolari · Syväjärvi

E10 · Pajala · Sieppijärvi · Pelkosenniemi

nberget · Tärendö · Lohiniva · 103 · 108

ällivare · 309 · F

Torneälven · Meltaus · PYHÄTUNTURI

MUDDUS · 21 · Hakkas · Kalixäl · Ounasjoki · E75

Korpilombolo · Pello · E

© ISTITUTO GEOGRAFICO DE AGOSTINI S.p.A. - Novara

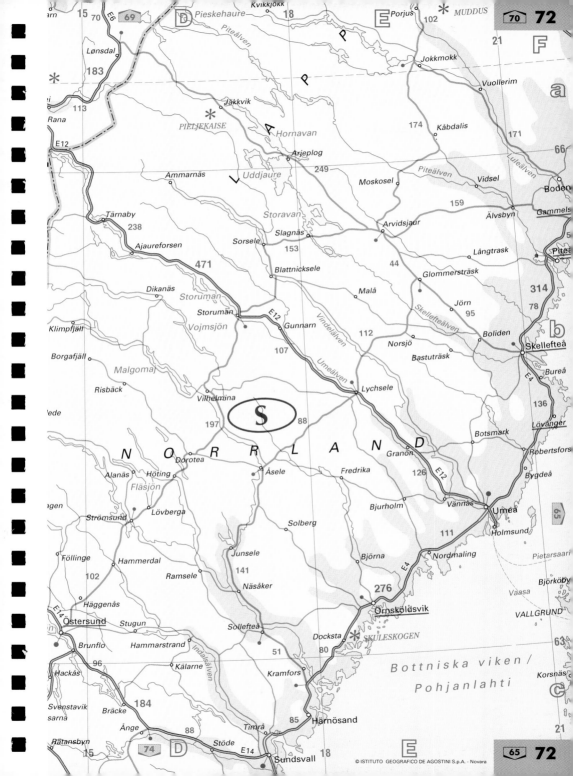

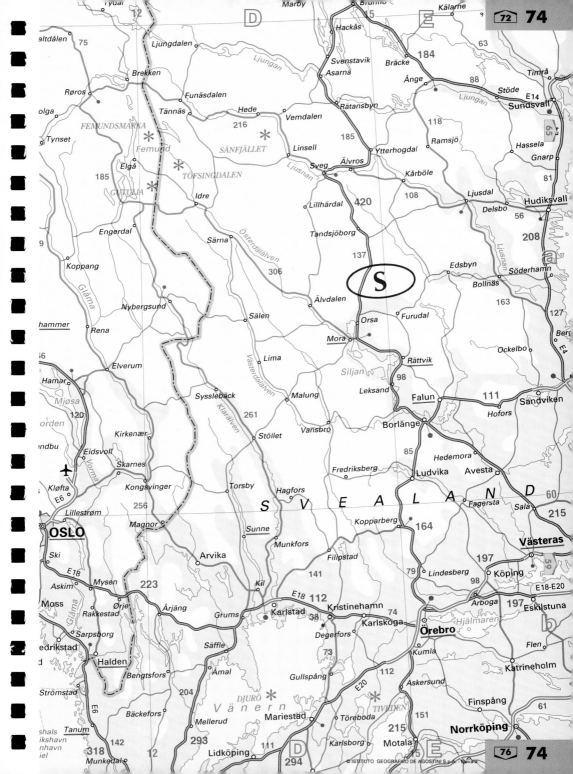

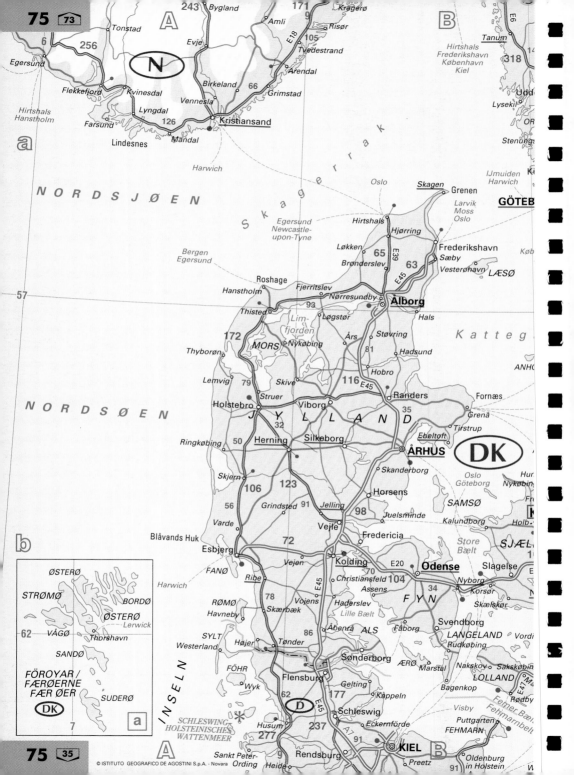

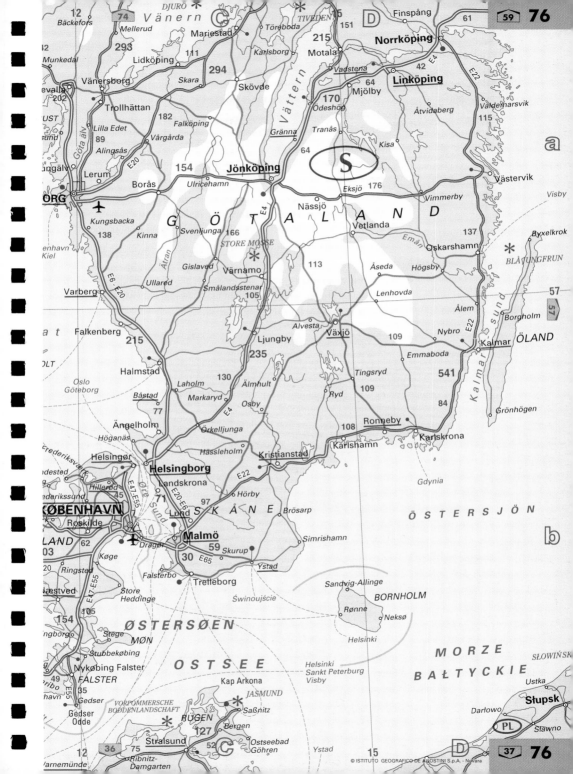

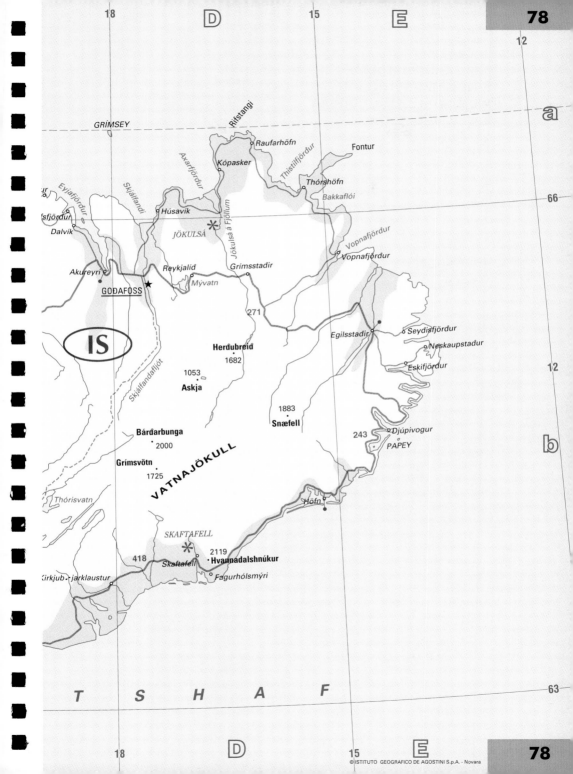

GRÍMSEY

Rifstangi

Raufarhöfn

Kópasker

Thistilfjördur

Fontur

Thórshöfn

Axarfjördur

Bakkaflói

Skjálfandi

Húsavík

Eyjafjördur

JÖKULSÁ

Jökulsá á Fjöllum

Vopnafjördur

-fjördur

Dalvík

Reykjalíd

Grímsstadir

Vopnafjördur

Akureyri

Mývatn

GODAFOSS

271

Egilsstadir

Seydisfjördur

IS

Neskaupstadur

Herdubreid

Eskifjördur

1682

1053

Skjálfandafljót

Askja

1883

Snæfell

243

Djúpivogur

Bárdarbunga

PAPEY

2000

Grímsvötn

1725

VATNAJÖKULL

Thórisvatn

Höfn

SKAFTAFELL

418

2119

Skaftafell

Hvannádalshnúkur

Kirkjub- -tjarklaustur

Fagurhólsmýri

T   S   H   A   F

©ISTITUTO GEOGRAFICO DE AGOSTINI S.p.A. - Novara

Distance chart
Distanze chilometriche
Distances kilométriques
Kilometrische Entfernungen
Distancias kilométricas

	Amsterdam	Athínai	Barcelona	Beograd	Berlin	Bern	Brest	Brindisi	Bruxelles	Bucureşti	Budapest	Calais	Dublin	Edinburg	Frankfurt/M	Gibraltar	Hamburg	Helsinki	İstanbul
Amsterdam	–	2746	1522	1829	671	826	1056	2093	199	2433	1432	365	937	1039	434	2265	448	1827	2802
Athínai	2746	–	2520	1162	2466	1971	3059	653	2568	1279	1559	2740	3455	3557	2327	3692	2755	4134	1166
Beograd	1829	1162	2027	–	1304	1422	2444	1329	1815	604	397	2031	2746	2848	1398	3199	1593	2972	973
Berlin	671	2466	1906	1304	–	962	1647	1911	750	1745	907	977	1570	1672	572	3017	289	1668	2277
Bern	826	1971	944	1422	962	–	1197	1318	657	2026	1164	878	1593	1695	416	2116	917	2296	2395
Helsinki	1827	4134	3154	2972	1668	2296	2864	3527	1967	3413	2575	2194	2736	2838	1880	4174	1379	–	3762
İstanbul	2802	1166	3000	973	2277	2395	3417	1333	2788	693	1370	3004	3719	3821	2371	4172	2566	3762	–
København	763	3070	2090	1908	604	1232	1800	2463	903	2349	1511	1130	1672	1774	816	3110	315	1064	2881
Köln	262	2499	1382	1570	555	588	1092	1846	224	2174	1173	451	1169	1271	172	2462	393	1772	2543
Lisboa	2287	3787	1267	3294	2839	2238	1877	3134	2088	3898	3251	2061	2776	2878	2347	661	2677	4056	4267
London	392	2910	1477	2201	1025	1048	925	2257	397	2805	1794	170	545	647	796	2409	812	2191	3174
Madrid	1561	3145	625	2652	2313	1569	1351	2492	1562	3256	2609	1535	2250	2352	1821	704	2153	3530	3625
Milano	1114	1632	963	1080	1062	339	1427	979	936	1648	1021	1108	1823	1925	695	2135	1239	2618	2053
Moskva	2486	3165	3721	2148	1815	2777	3462	3477	2594	1886	1960	2792	3385	3515	2387	4832	2104	1183	2579
Oslo	1358	3665	2685	2503	1199	1827	2395	3058	1498	2944	2106	1725	2267	2369	1411	3705	910	976	3476
Paris	501	2465	1032	1850	1053	603	594	1812	302	2468	1525	275	990	1092	561	1964	891	2270	2823
Roma	1702	1190	1330	1330	1520	927	2015	537	1524	1934	1271	1696	2411	2513	1283	2502	1757	3156	1870
Stockholm	1404	3711	2731	2549	1245	1873	2441	3104	1544	2990	2152	1771	2313	2415	1457	3751	956	423	3522
Warszawa	1256	2274	2430	1067	585	1547	2440	2396	1384	1190	670	1630	2155	2257	1157	3594	874	2253	2040
Wien	1175	1819	1818	657	647	904	1859	1444	1137	1098	260	1364	2097	2181	741	2990	936	2315	1630

Le distanze stradali, in chilometri, sono calcolate sui percorsi più brevi o rapidi (autostrade, strade principali) da centro abitato a centro abitato, a prescindere dalle condizioni meteorologiche stagionali.

Road distances, in kilometres, are calculated by the shortest or quickest routes (motorways, main roads) from centre to centre and do not take into account seasonal weather conditions.

Les distances routières, en kilomètres, sont calculées sur les routes les plus brèves ou rapides (autoroutes, routes principales) de localité à localité, sans tenir compte des conditions météorologiques saisonnières.

Entfernungsangaben, in Kilometern, sind auf den kurzesten oder schnellsten Routen berechnet (Autobahnen, Hauptstraßen), von Ortschaft bis Ortschaft, unabhängig von der jahreszeitlichen Wetterlage.

Las distancias kilométricas en carreteras son calculadas en los itinerarios más breves o rápidos (autopistas, carreteras principales) de localidad a localidad, prescindiendo de las condiciones meteorológicas estacionales.

København	Köln	La Coruña	Lisboa	London	Luxembourg	Lyon	Madrid	Marseille	Milano	Moskva	München	Narvik	Oslo	Paris	Praha	Roma	Sofija	Stockholm	Warszawa	Wien	Zagreb	Zürich
763	262	1995	2287	392	391	888	1561	1213	1114	2486	854	2813	1358	501	968	1702	2242	1404	1256	1175	1462	820
3070	2499	3491	3787	2910	2355	2085	3145	2657	1632	3165	1966	5120	3665	2465	2113	1190	882	3711	2274	1819	1577	1933
1908	1570	2998	3294	2201	1602	1533	2652	1572	1080	2148	1023	3958	2503	1850	951	1330	413	2549	1067	657	415	1297
604	555	2547	2839	1025	750	1272	2313	1542	1062	1815	598	2654	1199	1053	353	1520	1717	1245	585	647	1018	837
1232	588	1915	2238	1048	444	310	1569	635	339	2777	426	3282	1827	603	844	927	1835	1873	1547	904	1004	125
1064	1772	3764	4056	2191	1967	2520	3530	2845	2618	1183	2214	1676	976	2270	2021	3156	3385	423	2253	2315	2822	2290
2881	2543	3971	4267	3174	2575	2506	3625	2545	2053	2579	1996	4661	3476	2823	1924	1870	560	3522	2040	1630	1388	2270
–	708	2700	2992	1127	903	1456	2466	1781	1554	2419	1150	2050	595	1206	957	2072	2321	641	1189	1251	1758	1240
708	–	1992	2284	624	195	748	1758	1073	867	2370	592	2758	1303	498	706	1455	1983	1349	1160	913	1200	582
2992	2284	619	–	2231	2128	1899	642	1778	2230	4648	2537	5131	3587	1786	2821	2597	3717	3633	3418	3085	2895	2363
1127	624	1939	2231	–	591	898	1705	1223	1278	2840	1216	3177	1722	445	1330	1866	2614	1768	1610	1534	1824	1026
2466	1758	564	642	1705	1602	1259	–	1138	1588	4128	1987	4486	3031	1260	2295	1955	3065	3107	2898	2443	2253	1694
1554	867	1934	2230	1278	723	453	1588	508	–	2753	514	3604	2149	833	903	588	1493	2195	1523	879	665	301
2419	2370	4362	4648	2840	2565	3087	4128	3357	2753	–	2282	2678	2159	2868	1850	3169	2283	1606	1230	1908	2256	2531
595	1303	3295	3587	1722	1498	2021	3031	2376	2149	2159	1745	1455	–	1801	1552	2667	2916	553	1784	1846	2353	1821
1206	498	1494	1786	445	342	453	1260	778	833	2868	827	3256	1801	–	1035	1421	2263	1847	1638	1265	1435	581
2072	1455	2301	2597	1866	1311	1041	1955	875	588	3169	922	4122	2667	1421	1301	–	1586	2713	1921	1121	915	889
641	1349	3341	3633	1768	1544	2097	3107	2422	2195	1606	1791	1652	553	1847	1598	2713	2962	–	1830	1892	2399	1867
1189	1160	3132	3418	1610	1355	1857	2898	2031	1523	1230	1062	3239	1784	1847	620	1921	1480	1830	–	678	1026	1301
1251	913	2789	3085	1534	1017	1214	2443	1363	879	1908	438	3300	1846	1265	294	1121	1070	1892	678	–	371	779

International registration letters

Targhe automobilistiche internazionali

Plaques automobiles internationales

Internationale Kraftfahrzeugkennzeichen

Placas automovilísticas internacionales

Country name abbreviations used in the index
Sigle presenti nell'indice
Sigles contenus dans l'index
Im Index vorhandene Kennzeichen
Siglas contenidas en el índice

A	Aus.	Austria
AL	Alb.	Albania
AND	And.	Andorra
B	Bel.	Belgium
BG	Bulg.	Bulgaria
BIH	Bos. Erz.	Bosnia and Hercegovina
BY	R.B.	Belorussia
CH	Svizz.	Switzerland
CZ	Rep. Ceca	Czech Republic
D	D	Germany
DK	Dan.	Denmark
DZ	Alg.	Algeria
E	Sp.	Spain
EST	Est.	Estonia
F	Fr.	France
FIN	Finl.	Finland
FL	Liech.	Liechtenstein
GB	RU	United Kingdom of Great Britain and Northern Ireland
GR	Grecia	Greece
H	Ung.	Hungary
HR	Cro.	Croatia
I	It.	Italy
IRL	Eire	Republic of Ireland
IS	Isl.	Iceland
L	Luss.	Luxembourg
LT	Lit.	Lithuania
LV	Lett.	Latvia
M	Malta	Malta
MA	Mar.	Morocco
MC	PMC	Monaco
MD	Mold.	Moldova
MK	Maced.	Former Yugoslav Republic of Macedonia
N	Norv.	Norway
NL	P.B.	Netherlands
P	Port.	Portugal
PL	Pol.	Poland
RO	Rom.	Romania
RSM	RSM	San Marino
RUS	Russia	Russian Federation
S	Svezia	Sweden
SK	Slovac.	Slovak Republic
SLO	Slo.	Slovenia
TN	Tun.	Tunisia
TR	Tur.	Turkey
UA	Ucr.	Ukraine
V	SCV	Vatican City
YU	Iug.	Yugoslavia
	Eur.	Europe

PLACE NAME INDEX
INDICE DEI NOMI
INDEX DES NOMS
NAMENVERZEICHNIS
INDICE DE NOMBRES

How to use the index

All place names in the index are followed by a page number and coordinates which indicate the grid square in which it falls on the map page. Where there are two places with the same name, they will be distinguished in the index by an abbreviation of the country name in brackets afterwards.
In countries with dual languages, both versions of the place name are given in the index e.g.:

Brussel/Bruxelles.

Avvertenze per la ricerca

L'indice elenca in ordine alfabetico i nomi contenuti nella carta seguiti da lettere indicanti il riquadro della proiezione geografica in cui sono rintracciabili.
Se le lettere sono più di due, i nomi vanno ricercati nelle immediate vicinanze del reticolato geografico da esse individuato.
Per semplicità tutti i nomi contenuti in due pagine affiancate sono riferiti alla pagina di numero dispari.
I nomi dei centri abitati ed i casi di omonimia sono seguiti dalla sigla indicante lo Stato di appartenenza.
Poiché in alcuni Paesi sono parlate e scritte più lingue ufficiali, si è ritenuto necessario indicare nell'indice alcune di queste forme differenziate.
I nomi si presentano scritti sia come:

Bruxelles/Brussel
Antwerpen/Anvers

sia viceversa: *Brussel/Bruxelles*
Anvers/Antwerpen

I nomi fisici hanno sia la parte generica che l'articolo posposti al nome proprio.
Dei principali toponimi stranieri è riportata la forma italiana accompagnata dalla sigla (I).

Notices pour la recherche

L'index récense en suivant l'ordre alphabétique les noms contenus dans la carte, suivis par des lettres qui indiquent le carré de la projection géographique où sont retrouvables.
Dans le cas où les lettres soient plus que deux, les noms vont recherchés près du réseau géographique localisé par les lettres mêmes.
Pour simplicité tous les noms contenus dans deux pages l'une à côté de l'autre sont rapportés à la page avec nombre impair. Les noms des localités et les cas d'homonymie sont suivis par le sigle qui indique le Pays d'appartenance.
Comme dans certains pays plusieurs langues officielles sont reconnues, on a estimé nécessaire de faire figurer dans l'index les formes diverses que peut revêtir un nom.
Ainsi, de nombreux toponymes se présentent soit sous la forme:

Bruxelles/Brussel
Antwerpen/Anvers

soit sous la forme: *Brussel/Bruxelles*
Anvers/Antwerpen

Les noms physiques ont soit la partie générique, soit l'article mis après le nom propre.
Des principaux toponymes étrangers on indique la forme italienne avec le sigle (I).

Erläuterungen des Suchsystems

Der Index enthält die in der Karte vorhandenen Namen in alphabetischer Reihenfolge; jedem Namen folgen Buchstaben, die auf das Viereck der geographischen Projektion weisen, wo er aufzufinden ist.
Falls es mehr als zwei Buchstaben gibt, soll man die Namen in nächster Nähe des von ihnen bestimmten geographischen Kartennetzes suchen.
Zur Einfachheit sind alle in zwei nebeneinanderen Seiten enthaltenen Namen auf die Seite mit ungerader Zahl bezogen.
Die Ortsnamen und die Gleichnamigkeiten werden von dem zugehörigen Staatskennzeichen gefolgt.
Da in einigen Länder mehr Amtssprachen gesprochen werden, hat man nötig gehalten, manche dieser verschiedenen Namensformen in den Index aufzunehmen.
Die Namen sind deshalb folgenderweise vorhanden:

Bruxelles/Brussel
Antwerpen/Anvers

und hingegen als: *Brussel/Bruxelles*
Anvers/Antwerpen

Die Artikel sowie alle vor dem eigentlichen Namen stehenden Zusatzbezeichnungen werden nachgestellt und der Eigenname bei der Alphabetisierung berücksichtigt. Von den wichtigsten ausländischen Ortsnamen wird hier die italienische, von der Abkürzung (I) begleitete Form übertragen.

Instrucciones para la consulta

El índice presenta por el orden alfabético los nombres que figuran en el mapa, seguidos de letras que remiten al recuadro de la proyección geográfica donde aparecen. Si las letras son más de dos, los nombres van buscados en las immediatas proximidades del retículo geográfico individuado por ellas.
Para simplicidad todos los nombres contenidos en dos páginas juntas éstan referidos a la página de número impar.
Los topónimos y los casos de homonimia van seguidos de la sigla que indica el País de pertenencia.
Dado que en algunos Países coexisten diversas lenguas oficiales, se ha creído conveniente hacer figurar en el índice estas formas diferenciadas.
Los topónimos se presentan escritos tanto bajo la forma:

Bruxelles/Brussel
Antwerpen/Anvers

como a la inversa: *Brussel/Bruxelles*
Anvers/Antwerpen

Los nombres físicos han la parte genérica y el artículo pospuestos al nombre propio.
De los principales topónimos extranjeros se indica la forma italiana acompañada de la sigla (I).

A

Aachen [D] **7** CDb
Aalen [D] **33** Ba
Aalst / Alost [Bel.] **7** Cab
Äänekoski [Finl.] **65** Dc
Aapajärvi [Finl.] **67** Db
Aarlen / Arlon [Bel.] **11** Ba
Abano Terme [It.] **31** Ba
Abbasanta [It.] **29** Ab
Abbeville [Fr.] **5** Dc
Abelvær [Norv.] **71** Bb
Åbenrå [Dan.] **75** Bb
Aberdeen [RU] **1** Da
Abergavenny [RU] **5** BCb
Aberystwyth [RU] **5** Bb
Abetone [It.] **31** Bb
Abide [Tur.] **47** Bb
Abington [RU] **1** Cb
Abisko [Svezia] **69** Cb
Abisko [Svezia] **69** Cb
Åbo / Turku [Finl.] **59** Ca
Abony [Ung.] **39** Bb
Abrántes [Port.] **19** Bb
Abruzzo **29** Cab
Accéglio [It.] **13** Cb
Achill **3** Aab
Achill Head **3** Aab
Aci Gölü **47** Cc
Acipayam [Tur.] **47** Cc
Acireale [It.] **25** BCb
Açores, Arquipélago dos- =
   Azzorre, Arcipelago
   delle- (I) **21** ins.a
Acquaviva delle Fonti [It.]
   27 Cb
Acqui Terme [It.] **31** Ba
A Cruña / La Coruña [Sp.]
   19 Ba
Adamclisi [Rom.] **49** Ca
Adda **31** Ba
Adelboden [Svizz.] **33** Ab
Adige **31** Ca
Adjud [Rom.] **51** BCb
Admont [Aus.] **33** Cb
Adour **15** BCb
Adra [Sp.] **21** CDb
Adrano [It.] **25** Bb
Adria [It.] **31** BCab
Adriano, Vallo di- (I) =
   Hadrian's Wall **3** Ca
Adriatico, Mar- **27** BCa
Adriatico, Mar- (I) = Jadransko
   More **27** BCa
Ærø **35** Ca
Aféa **45** Bb
Afsluitdijk **7** Ca
Agde [Fr.] **13** Bb
Agen [Fr.] **15** Cb
Aggteler **39** Ba
Agnita [Rom.] **51** Bb
Ágreda [Sp.] **17** Bab
Agrigento [It.] **25** Bb
Agrínion [Grecia] **43** Bc
Agropoli [It.] **29** CDb
Águeda [Port.] **19** Bb
Aguilar de la Frontera [Sp.]
   21 Cb
Águilas [Sp.] **23** Bb
Ahtopol [Bulg.] **49** Ca
Ahtyrka [Ucr.] **53** Db
Ahvenanmaa / Åland = Åland,
   Isole- (I) **59** Ba
Aigle [Svizz.] **11** Cb
Aigues-Mortes [Fr.] **13** Bb
Aigues Tortes **17** Ca
Ainaži / Ajnaži [Lett.] **59** Db
Aínos **43** Ac
Ainsa [Sp.] **17** BCa
Aire-sur-l'Adour [Fr.] **15** Bb
Airolo [Svizz.] **33** Ab
Aiud [Rom.] **51** Ab

Aix-en-Provence [Fr.] **13** Bb
Aix-les-Bains [Fr.] **13** BCa
Aiyaíon Pélagos = Egeo,
   Mar- (I) **47** Bb
Aíyina = Egina (I) **45** Ab
Aíyinion [Grecia] **43** Bb
Aíyion [Grecia] **45** Ab
Aízkraukle [Lett.] **57** Db
Ajaccio [Fr.] **13** Cbc
Ajaureforsen [Svezia] **71** Db
Ajdovščina [Slo.] **31** Ca
Ajka [Ung.] **39** Ab
Ajnaži / Ainaži [Lett.] **59** Db
Ajtos [Bulg.] **49** Ca
Akajaure **69** Bb
Äkäslompolo [Finl.] **67** BCb
Akbou [Alg.] **23** Db
Ak Dağ **45** Cb
Akharnaí [Grecia] **45** Ab
Akhelóös **43** Bb
Akhisar [Tur.] **45** Cab
Akköy [Tur.] **45** Cb
Aknoul [Mar.] **21** Cc
Akranes [Isl.] **77** Bb
Akrítas, Ákra- = Gallo,
   Capo- (I) **45** Ab
Akureyri [Isl.] **77** Cb
Alacant / Alicante [Sp.] **23** Bb
Alagna Valsesia [It.] **31** Aa
Alagón **19** Bb
Alajärvi [Finl.] **65** Cbc
Alanás [Svezia] **71** Bb
Åland / Ahvenanmaa = Åland,
   Isole- (I) **59** Ba
Åland, Isole- (I) = Ahvenanmaa /
   Åland **59** Ba
Åland, Isole- (I) = Åland /
   Ahvenanmaa **59** Ba
Alaşehir [Tur.] **45** Cb
Alassio [It.] **31** Ab
Alatri [It.] **29** Cb
Alavo / Alavus [Finl.] **65** Cc
Alavus / Alavo [Finl.] **65** Cc
Alba [It.] **31** Ab
Albacete [Sp.] **23** Bab
Albaida [Sp.] **23** Bab
Alba Iulia [Rom.] **51** Ab
Albano Laziale [It.] **29** Cb
Albarracín [Sp.] **17** Bb
Albenga [It.] **31** Ab
Albergaria-a-Velha [Port.]
   19 Bb
Alberobello [It.] **27** Cb
Albert [Fr.] **7** Bb
Albertville [Fr.] **13** Ca
Albi [Fr.] **15** Cb
Albocácer / Albocásser [Sp.]
   23 BCa
Albocásser / Albocácer [Sp.]
   23 BCa
Alborán, Isla de- **21** CDc
Ålborg [Dan.] **75** Bab
Albufeira [Port.] **21** Bb
Alburquerque [Sp.] **21** Ba
Alcácer do Sal [Port.] **21** Bb
Alcalá de Guadaira [Sp.] **21** Cb
Alcalá de Henares [Sp.] **19** Cb
Alcalá la Real [Sp.] **21** Cb
Alcamo [It.] **25** Bb
Alcañices [Sp.] **19** Bb
Alcañiz [Sp.] **17** BCb
Alcántara [Sp.] **19** Bb
Alcántara, Embalse de- **19** Bb
Alcaraz [Sp.] **23** Bb
Alcaudete [Sp.] **21** Cb
Alcázar de San Juan [Sp.]
   21 Ca
Alcira / Alzira [Sp.] **23** Bab
Alcobaça [Port.] **19** ABb
Alcoi / Alcoy [Sp.] **23** Bb
Alcolea del Pinar [Sp.] **17** Bb
Alcoutim [Port.] **21** Bb
Alcoy / Alcoi [Sp.] **23** Bb

Alcúdia [Sp.] **23** CDa
Alderney **9** Ba
Alegranza **23** ins.a
Alehovština [Russia] **61** Ca
Aleksin [Russia] **55** Eb
Aleksinac [Iug.] **41** Db
Álem [Svezia] **75** Dab
Alençon [Fr.] **9** BCa
Alentejo **21** Bb
Aléria [It.] **13** Dbc
Alès [Fr.] **13** Bb
Aleşd [Rom.] **39** Cb
Alessandria [It.] **31** Aab
Alessandria [It.] **31** Aab
Ålesund [Norv.] **73** Ba
Alexandria [Rom.] **49** Ba
Alexandroúpolis [Grecia] **47** Bb
Al Faḥḥ [Tun.] **25** Ab
Alfaro [Sp.] **17** Bab
Alfatar [Bulg.] **49** Ca
Ålgård [Norv.] **73** Ab
Algarve **21** Bb
Algeciras [Sp.] **21** Cbc
Alghero [It.] **29** Ab
Alhama de Granada [Sp.]
   21 Cb
Al Hoceima [Mar.] **21** Cc
Aliağa [Tur.] **45** BCb
Aliákmon **43** Bb
Alibunar [Iug.] **41** CDab
Alicante / Alacant [Sp.] **23** Bb
Alicudi **25** Bb
Alingsås [Svezia] **75** Ca
Alitus / Alytus [Lit.] **57** CDb
Aljezur [Port.] **21** Bb
Aljustrel [Port.] **21** Bb
Alkmaar [P.B.] **7** Ca
Allgäu / Kempten [D] **33** Bb
Allier **11** Bb
Allos [Fr.] **13** Cb
Almada [Port.] **21** ABb
Almadén [Sp.] **21** Cb
Almagro [Sp.] **21** Cab
Al Mahdīyah [Tun.] **25** Ac
Almansa [Sp.] **23** Bab
Al Marsá [Tun.] **25** Ab
Almazán [Sp.] **17** Bb
Almeirim [Port.] **21** Ba
Almelo [P.B.] **7** Da
Almendra, Embalse de- **19** Bb
Almendralejo [Sp.] **21** Bb
Almería [Sp.] **23** Bb
Almirós [Grecia] **43** Bc
Almodôvar [Port.] **21** Bb
Almodóvar del Campo [Sp.]
   21 Cb
Al Muknin [Tun.] **25** Ac
Al Munastīr [Tun.] **25** Ac
Almuñécar [Sp.] **21** Cb
Almuradiel [Sp.] **21** Cb
Alnwick [RU] **3** Da
Alónnisos [Grecia] **43** BCbc
Alónnisos [Grecia] **43** BCb
Alora [Sp.] **21** Cb
Alost / Aalst [Bel.] **7** Cab
Alpalhão [Port.] **21** Ba
Alpen = Alpi (I) **33** BCb
Alpes = Alpi (I) **33** Bb
Alpi **33** Bb
Alpi = Alpen **33** BCb
Alpi (I) = Alpes **33** Bb
Alpi Transilvaniche (I) =
   Carpaţii Meridionali **41** Dab
Al Qayrawān [Tun.] **25** Ac
Als **75** Bb
Alsace = Alsazia (I) **33** Aa
Alsasua / Altsasu [Sp.] **17** Ba
Alsazia (I) = Alsace **33** Aa
Alsfeld [D] **35** Cc
Alsten **71** Cab
Alta [Norv.] **69** Da
Altaelva **69** Da
Altafjorden **69** Da

Altamira, Cuevas de- =
   Altamira, Grotte di- (I) **19** Ca
Altamira, Grotte di- (I) =
   Altamira, Cuevas de- **19** Ca
Altamura [It.] **27** Cb
Altdorf [Svizz.] **33** Ab
Altenburg [D] **35** Dbc
Altenkirchen (Westerwald) [D]
   35 Bc
Altmark / Osterburg [D] **35** Cb
Altmühl **33** Ba
Altötting [D] **33** Ca
Altsasu / Alsasua [Sp.] **17** Ba
Alüksne [Lett.] **55** Ba
Alvdal [Norv.] **73** Ca
Älvdalen [Svezia] **73** Da
Alvesta [Svezia] **75** Cab
Älvkarleby [Svezia] **59** Aa
Álvros [Svezia] **73** Da
Älvsbyn [Svezia] **71** EFb
Alytus / Alitus [Lit.] **57** CDb
Alzira / Alcira [Sp.] **23** Bab
Amadora [Port.] **21** Ab
Åmål [Svezia] **73** Db
Amalfi [It.] **29** Cb
Amaliás [Grecia] **43** Bc
Amantea [It.] **25** Cab
Amarante [Port.] **19** Bb
Amatrice [It.] **29** Ca
Ámbelos, Ákra- **43** BCb
Amberg [D] **33** BCa
Ambert [Fr.] **13** Ba
Amboise [Fr.] **9** Cb
Amburgo (I) = Hamburg [D]
   35 Cb
Ameland **7** Ca
Amersfoort [P.B.] **7** Ca
Amfilokhía [Grecia] **43** Bbc
Ámfissa [Grecia] **45** Ab
Amiens [Fr.] **7** Bb
Amli [Norv.] **73** Bb
Ämmänsaari [Finl.] **63** Ab
Ammarnäs [Svezia] **71** Dab
Amorgós [Grecia] **45** Bb
Amorgós [Grecia] **45** Bb
Åmot [Norv.] **73** Bb
Amsterdam [P.B.] **7** Ca
Amstetten [Aus.] **33** CDab
Anáfi **45** Bb
Anagni [It.] **29** Cb
An Baile Meánach / Ballymena
   [RU] **3** Ba
An Cabhán / Cavan [Eire]
   3 Bab
An Caisleán Nua / Newcastle
   [RU] **3** BCa
An Chathair / Caher [Eire]
   3 Bb
An Cóbh / Cóbh [Eire] **3** Bb
An Daingean / Dingle [Eire]
   3 Ab
Åndalsnes [Norv.] **73** Ba
Andalucía = Andalusia (I)
   21 Cb
Andalusia (I) = Andalucía
   21 Cb
Andenes [Norv.] **69** Ba
Änderalen **69** Ba
Andermatt [Svizz.] **33** Ab
Andernach [D] **7** Db
Andfjorden **69** Ba
Andikíthira = Cerigotto (I)
   45 Abc
Andímilos **45** Bb
Andíparos **45** Bb
Andorra la Vella [And.] **17** Ca
Andover [RU] **5** Cb
Andøya **69** Bab
Andraitx / Andratx [Sp.] **23** Ca
Andratx / Andraitx [Sp.] **23** Ca
Andria [It.] **27** Cb
Andrijevica [Iug.] **41** Cb

Andro (I) = Ándros [Grecia]
   45 Bb
Ándros [Grecia] **45** Bb
Ándros [Grecia] = Andro (I)
   45 Bb
Andselv [Norv.] **69** Cab
Andújar [Sp.] **21** Cb
Aneto, Pico de- **17** Ca
Ånge [Svezia] **73** Ea
Ångelholm [Svezia] **75** Cb
Angermünde [D] **35** Db
Angers [Fr.] **9** Bb
Anglès [Sp.] **17** Cab
Anglesey **5** Ba
Angoulême [Fr.] **15** Ca
Angra do Heoriosmo [Port.]
   21 ins.a
Anholt / Köthen [D] **35** CDb
Anholt **75** Bb
Anina [Rom.] **41** Dab
Anjalankoski [Finl.] **59** DEa
Anklam [D] **35** Dab
An Longfort / Longford [Eire]
   3 Bb
An Muileann gCearr /
   Mullingar [Eire] **3** Bb
Ånn [Svezia] **71** Cb
Annaberg-Buchholz [D] **35** Dc
An Nafīḍah [Tun.] **25** Abc
Annecy [Fr.] **11** BCb
Annenski Most [Russia] **61** Ca
Annonay [Fr.] **13** Ba
An Omaigh / Omagh [RU] **3** Ba
Áno Viánnos [Grecia] **45** Bc
An Ráth / Ráth Luirc [Eire]
   3 Bb
Ansbach [D] **33** Ba
An Sciobairín / Skibbereen
   [Eire] **3** Ab
An Srath Bán / Strabane [RU]
   3 Ba
Antequera [Sp.] **21** Cb
Antibes [Fr.] **13** Cb
An tInbhear Mór / Arklow [Eire]
   3 BCb
an t-Iúr / Newry [RU] **3** Ba
Antopol [R.B.] **53** Aa
Antrim / Aontroim [RU] **3** Ba
An Tulach Mhór / Tullamore
   [Eire] **3** Bb
Antwerpen / Anvers [Bel.] =
   Anversa (I) **7** Ca
Anvers / Antwerpen [Bel.] =
   Anversa (I) **7** Ca
Anversa (I) = Antwerpen /
   Anvers [Bel.] **7** Ca
Anversa (I) = Anvers /
   Antwerpen [Bel.] **7** Ca
Anzio [It.] **29** Cb
Aontroim / Antrim [RU] **3** Ba
Aosta / Aoste [It.] **13** Ca
Aoste / Aosta [It.] **13** Ca
Apatin [Iug.] **41** Ca
Apatity [Russia] **67** Fb
Apeldoorn [P.B.] **7** CDa
Aphrodisias **45** Cb
Apennini **29** Ca
Appenzell [Svizz.] **33** Cb
Apt [Fr.] **13** Cb
Aquileia [It.] **31** Ca
Aracena [Sp.] **21** Cb
Arad [Rom.] **41** Da
Aragón = Aragona (I) **17** Bb
Aragona (I) = Aragón **17** Bb
Aranda de Duero [Sp.] **19** Cb
Arandelovac [Iug.] **41** Cb
Aran Island **3** Aa
Aran Islands **3** Ab
Aranjuez [Sp.] **19** Cb
Arbatax [It.] **29** Bb
Arboga [Svezia] **73** Eb
Arbroath [RU] **1** Db
Arcachon [Fr.] **15** Bb

Arcangelo (I) = Arhangelsk [Russia] **63** Eb
Arciz [Ucr.] **51** Cb
Arda **47** Bb
Árdhas **47** Bb
Ard Mhacha / Armagh [RU] **3** Ba
Ardrossan [RU] **1** Cb
Ardvasar [RU] **1** BCab
Åre [Svezia] **71** Ab
Arenas de San Pedro [Sp.] **19** Cb
Arendal [Norv.] **75** Aa
Arenys de Mar / Arénys de Mar [Sp.] **17** Cb
Arénys de Mar / Arenys de Mar [Sp.] **17** Cb
Areópolis [Grecia] **45** Ab
Arévalo [Sp.] **19** Cb
Arezzo [It.] **31** BCb
Argelès-sur-Mer [Fr.] **17** CDa
Argenta [It.] **31** BCb
Argentan [Fr.] **9** BCa
Argenton-sur-Creuse [Fr.] **9** Cb
Árgos [Grecia] **45** Ab
Argostólion [Grecia] **43** Ac
Arhangelsk [Russia] = Arcangelo (I) **63** Eb
Århus [Dan.] **75** Bb
Ariano Irpino [It.] **27** Cb
Ariège **17** Ca
Årjäng [Svezia] **73** CDb
Arjeplog [Svezia] **71** DEab
Arklow / An tInbhear Mór [Eire] **3** BCb
Arkona, Kap– **35** Da
Arlberg **33** Bb
Arles [Fr.] **13** Bb
Arlon / Aarlen [Bel.] **11** Ba
Armagh / Ard Mhacha [RU] **3** Ba
Arnaía [Grecia] **43** Bb
Arnhem [P.B.] **7** CDa
Arno **31** Bb
Arnøy **69** Ca
Arnstadt [D] **35** Cc
Arona [It.] **31** Aa
Arraiolos [Port.] **21** Bb
Arran, Island of– **1** Cb
Arras [Fr.] **7** Bb
Arrecife [Sp.] **23** ins.a
Års [Dan.] **75** Bb
Árta [Grecia] **43** ABbc
Artá / Artà [Sp.] **23** Da
Artà / Artá [Sp.] **23** Da
Artesa de Segre [Sp.] **17** Cab
Arucas [Sp.] **23** ins.a
Arvidsjaur [Svezia] **71** Eb
Arvika [Svezia] **73** Db
Arzúa [Sp.] **19** Ba
Asarna [Svezia] **73** Da
Aschaffenburg [D] **33** ABa
Aschersleben [D] **35** Cb
Ascoli Piceno [It.] **29** Ca
Åseda [Svezia] **75** Dab
Åsele [Svezia] **71** Eb
Asenovgrad [Bulg.] **47** Bab
Ashford [RU] **5** Dbc
Asiago [It.] **31** Ba
Asikkala [Finl.] **59** Da
Asilah [Mar.] **21** BCc
Asinara [It.] **29** Ab
Asinara [It.] **29** Ab
Askersund [Svezia] **73** DEb
Askim [Norv.] **73** Cb
Askja **77** Db
Askvoll [Norv.] **73** Aa
Aspromonte **25** Cb
Assen [P.B.] **7** Da
Assens [Dan.] **75** Bb
Assia (I) = Hessen **35** Cc
Assisi [It.] **29** Ca

Assos **47** Bb
Astakós [Grecia] **43** ABc
Asti [It.] **31** Aab
Astipálaia [Grecia] **45** Bb
Astipálaia [Grecia] **45** Bb
Astorga [Sp.] **19** BCa
Atalándi [Grecia] **45** Ab
Atene (I) = Athínai [Grecia] **45** Ab
Athínai [Grecia] = Atene (I) **45** Ab
Athlone / Baile Átha Luain [Eire] **3** Bb
Áthos **47** Bb
Atienza [Sp.] **17** Bb
Atlanteren = Atlantico, Oceano– (I) **71** ABab
Atlántico, Océano– = Atlantico, Oceano– (I) **19** Aa
Atlántico, Oceano– = Atlantico, Oceano– (I) **19** Ab
Atlantico, Oceano– (I) = Atlanteren **71** ABab
Atlántico, Oceano– (I) = Atlántico, Océano– **19** Ab
Atlántico, Océano– (I) = Atlántico, Oceano– **19** Aa
Atlantico, Oceano– (I) = Atlantic Ocean **1** ABa
Atlantico, Oceano– (I) = Atlantique, Océan– **15** ABa
Atlantic Ocean = Atlantico, Oceano– (I) **1** ABa
Atlantique, Océan– = Atlantico, Oceano– (I) **15** ABa
Ätran **75** Ca
Åtvidaberg [Svezia] **75** Da
Aubagne [Fr.] **13** Bb
Aube **11** Ba
Aubenas [Fr.] **13** Bb
Aubigny-sur-Nère [Fr.] **9** Cb
Aubusson [Fr.] **15** Ca
Auch [Fr.] **15** Cb
Aude **17** Ca
Audenarde / Oudenaarde [Bel.] **7** Cab
Audierne [Fr.] **9** Aab
Aue [D] **35** Dc
Augsburg [D] = Augusta (I) **33** Ba
Augusta [It.] **25** Cb
Augusta (I) = Augsburg [D] **33** Ba
Augustów [Pol.] **57** Cbc
Aukštaitija **57** Db
Aulla [It.] **31** Bb
Aumale [Fr.] **9** Ca
Aure [Norv.] **71** Ab
Aurich [D] **35** Bb
Aurillac [Fr.] **15** Cab
Aurlandsvangen [Norv.] **73** Ba
Austvågøy **69** Ab
Autun [Fr.] **11** Bb
Auxerre [Fr.] **11** Bb
Avallon [Fr.] **11** Bb
Aveiro [Port.] **19** Bb
Avellino [It.] **29** Cb
Aven Armand **13** Bb
Averøya **73** Ba
Aversa [It.] **29** Cb
Avesnes-sur-Helpe [Fr.] **7** Cb
Avesta [Svezia] **73** Ea
Aveyron **15** Cb
Avezzano [It.] **29** Cab
Avignon [Fr.] = Avignone (I) **13** Bb
Avignone (I) = Avignon [Fr.] **13** Bb
Ávila [Sp.] **19** Cb
Avilés [Sp.] **19** Ca
Avis [Port.] **21** Bab
Avranches [Fr.] **9** Ba
Axarfjörður **77** Da

Axiós **43** Bb
Ax-les-Thermes [Fr.] **17** Ca
Aydın [Tur.] **45** Cb
Ayerbe [Sp.] **17** Ba
Áyion Óros **47** Bb
Áyios Evstrátios **47** Bb
Áyios Kírikos [Grecia] **45** Bb
Áyios Nikólaos [Grecia] **45** Bc
Ayora [Sp.] **23** Bab
Ayr [RU] **3** Ca
Ayvacık [Tur.] **47** Bb
Ayvalık [Tur.] **47** Bb
Azahar, Costa del– **17** BCb
Azaila [Sp.] **17** Bb
Azambuja [Port.] **21** ABab
Azay–le–Rideau [Fr.] **9** Cb
Azpeitia [Sp.] **17** Ba
Azur, Côte d'– = Azzurra, Costa– (I) **13** Cb
Azzorre, Arcipelago delle– (I) = Açores, Arquipélago dos– **21** ins.a
Azzurra, Costa– (I) = Azur, Côte d'– **13** Cb

B

Baba Burun **47** Bb
Babadag [Rom.] **49** Ca
Babaeski [Tur.] **47** BCb
Babia Góra **39** Ba*
Bacău [Rom.] **51** BCb
Baccarat [Fr.] **11** Ca
Bačka Palanka [Iug.] **41** Ca
Bačka Topola [Iug.] **41** Ca
Bäckefors [Svezia] **73** CDb
Bačkovski Manastir **47** Bab
Bácsalmás [Ung.] **41** Ca
Badajoz [Sp.] **21** Bab
Badalona [Sp.] **17** Cb
Bad Aussee [Aus.] **33** Cb
Bad Doberan [D] **35** CDab
Baden [Aus.] **39** Aab
Baden [Svizz.] **33** Ab
Baden–Baden [D] **33** Aa
Badgastein [Aus.] **33** Cb
Bad Hall [Aus.] **33** Cab
Bad Hersfeld [D] **35** Cbc
Bad Homburg von der Höhe [D] **33** Aa
Bad Ischl [Aus.] **33** Cb
Bad Kissingen [D] **33** Ba
Bad Kreuznach [D] **33** Aa
Bad Mergentheim [D] **33** Ba
Bad Muskau [D] **35** Db
Bad Neustadt an der Saale [D] **35** Cc
Bad Ragaz [Svizz.] **33** Bb
Bad Reichenhall [D] **33** Cb
Bad Segeberg [D] **35** Cab
Bad Tölz [D] **33** Bb
Baena [Sp.] **21** Cb
Baeza [Sp.] **21** Cb
Bagenkop [Dan.] **35** Ca
Bagheria [It.] **25** Bb
Bagn [Norv.] **73** Ca
Bagnères-de-Bigorre [Fr.] **17** BCa
Bagnères-de-Luchon [Fr.] **17** Ca
Bagni di Lucca [It.] **31** Bb
Bagno di Romagna [It.] **31** BCb
Bagnoles-de-l'Orne [Fr.] **9** Ba
Bagrationovsk [Russia] **57** Bb
Bahuşi [Rom.] **51** Bb
Baia Mare [Rom.] **39** Cb
Baile an Chaistil / Ballycastle [RU] **3** Ba
Baile an Róba / Ballinrobe [Eire] **3** Ab

Baile Átha Cliath / Dublin [RU] = Dublino (I) **3** Bb
Baile Átha Luain / Athlone [Eire] **3** Bb
Bäileşti [Rom.] **49** Aa
Băile Tuşnad [Rom.] **51** Bb
Bain-de-Bretagne [Fr.] **9** Bb
Baiona / Bayona [Sp.] **19** ABab
Baixo Alentejo / Torrão [Port.] **21** Bb
Baja [Ung.] **41** Ca
Bakkaflói **77** Ea
Balaguer [Sp.] **17** Cb
Balassagyarmat [Ung.] **39** Bab
Balaton = Balaton, Lago– (I) **39** Ab
Balaton, Lago– (I) = Balaton **39** Ab
Balatonfüred [Ung.] **39** ABb
Balatonkeresztúr [Ung.] **39** Ab
Balcani (I) = Stara Planina **49** ABa
Balčik [Bulg.] **49** Ca
Baleares, Islas– **23** CDa
Balıkesir [Tur.] **47** Cb
Balkan **49** Ba
Ballagen [Norv.] **69** Bb
Ballina / Béal an Átha [Eire] **3** Aab
Ballinasloe [Eire] **3** Bb
Ballinrobe / Baile an Róba [Eire] **3** Ab
Ballycastle / Baile an Chaistil [RU] **3** Ba
Ballygawley [RU] **3** Ba
Ballyhaunis [Eire] **3** Bb
Ballymena / An Baile Meánach [RU] **3** Ba
Balmazújváros [Ung.] **39** Cb
Balmoral Castle **3** Cab
Balta [Ucr.] **51** Cab
Baltasound [RU] **1** ins.a
Bălţi [Mold.] **51** Cb
Baltico, Mar– (I) = Baltijas jūra **57** Bab
Baltico, Mar– (I) = Baltijos jura **57** Bab
Baltico, Mar– (I) = Baltijskoje more **75** Db
Baltico, Mar– (I) = Balti meri **59** BCb
Baltico, Mar– (I) = Bałtyckie, Morze– **57** ABb
Baltico, Mar– (I) = Itämeri **59** BCb
Baltico, Mar– (I) = Östersjön **75** Dab
Baltico, Mar– (I) = Østersøen **75** Cb
Baltico, Mar– (I) = Ostsee **75** Cb
Baltijas jūra = Baltico, Mar– (I) **57** Bab
Baltijos jura = Baltico, Mar– (I) **57** Bab
Baltijsk [Russia] **57** Bb
Baltijskoje more = Baltico, Mar– (I) **75** Db
Balti meri = Baltico, Mar– (I) **59** BCb
Bałtyckie, Morze– = Baltico, Mar– (I) **57** ABb
Balya [Tur.] **47** Cb
Bamberg [D] **33** Ba
Banat = Banato (I) **41** CDa
Banato (I) = Banat **41** CDa
Banaz [Tur.] **47** Cc
Banbury [RU] **5** Cb
Bande [Sp.] **19** Bab
Bandırma [Tur.] **47** Cb
Banff [RU] **1** Da
Bangor [RU] **5** Bb
Bangor / Beannchar [RU] **3** Ca

Banja Luka [Bos.Erz.] **41** Bb
Bann **3** Ba
Banská Bystrica [Slovac.] **39** Ba
Banská Štiavnica [Slovac.] **39** Ba
Bantry / Beanntraí [Eire] **3** Ab
Banzart [Tun.] **25** Ab
Bar [Iug.] **41** Cb
Baradla **39** Bab
Baranoviči [R.B.] **53** Aa
Barbastro [Sp.] **17** BCab
Barbate de Franco [Sp.] **21** BCb
Barbezieux–Saint–Hilaire [Fr.] **15** BCa
Barcellona (I) = Barcelona [Sp.] **17** Cb
Barcellona Pozzo di Gotto [It.] **25** Cb
Barcelona [Sp.] = Barcellona (I) **17** Cb
Barcelonnette [Fr.] **13** Cb
Barcelos [Port.] **19** Bb
Barcs [Ung.] **41** Ba
Bárðarbunga **77** Db
Bardejov [Slovac.] **39** Ca
Bardonecchia [It.] **13** Cab
Barencevo mcre = Barents, Mare di– (I) **67** EFa
Barents, Mare di– (I) = Barencevo more **67** EFa
Barents, Mare di– (I) = Barentshavet **67** EFa
Barentshavet = Barents, Mare di– (I) **67** EFa
Barfleur, Pointe de– **9** Ba
Bari [It.] **27** Cb
Barika [Alg.] **23** Dc
Bar–le–Duc [Fr.] **11** Ba
Barletta [It.] **27** Cb
Barlovento [Sp.] **23** ins.a
Barnard Castle [RU] **3** Da
Barneville-Carteret–Carteret [Fr.] **9** Ba
Barnstaple [RU] **5** Bbc
Barra **1** Bab
Barrancos [Port.] **21** Bb
Barreiro [Port.] **21** ABb
Barrow **3** Ba
Barrow-in-Furness [RU] **3** Cab
Barry [RU] **5** Bb
Bar-sur-Aube [Fr.] **11** Ba
Bar-sur-Seine [Fr.] **11** Bab
Bartoszyce [Pol.] **57** Bb
Basel [Svizz.] = Basilea (I) **33** Ab
Basilea (I) = Basel [Svizz.] **33** Ab
Basingstoke [RU] **5** Cb
Baška Voda [Cro.] **41** Bb
Bassano del Grappa [It.] **31** Ba
Båstad [Svezia] **75** Cb
Bastenaken / Bastogne [Bel.] **7** Cab
Bastia [Fr.] **13** Db
Bastogne / Bastenaken [Bel.] **7** Cab
Bastuträsk [Svezia] **71** Eb
Batak [Bulg.] **47** Bab
Batalha [Port.] **19** ABb
Batecki [Russia] **61** Bb
Bath [RU] **5** Cb
Båtsfjord [Norv.] **69** Fa
Battipaglia [It.] **29** CDb
Baugé [Fr.] **9** BCb
Bauska [Lett.] **57** Bb
Bautzen / Budyšin [D] **35** Db
Baviera (I) = Bayern **33** Ba
Bayern = Baviera (I) **33** Ba
Bayeux [Fr.] **9** Ba
Bayındır [Tur.] **45** Cb

Bayona / Baiona [Sp.] **19** ABab
Bayonne [Fr.] **17** Ba
Bayreuth [D] **33** Ba
Baza [Sp.] **23** Bb
Béal an Átha / Ballina [Eire] **3** Aab
Béal Feirste / Belfast [RU] **3** Ca
Beannchar / Bangor [RU] **3** Ca
Beanntraí / Bantry [Eire] **3** Ab
Beaugency [Fr.] **9** Cb
Beaune [Fr.] **11** Bb
Beauvais [Fr.] **9** Ca
Beauvoir-sur-Mer [Fr.] **9** Bb
Bečej [Iug.] **41** Cab
Becerreá [Sp.] **19** Ba
Bechet [Rom.] **49** ABa
Beclean [Rom.] **51** Bb
Bedford [RU] **5** Cb
Beelitz [D] **35** Db
Beeskow [D] **35** Db
Begna **73** Ca
Begoml [R.B.] **55** Bb
Beiarn [Norv.] **69** Ab
Beiuş [Rom.] **39** Cb
Beja [Port.] **21** Bb
Béjaïa [Alg.] **23** Db
Béjaïa, Golfe de– **23** Db
Béjar [Sp.] **19** Cb
Békés [Ung.] **39** BCb
Békéscsaba [Ung.] **39** BCb
Bela Crkva [Iug.] **41** Dab
Belaja Cerkov [Ucr.] **53** BCb
Bela Palanka [Iug.] **41** Dab
Belev [Russia] **55** DEc
Belfast / Béal Feirste [RU] **3** Ca
Belfort [Fr.] **11** Cb
Belgorod–Dnestrovski [Ucr.] **51** Db
Belgrado (I) = Beograd [Iug.] **41** Cb
Beli Manastir [Cro.] **41** Ca
Bellagio [It.] **31** Ba
Bellegarde-sur-Valserine [Fr.] **11** Bb
Belle Ile **9** Ba
Belley [Fr.] **13** Ba
Bellinzona [Svizz.] **31** Ba
Belluno [It.] **31** Ca
Belmonte [Sp.] **23** Ba
Belmullet [Eire] **3** Aa
Belogradčik [Bulg.] **41** Db
Beloje more = Bianco, Mar– (I) **63** DEab
Beloje ozero = Bianco, Lago– (I) **61** Da
Belomorsk [Russia] **63** Cb
Belovežskaja Pušča **37** CDb
Belozersk [Russia] **61** Dab
Beluša [Slovac.] **39** Ba
Bely [Russia] **55** CDb
Belyniči [R.B.] **55** Bbc
Benabarre / Benavarri [Sp.] **17** Cab
Benasc / Benasque [Sp.] **17** Ca
Benasque / Benasc [Sp.] **17** Ca
Benavarri / Benabarre [Sp.] **17** Cab
Benavente [Sp.] **19** Cab
Benbecula **1** Ba
Benešov [Rep.Ceca] **33** Ca
Benevento [It.] **29** Cb
Bengtsfors [Svezia] **73** Db
Benidorm [Sp.] **23** BCb
Benkovac [Cro.] **41** Bb
Beograd [Iug.] = Belgrado (I) **41** Cb
Berati [Alb.] **43** Ab
Berchtesgaden **33** Cb
Berchtesgaden [D] **33** Cb
Berck–Plage [Fr.] **5** Dc
Berdičev [Ucr.] **53** Bb
Beregovo [Ucr.] **39** Ca

Berettyóújfalu [Ung.] **39** Cb
Bereza [R.B.] **53** Aa
Berezan [Ucr.] **53** Cb
Berezina **53** Ba
Berga [Sp.] **17** Cab
Bergama [Tur.] **47** Cb
Bergamo [It.] **31** Ba
Bergby [Svezia] **59** Aa
Bergen [Norv.] **73** Aa
Bergen / Mons [Bel.] **7** Cb
Bergen / Rügen [D] **35** Da
Bergen op Zoom [P.B.] **7** Ca
Bergerac [Fr.] **15** Cab
Berkåk [Norv.] **73** Ca
Berkovica [Bulg.] **49** Aa
Berlengas, Ilhas– **21** Aa
Berlevåg [Norv.] **69** Fa
Berlin [D] = Berlino (I) **35** Db
Berlino (I) = Berlin [D] **35** Db
Bern / Berne [Svizz.] = Berna (I) **33** Ab
Berna (I) = Bern / Berne [Svizz.] **33** Ab
Berna (I) = Berne / Bern [Svizz.] **33** Ab
Bernau bei Berlin [D] **35** Db
Bernay [Fr.] **9** Ca
Bernburg / Saale [D] **35** Cb
Berne / Bern [Svizz.] = Berna (I) **33** Ab
Bernina **33** Bb
Beroun [Rep.Ceca] **33** Ca
Bersenbrück [D] **35** Bb
Berwick-upon-Tweed [RU] **1** Db
Besançon [Fr.] **11** BCb
Betancuria [Sp.] **23** ins.a
Betanzos [Sp.] **19** Ba
Béthune [Fr.] **7** Bb
Beverley [RU] **5** Cb
Beykoz [Tur.] **47** Cb
Bežeck [Russia] **61** Db
Béziers [Fr.] **17** Ba
Biała Podlaska [Pol.] **37** Cb
Białobrzegi [Pol.] **37** BCb
Białogard [Pol.] **37** Aa
Białowieża [Pol.] **37** Cb
Białowieża [Pol.] **37** CDb
Białystok [Pol.] **37** Cb
Bianco, Lago– (I) = Beloje ozero **61** Da
Bianco, Mar– (I) = Beloje more **63** DEab
Bianco, Monte– **13** Ca
Bianco, Monte– (I) = Blanc, Mont– **13** Ca
Biarritz [Fr.] **17** Ba
Biberach an der Riß [D] **33** Bab
Bicaz [Rom.] **51** Bb
Bideford [RU] **5** Bbc
Biebrza **37** Cb
Biel / Bienne [Svizz.] **11** Cb
Bielefeld [D] **35** Bb
Biella [It.] **31** Aa
Bielsko-Biała [Pol.] **39** Ba
Bielsk Podlaski [Pol.] **37** Cb
Bienne / Biel [Svizz.] **11** Cb
Bieszczady **39** Ca
Biga [Tur.] **47** Cb
Bigadiç [Tur.] **47** Cb
Bihać [Cro.] **41** Bb
Bijeljina [Bos.Erz.] **41** Cb
Bijelo Polje [Iug.] **41** Cb
Bilbao / Bilbo [Sp.] **17** ABa
Bilbo / Bilbao [Sp.] **17** ABa
Bileća [Bos.Erz.] **41** Cb
Bilecik [Tur.] **47** Cb
Biłgoraj [Pol.] **37** Cc
Bilto [Norv.] **69** Da
Bingen [D] **33** Aa
Biograd na Moru [Cro.] **41** Bb
Biogradska Gora **41** Cb
Biorra / Birr [Eire] **3** Bb

Birkeland [Norv.] **75** Aa
Birkenhead [RU] **5** BCb
Bîrlad [Rom.] **51** Cb
Birmingham [RU] **5** Cb
Birr / Biorra [Eire] **3** Bb
Birsay [RU] **1** Ca
Birżai / Biržai [Lit.] **57** Db
Biržaj / Biržai [Lit.] **57** Db
Biscaglia, Golfo di– (I) = Vizcaya, Golfo de– **15** Bb
Bishop's Stortford [RU] **5** Cbb
Biskupiec [Pol.] **57** BCbc
Bistrița [Rom.] **51** Bb
Bitburg [D] **7** Db
Bitola [Maced.] **43** Bb
Bitonto [It.] **27** Cb
Bitterfeld [D] **35** Db
Bitti [It.] **29** Bb
Bjala [Bulg.] **49** Ba
Bjargtangar **77** Ab
Bjelovar [Cro.] **41** Ba
Bjerkvik [Norv.] **69** Bb
Björköby [Finl.] **65** Cb
Björna [Svezia] **71** Eb
Björneborg / Pori [Finl.] **59** Ca
Bjørnevatn [Norv.] **69** Fa
Bjurholm [Svezia] **71** Eb
Blackburn [RU] **5** Cb
Blackpool [RU] **5** Bb
Blackwater **3** ABb
Blagojevgrad [Bulg.] **43** Bab
Blaj [Rom.] **51** ABb
Blågungfrun **75** Da
Blanc, Mont– = Bianco, Monte– (I) **13** Ca
Blanca, Costa– **23** Bb
Blanes [Sp.] **17** Cb
Blankenberge [Bel.] **7** Ca
Blansko [Rep.Ceca] **39** Aa
Blattnicksele [Svezia] **71** Db
Blåvands Huk **75** Ab
Blaye [Fr.] **15** Bab
Bled [Slo.] **33** Cb
Blois [Fr.] **9** Cb
Blönduós [Isl.] **77** Cb
Blyth [RU] **5** Cb
Bø [Norv.] **69** Ab
Bobbio [It.] **31** Bb
Bobolice [Pol.] **37** Aab
Bobrovica [Ucr.] **53** Cb
Bobrowniki [Pol.] **37** CDb
Bobrujsk [R.B.] **53** Ba
Bocholt [D] **7** Da
Bochum [D] **7** Da
Bocognano [Fr.] **13** CDbc
Boden [Svezia] **65** Cb
Bodensee = Costanza, Lago di– (I) **33** Bb
Bodmin [RU] **5** Bc
Bodø [Norv.] **69** Ab
Bodrum [Tur.] **45** Cb
Boglärlelle [Ung.] **39** Ab
Bognes [Norv.] **69** Bb
Böhmerwald = Selva Boema (I) **33** Ca
Böhönye [Ung.] **39** Ab
Boknafjorden **73** Ab
Bol [Cro.] **41** Bb
Bolbec [Fr.] **9** Ca
Bolesławiec [Pol.] **37** Ab
Bolgrad [Ucr.] **51** Cb
Boliden [Svezia] **71** Eb
Boljevac [Iug.] **41** Db
Bollnäs [Svezia] **59** Aa
Bologna [It.] **31** Bb
Bolšaja Berestovica [R.B.] **37** Db
Bolsena [It.] **29** BCa
Bolsena, Lago–di (I) **29** BCa
Bolšoj Klimecki, ostrov– **61** Ca
Bolton [RU] **5** Cb
Bolungarvik [Isl.] **77** Bab
Bolva **55** Dc

Bolzano / Bozen [It.] **33** Bb
Bømlo **73** Ab
Bon, Capo– (I) = Ţib, Ra's aţ– **25** Ab
Bonifacio [Fr.] **13** Dc
Bonifacio, Bocche di– **29** ABb
Bonn [D] **7** Db
Bonnåsjøen [Norv.] **69** Bb
Bono [It.] **29** ABb
Bor [Iug.] **41** Db
Bor [Rep.Ceca] **33** Ca
Borås [Svezia] **75** Ca
Borba [Port.] **21** Bb
Bordeaux [Fr.] **15** Bb
Bordighera [It.] **31** Ab
Bordj Bou Arreridj [Alg.] **23** Dbc
Bordø **75** ins.a
Borgå / Porvoo [Finl.] **59** Da
Borgafjäll [Svezia] **71** CDb
Borgarnes [Isl.] **77** Bb
Børgefjell **71** Cb
Borgholm [Svezia] **75** Dab
Borgogna (I) = Bourgogne **11** Bb
Borgomanero [It.] **31** Aa
Borgo Val di Taro [It.] **31** Bb
Borisov [R.B.] **55** Bb
Borispol [Ucr.] **53** Cb
Borjas Blancas [Sp.] **17** Cb
Borken [D] **7** Da
Borkum **7** Da
Borlänge [Svezia] **73** Ea
Bormio [It.] **33** Bb
Borna [D] **35** Dbc
Bornholm **75** Db
Borodinskoje [Russia] **61** Aa
Borodjanka [Ucr.] **53** BCb
Borovan [Bulg.] **49** Aa
Boroviči [Russia] **61** Cb
Borşa [Rom.] **51** Bb
Børselv [Norv.] **69** Ea
Bort-les-Orgues [Fr.] **15** Ca
Bosa Marina [It.] **29** Ab
Bosanska Dubica [Bos.Erz.] **41** Ba
Bosanska Gradiška [Bos.Erz.] **41** Bab
Bosanska Krupa [Bos.Erz.] **41** Bab
Bosanski Brod [Bos.Erz.] **41** BCab
Bosanski Novi [Bos.Erz.] **41** Bab
Bosanski Petrovac [Bos.Erz.] **41** Bb
Bosanski Šamac [Bos.Erz.] **41** Cab
Bosansko Grahovo [Bos.Erz.] **41** Bb
Bosforo (I) = İstambul boğazı **47** Cb
Bosna **41** Cab
Boston [RU] **5** CDb
Botev **49** Ba
Botevgrad [Bulg.] **49** Aa
Botngard [Norv.] **73** Bb
Botnia, Golfo di– (I) = Bottniska viken **71** BCbc
Botnia, Golfo di– (I) = Pohjanlahti **65** BCbc
Botoşani [Rom.] **51** Bb
Botrange **7** CDb
Botsmark [Svezia] **71** Eb
Bottniska viken = Botnia, Golfo di– (I) **71** BCbc
Bouillon [Bel.] **11** Ba
Boulogne-sur-Mer [Fr.] **5** Dc
Bourbonne-les-Bains [Fr.] **11** Bab
Bourganeuf [Fr.] **15** Ca
Bourg-en-Bresse [Fr.] **11** Bb
Bourges [Fr.] **9** Cb

Bourg Madame [Fr.] **17** Ca
Bourgogne = Borgogna (I) **11** Bb
Bourg-St.-Maurice [Fr.] **13** Ca
Bournemouth [RU] **5** Cc
Bovec [Slo.] **33** Cb
Boyle / Mainistir na Búille [Eire] **3** Bab
Boyne **3** Bb
Bozcaada **47** Bb
Bozdoğan [Tur.] **45** Cb
Bozen / Bolzano [It.] **33** Bb
Bra [It.] **31** Ab
Brač **41** Bb
Bracciano, Lago di– **29** Cab
Bräcke [Svezia] **73** Ea
Brad [Rom.] **51** Ba
Bradford [RU] **5** Cb
Braemar [RU] **1** Cab
Braga [Port.] **19** Bb
Bragança [Port.] **19** Bb
Brahestad / Raahe [Finl.] **65** Cb
Bräila [Rom.] **51** Cb
Brandbu [Norv.] **73** Ca
Brandeburgo (I) = Brandenburg **35** Db
Brandenburg / Havel [D] **35** Db
Brandenburg = Brandeburgo (I) **35** Db
Braniewo [Pol.] **57** Bb
Brańsk [Pol.] **37** Cb
Brantôme [Fr.] **15** Ca
Braslav [R.B.] **55** Bb
Braşov [Rom.] **51** Bb
Bratislava [Slovac.] **39** Aa
Braunau am Inn [Aus.] **33** Ca
Braunschweig [D] **35** Cb
Brava, Costa– **17** CDb
Bray / Brè [Eire] **3** BCb
Bray Head **3** Ab
Brčko [Bos.Erz.] **41** Cab
Brè / Bray [Eire] **3** BCb
Břeclav [Rep.Ceca] **39** Aa
Brecon [RU] **5** Bb
Brecon Beacons **5** Bb
Breda [P.B.] **7** Ca
Bregenz [Aus.] **33** Bb
Breiðafjörður **77** Bb
Breivikeidet [Norv.] **69** Ca
Brekken [Norv.] **73** CDa
Brekstad [Norv.] **73** Ca
Brema (I) = Bremen [D] **35** Bb
Bremangerlandet **73** Aa
Bremen [D] = Brema (I) **35** Bb
Bremerhaven [D] **35** Bb
Brennero, Passo del– **33** Bb
Brennero, Passo del– (I) = Brennerpaß **33** Bb
Brennerpaß = Brennero, Passo del– (I) **33** Bb
Brenta **31** Ba
Brescia [It.] **31** Ba
Breslavia (I) = Wrocław [Pol.] **37** Abc
Bressanone / Brixen [It.] **33** Bb
Bressay **1** ins.a
Bressuire [Fr.] **9** Bb
Brest [Fr.] **9** Bb
Brest [R.B.] **37** Cb
Bretagna (I) = Bretagne **9** ABab
Bretagne = Bretagna (I) **9** ABab
Breuil-Cervinia, Valtournenche– [It.] **31** Aa
Brežice [Slo.] **41** Ba
Brezno [Slovac.] **39** Ba
Briançon [Fr.] **13** Ba
Briceni [Mold.] **51** BCa
Bridgwater [RU] **5** Bb
Bridlington [RU] **5** Dab
Bridport [RU] **5** Cc
Brienne-le-Château [Fr.] **11** Ba
Brig [Svizz.] **31** Aa

Brighton [RU] **5** CDbc
Brignoles [Fr.] **13** BCb
Brindisi [It.] **27** CDb
Brioude [Fr.] **13** Ba
Bristol [RU] **5** Cb
Bristol, Canale di– (I) = Bristol
  Channel **5** Bb
Bristol Channel = Bristol,
  Canale di– (I) **5** Bb
Brive–la–Gaillarde [Fr.] **15** Cab
Briviesca [Sp.] **19** Ca
Brixen / Bressanone [It.] **33** Bb
Brjansk [Russia] **53** Da
Brno [Rep.Ceca] **39** Aa
Brodick [RU] **1** Cb
Brodnica [Pol.] **37** Bb
Brody [Ucr.] **53** Ab
Brønderslev [Dan.] **75** Ba
Brønnøysund [Norv.] **71** Cb
Brora [RU] **1** Ca
Brósarp [Svezia] **75** Cb
Brough [RU] **3** Da
Brovary [Ucr.] **53** Cb
Brozas [Sp.] **19** Bb
Bruchsal [D] **33** Aa
Bruck an der Leitha [Aus.]
  39 Aab
Bruck an der Mur [Aus.] **33** Cb
Bruges / Brugge [Bel.] **7** Ca
Brugge / Bruges [Bel.] **7** Ca
Bruneck / Brunico [It.] **33** BCb
Brunflo [Svezia] **71** Cbc
Brunico / Bruneck [It.] **33** BCb
Brunkeberg [Norv.] **73** Bb
Bruntál [Rep.Ceca] **39** Aa
Brussel / Bruxelles [Bel.] **7** Ca
Bruxelles / Brussel [Bel.] **7** Ca
Brzeg [Pol.] **37** Abc
Bučač [Ucr.] **51** Ba
Bucarest (I) = Bucureşti [Rom.]
  49 Ba
Bucegi **51** Bb
Buchen (Odenwald) [D] **33** Ba
Bucureşti [Rom.] = Bucarest (I)
  49 Ba
Bud [Norv.] **73** Ba
Budapest [Ung.] **39** Bb
Búðardalur [Isl.] **77** Bb
Bude [RU] **5** Bc
Budeşti [Rom.] **49** Ba
Budva [Iug.] **41** Cb
Budyšin / Bautzen [D] **35** Db
Bug **37** Cb
Bug Meridionale (I) = Južny
  Bug **51** Db
Bugojno [Bos.Erz.] **41** Bb
Bujaraloz [Sp.] **17** BCb
Buje [Cro.] **31** Ca
Bükk **39** Bab
Buldan [Tur.] **45** Cb
Bulle [Svizz.] **11** Cb
Bunbeg [Eire] **3** Ba
Buncrana [Eire] **3** Ba
Bun Dobhráin / Bundoran [Eire]
  3 Ba
Bundoran / Bun Dobhráin [Eire]
  3 Ba
Bureå [Svezia] **65** Cb
Burfjord [Norv.] **69** Da
Burgas [Bulg.] **49** Ca
Burg bei Magdeburg [D]
  35 CDb
Burglengenfeld [D] **33** BCa
Burgos [Sp.] **19** Ca
Burgsvik [Svezia] **57** Bab
Burhaniye [Tur.] **47** BCb
Burnley [RU] **5** Cb
Burreli [Alb.] **43** Ab
Bursa [Tur.] **47** Cb
Burton–upon–Trent [RU] **5** Cb
Burwick [RU] **1** CDa
Bury Saint Edmunds [RU] **5** Cb
Busk [Ucr.] **39** Da

Busko–Zdrój [Pol.] **37** Bc
Busto Arsizio [It.] **31** ABa
Butera [It.] **25** Bb
Buthrotum **43** Ab
Büyük Menderes **45** Cb
Buzău [Rom.] **51** Cb
Buzău [Rom.] **51** Bc
Bydgoszcz [Pol.] **37** ABb
Bygdeå [Svezia] **71** EFb
Bygdin [Norv.] **73** Ba
Bygland [Norv.] **73** Bb
Bykle [Norv.] **73** Bb
Bytom [Pol.] **37** Bc
Bytów [Pol.] **37** Aa
Byxelkrok [Svezia] **75** Da

C

Cabeza de Buey [Sp.] **21** Cb
Cabrera, Isla– **23** CDab
Čačak [Iug.] **41** Cb
Caccia, Capo– **29** Ab
Cáceres [Sp.] **21** Ba
Čadca [Slovac.] **39** Ba
Cadice (I) = Cádiz [Sp.] **21** Bb
Cadice, Golfo di– (I) = Cádiz,
  Golfo de– **21** Bb
Cádiz [Sp.] = Cadice (I) **21** Bb
Cádiz, Golfo de– = Cadice,
  Golfo di– (I) **21** Bb
Caen [Fr.] **9** Ba
Caernarfon [RU] **5** Bb
Cagliari [It.] **29** Bb
Cagnes–sur–Mer [Fr.] **13** Ca
Caher / An Chathair [Eire] **3** Bb
Cahersiveen / Cathair
  Saidhbhín [Eire] **3** Ab
Cahors [Fr.] **15** Cb
Cahul [Mold.] **51** Cb
Cairo Montenotte [It.] **31** Ab
Caiseal / Cashel [Eire] **3** Bb
Caisleán an Bharraigh /
  Castlebar [Eire] **3** Aab
Čakor **41** Cb
Čakovec [Cro.] **39** Aa
Calabria **25** Ca
Calafat [Rom.] **49** Ba
Calahorra [Sp.] **17** Ba
Calais [Fr.] **5** Dbc
Calais, Pas de– = Calais, Passo
  di– (I) **5** Dbc
Calais, Passo di– (I) = Calais,
  Pas de– **5** Dbc
Calamocha [Sp.] **17** Bb
Călăraşi [Mold.] **51** Cb
Călăraşi [Rom.] **49** Ca
Cala Ratjada [Sp.] **23** Da
Calatayud [Sp.] **17** Bb
Calcide (I) = Khálki **45** Cb
Caldas da Rainha [Port.]
  21 ABa
Caldera de Taburiente **23** ins.a
Călimăneşti [Rom.] **51** Bb
Čalna [Russia] **61** Ca
Calp / Calpe [Sp.] **23** BCb
Calpe / Calp [Sp.] **23** BCb
Caltagirone [It.] **25** Bb
Caltanissetta [It.] **25** Bb
Calvi [Fr.] **13** Cb
Camarat, Cap– **13** Cb
Camariñas [Sp.] **19** Aa
Cambados [Sp.] **19** Ba
Cambo–les–Bains [Fr.] **17** Ba
Cambrai [Fr.] **7** Cb
Cambridge [RU] **5** CDb
Camenca [Mold.] **51** Cab
Camerino [It.] **29** Ca
Caminha [Port.] **19** ABab
Campbeltown [RU] **3** Ca
Campillos [Sp.] **21** Cb
Campobasso [It.] **29** Cb

Çan [Tur.] **47** BCb
Cañadas del Teide **23** ins.a
Çanakkale [Tur.] **47** Bb
Çanakkale bogazı = Dardanelli (I)
  47 Bb
Canale, Isole del– (I) = Channel
  Islands **9** Ba
Canarias, Islas– = Canarie,
  Isole– (I) **23** ins.a
Canarie, Isole– (I) = Canarias,
  Islas– **23** ins.a
Cañaveras [Sp.] **17** Bb
Canazei [It.] **33** Bb
Cañete [Sp.] **23** Ba
Cangas de Narcea [Sp.] **19** Ba
Cangas de Onís [Sp.] **19** Ca
Canicattì [It.] **25** Bb
Cañizal [Sp.] **19** Cb
Cannes [Fr.] **13** Cb
Canosa di Puglia [It.] **27** Cb
Cantabria, Cordigliera– (I) =
  Cantábrica, Cordillera–
  19 Ca
Cantábrica, Cordillera– =
  Cantabria, Cordigliera– (I)
  19 Ca
Canterbury [RU] **5** Db
Caorle [It.] **31** Ca
Capraia **29** Ba
Caprera **29** Bb
Capri **29** Cb
Capua [It.] **29** Cb
Caracal [Rom.] **49** Ba
Cara Droma Rúisc / Carrick–on–
  Shannon [Eire] **3** Bab
Caracava [Sp.] **23** Bb
Carballo [Sp.] **19** Ba
Carbon, Cap– **23** Cb
Carbonara, Capo– **29** Bbc
Carbonia **29** Abc
Carcassonne [Fr.] **17** Ca
Çardak [Tur.] **47** Cc
Cardiff [RU] **5** Bb
Cardigan [RU] **5** Bb
Cardigan, Baia di– (I) =
  Cardigan Bay **5** Bb
Cardigan Bay = Cardigan, Baia
  di– (I) **5** Bb
Carei [Rom.] **39** Cb
Carelia (I) = Karelija **63** BCb
Carentan [Fr.] **9** Ba
Cargèse [Fr.] **13** Cbc
Carhaix–Plouguer [Fr.] **9** Aa
Cariati [It.] **25** Ca
Cariñena [Sp.] **17** Bb
Carinzia (I) = Kärnten **33** Cb
Carlisle [RU] **3** CDa
Carlow / Ceatharlach [Eire]
  3 Bb
Carloway [RU] **1** Ba
Carmarthen [RU] **5** Bb
Carmona [Sp.] **21** Cb
Carnac [Fr.] **9** ABb
Carnsore Point **3** Bb
Carpáţii Meridionali = Alpi
  Transilvaniche (I) **41** Dab
Carpáţii Orientali = Carpazi
  Orientali (I) **51** Bab
Carpazi Occidentali (I) =
  Karpaty [Eur.] **39** BCa
Carpazi Orientali (I) = Carpáţii
  Orientali **51** Bab
Carpentras [Fr.] **13** Bb
Carpi [It.] **31** Bb
Carrantuohill **3** Ab
Carrara [It.] **31** Bb
Carrick–on–Shannon / Cara
  Droma Rúisc [Eire] **3** Bab
Carrión de los Condes [Sp.]
  19 Ca
Cartagena [Sp.] **23** Bb
Carvoeiro, Cabo– **21** Aa

Casale Monferrato [It.] **31** Aab
Casas–Ibáñez [Sp.] **23** Ba
Cascais [Port.] **21** Ab
Cascia [It.] **29** Ca
Caserta [It.] **29** Cb
Cashel / Caiseal [Eire] **3** Bb
Čáslav [Rep.Ceca] **33** Da
Caso (I) = Kásos **45** BCc
Caspe [Sp.] **17** BCb
Cassandra (I) = Kassándra
  43 Bb
Cassino [It.] **29** Cb
Castel di Sangro [It.] **29** Cb
Castellammare di Stabia [It.]
  29 Cb
Castellana Grotte [It.] **27** Cb
Castellane [Fr.] **13** Ca
Castellón de la Plana [Sp.]
  23 BCa
Castelnaudary [Fr.] **17** Ca
Castelnau–de–Médoc [Fr.]
  15 Bab
Castelo Branco [Port.] **19** Bb
Castelsardo [It.] **29** Ab
Castelvetrano [It.] **25** Bb
Castets [Fr.] **15** Bb
Castiglione della Pescaia [It.]
  29 Ba
Castilla la Nueva = Nuova
  Castiglia (I) **19** Cb
Castilla la Vieja = Vecchia
  Castiglia (I) **19** Cb
Castlebar / Caisleán an
  Bharraigh [Eire] **3** Aab
Castlebay [RU] **1** Bab
Castle Douglas [RU] **3** Ca
Castletown [RU] **3** Cab
Castres [Fr.] **17** Ca
Castro Daire [Port.] **19** Bb
Castropol [Sp.] **19** Ba
Castro Verde [Port.] **21** Bb
Castrovillari [It.] **25** Ca
Castuera [Sp.] **21** Cb
Cataluña **17** Cb
Catania [It.] **25** Cb
Catanzaro [It.] **25** Cab
Catanzaro–Marina di Catanzaro
  [It.] **25** Cb
Cathair na Mart / Westport
  [Eire] **3** Aab
Cathair Saidhbhín /
  Cahersiveen [Eire] **3** Ab
Căuşanii [Mold.] **51** Cb
Cauterets [Fr.] **17** BCa
Çavadarhısar [Tur.] **47** Cbc
Cavalese [It.] **31** Ba
Cavan / An Cabhán [Eire]
  3 Bab
Cavcat [Cro.] **41** Cb
Cazalla de la Sierra [Sp.]
  21 Cb
Ceahlău **51** Bb
Ceatharlach / Carlow [Eire]
  3 Bb
Cebreros [Sp.] **19** Cb
Čechy **33** Ca
Cecina [It.] **31** Bb
Cefalonia (I) = Kefallinía **43** Ac
Cefalù [It.] **25** Bb
Cegléd [Ung.] **39** Bb
Čehov [Russia] **55** Eb
Celje [Slo.] **41** Ba
Celldömölk [Ung.] **39** Ab
Celle [D] **35** Cb
Celorico da Beira [Port.]
  19 Bb
Celtico, Mar– (I) = Celtic Sea
  3 Bb

Celtic Sea = Celtico, Mar– (I)
  3 Bb
Central, Massif– = Centrale,
  Massiccio– (I) **13** ABab
Centrale, Massiccio– (I) =
  Central, Massif– **13** ABab
Cerbère [Fr.] **17** CDa
Čerepovec [Russia] **61** Db
Ceresole Reale [It.] **13** Ca
Céret [Fr.] **17** Ca
Cergy–Pontoise [Fr.] **9** Ca
Cerignola [It.] **29** Cb
Cerigo (I) = Kíthira [Grecia]
  45 Ab
Cerigotto (I) = Andikíthira
  45 Abc
Čerkassy [Ucr.] **53** Cb
Cernavoda [Rom.] **49** Ca
Černigov [Ucr.] **53** Ca
Cernjahov [Ucr.] **53** Bb
Černjahovsk [Russia] **57** Cb
Černobyl [Ucr.] **53** Ca
Černoje more = Nero, Mar– (I)
  51 Db
Černo More = Nero, Mar– (I)
  51 Db
Černomorskoje [Ucr.] **51** Db
Černovcy [Ucr.] **51** Ba
Červen [R.B.] **55** Bc
Červen Briag [Bulg.] **49** ABa
Cervera [Sp.] **17** Cb
Cervera di Pisuerga [Sp.]
  19 Ca
Ceveteri [It.] **29** BCab
Cervia [It.] **31** Cb
Cervino **31** Aa
Červonograd [Ucr.] **37** Dc
Cesena [It.] **31** Cb
Cesenatico [It.] **31** Cb
Cesis / Cēsis [Lett.] **57** Da
Cēsis / Cesis [Lett.] **57** Da
Česká Lípa [Rep.Ceca] **35** Dc
České Budějovice [Rep.Ceca]
  33 Ca
Český Krumlov [Rep.Ceca]
  33 Ca
Český Těšín [Rep.Ceca] **39** Ba
Çeşme [Tur.] **45** Bb
Cetinje [Iug.] **41** Cb
Ceuta [Sp.] **21** Cbc
Cevenne (I) = Cévennes [Fr.]
  13 Bb
Cévennes [Fr.] **13** Bb
Cévennes [Fr.] = Cevenne (I)
  13 Bb
Chalais [Fr.] **15** BCa
Challans [Fr.] **9** Ca
Châlons–sur–Marne [Fr.]
  11 Ba
Chalon–sur–Saône [Fr.] **11** Bb
Cham [D] **33** Ca
Chambéry [Fr.] **13** BCa
Chambord [Fr.] **9** Cb
Chamonix–Mont–Blanc [Fr.]
  11 Cb
Champagne **11** Ba
Champagnole [Fr.] **11** BCb
Channel Islands = Canale, Isole
  del– (I) **9** Ba
Chantada [Sp.] **19** Ba
Chantilly [Fr.] **9** Ca
Chantonnay [Fr.] **9** Cb
Charente **15** Ca
Charleroi [Bel.] **7** Cb
Charlestown [Eire] **3** Bab
Charleville–Mézières [Fr.]
  11 Ba
Chartres [Fr.] **9** Ca
Château–Arnoux [Fr.] **13** BCb
Châteaubriant [Fr.] **9** Bb
Château–Chinon [Fr.] **11** Bb
Château–du–Loir [Fr.] **9** Cb
Châteaudun [Fr.] **9** Cab

Château-Gontier [Fr.] **9** Bab
Châteauneuf-sur-Loire [Fr.]
  9 Cab
Château-Renault [Fr.] **9** Cb
Châteauroux [Fr.] **9** Cb
Château-Salins [Fr.] **11** Ca
Château-Thierry [Fr.] **11** Ba
Châtellerault [Fr.] **9** Cb
Châtillon-sur-Seine [Fr.]
  11 Bab
Chaumont [Fr.] **11** Bab
Chauny [Fr.] **11** Ba
Chauvigny [Fr.] **9** Cb
Chaves [Port.] **19** Bb
Cheb [Rep.Ceca] **33** Ca
Chechaouene [Mar.] **21** Cc
Cheile Nerej–Beuşniţa **41** Dab
Chełm [Pol.] **37** Cbc
Chełmno [Pol.] **37** Bb
Chelmsford [RU] **5** Db
Chełmża [Pol.] **37** Bb
Cheltenham [RU] **5** Cb
Chelva [Sp.] **23** Ba
Chemillé [Fr.] **9** Bb
Chemnitz (Karl–Marx–Stadt)
  [D] **35** Dc
Chenonceaux [Fr.] **9** Cb
Cher **9** Cb
Cherbourg [Fr.] **9** Ba
Chester [RU] **5** BCb
Chesterfield [RU] **5** Cb
Chianciano Terme [It.] **29** Ba
Chiavari [It.] **31** Ba
Chiavenna [It.] **31** Ba
Chichester [RU] **5** Cbc
Chiclana de la Frontera [Sp.]
  21 BCb
Chieti [It.] **29** Ca
Chinon [Fr.] **9** Cb
Chio (I) = Khíos [Grecia] **45** Bb
Chioggia [It.] **31** Ca
Chippenham [RU] **5** Cb
Chişinău [Mold.] **51** Cb
Chişineu Criş [Rom.] **39** Cb
Chiva [Sp.] **23** Ba
Chivasso [It.] **31** Aa
Chodzież [Pol.] **37** Ab
Chojna [Pol.] **35** Db
Chojnice [Pol.] **37** Ab
Chojnów [Pol.] **37** Ab
Cholet [Fr.] **9** Bb
Chomutov [Rep.Ceca] **35** Dc
Chorzele [Pol.] **37** BCb
Choşebuz / Cottbus [D] **35** Db
Choszczno [Pol.] **37** Ab
Christchurch [RU] **5** Cc
Christiansfeld [Dan.] **75** Bb
Chrudim [Rep.Ceca] **39** Aa
Chrzanów [Pol.] **39** Ba
Chur / Cuera [Svizz.] **33** Bb
Cicladi (I) = Kikládhes **45** Bb
Ciechanów [Pol.] **37** Bb
Cieszanów [Pol.] **39** Ca
Cieszyn [Pol.] **39** Ba
Cieza [Sp.] **23** Bb
Cifuentes [Sp.] **17** Bb
Cijara, Embalse de– **21** Ca
Cilento e Vallo di Diano **27** Cb
Cill Airne / Killarney [Eire]
  3 Ab
Cill Chainnigh / Kilkenny [Eire]
  3 Bb
Cill Chaoi / Kilkee [Eire] **3** Ab
Cill Dara / Kildare [Eire] **3** Bb
Cill Mhantáin / Wicklow [Eire]
  3 BCb
Cîmpeni [Rom.] **39** Cb
Cîmpia Turzii [Rom.] **39** CDb
Cîmpina [Rom.] **51** Bbc
Cîmpulung [Rom.] **51** Bb
Cîmpulung Moldovenesc
  [Rom.] **51** Bb
Cinca **17** Cb

Çine [Tur.] **45** Cb
Cinto, Monte– **13** CDb
Cionn tSáile / Kinsale [Eire]
  3 Bb
Circeo **29** Cb
Cirencester [RU] **5** Cb
Cirò Marina [It.] **25** Ca
Čirpan [Bulg.] **49** Ba
Cisa, Passo della– **31** Bb
Cisnădie [Rom.] **51** ABb
Cistierna [Sp.] **19** Ca
Città del Vaticano [SCV]
  29 Cab
Città di Castello [It.] **31** Cb
Ciudadela / Ciutadella [Sp.]
  23 Da
Ciudad Real [Sp.] **21** Cab
Ciudad-Rodrigo [Sp.] **19** Bb
Ciudi, Lago dei– (I) = Čudskoje
  ozero **59** Eb
Ciudí, Lago dei– (I) = Peipsi
  järv **59** Eb
Ciutadella / Ciudadela [Sp.]
  23 Da
Cividale del Friuli [It.] **31** Ca
Civita Castellana [It.] **29** Ca
Civitanova Marche [It.] **31** Cb
Civitavecchia [It.] **29** Bab
Çivril [Tur.] **47** Cc
Cjurupinsk [Ucr.] **51** Ba
Čortkov [Ucr.] **51** Ba
Clacton–on–Sea [RU] **5** Db
Clamecy [Fr.] **11** Bb
Clermont [Fr.] **9** Ca
Clermont–Ferrand [Fr.]
  13 ABa
Clifden [Eire] **3** Ab
Cliffs of Moher **3** Ab
Cloich na Coillte / Clonakilty
  [Eire] **3** ABb
Clonakilty / Cloich na Coillte
  [Eire] **3** ABb
Clonmel / Cluain Meala [Eire]
  3 Bb
Cloppenburg [D] **35** Bb
Cluain Meala / Clonmel [Eire]
  3 Bb
Cluj Napoca [Rom.] **39** Cb
Cluses [Fr.] **11** Cb
Clyde, Firth of– **1** Cb
Cnosso (I) = Knosós **45** Bc
Cóbh / An Cóbh [Eire] **3** Bb
Coburg [D] **33** Ba
Coesfeld [D] **7** Da
Cognac [Fr.] **15** Ba
Cogne [It.] **13** Ca
Coimbra [Port.] **19** Bb
Colchester [RU] **5** Db
Coleraine / Cúil Raithin [RU]
  3 Ba
Coll **1** Bb
Collioure [Fr.] **17** CDa
Colmar [Fr.] **11** Cab
Colmenar Viejo [Sp.] **19** Cb
Colonia (I) = Köln [D] **7** Dab
Colonsay **1** Bb
Columbretes, Islas– **23** Ca
Colwyn Bay [RU] **5** Bb
Comacchio [It.] **31** BCb
Comăneşti [Rom.] **51** Bb
Combeaufontaine [Fr.] **11** BCb
Comino, Capo– **29** Bb
Como [It.] **31** ABa
Como, Lago di– **31** Ba
Compiègne [Fr.] **11** Ba
Comrat [Mold.] **51** Cb
Concarneau [Fr.] **9** Aab
Condom [Fr.] **15** Cb
Conegliano [It.] **31** Ca
Confolens [Fr.] **15** Ca
Connemara **3** Ab
Constanţa [Rom.] = Costanza (I)
  49 Ca
Contreras, Embalse de– **23** Ba

Copenaghen (I) = København
  [Dan.] **75** Cb
Corabia [Rom.] **49** Ba
Corbeil–Essonnes [Fr.] **9** Ca
Corbigny [Fr.] **11** Bb
Corcaigh / Cork [Eire] **3** Bb
Corcubión [Sp.] **19** Aa
Córdoba [Sp.] **21** Cb
Corfú (I) = Kérkira [Grecia]
  43 Ab
Coria [Sp.] **19** Bb
Corinto, Golfo di– (I) =
  Korinthiakós Kólpos **45** Ab
Cork / Corcaigh [Eire] **3** Bb
Corleone [It.] **25** Bb
Çorlu [Tur.] **47** Cc
Cornovaglia (I) = Cornwall
  5 Bc
Cornwall = Cornovaglia (I)
  5 Bc
Corralejo [Sp.] **23** ins.a
Correnti, Isola delle– **25** Cc
Corrib, Lough– **3** Ab
Corse = Corsica (I) **13** CDbc
Corse, Cap– = Corso, Capo– (I)
  13 Db
Corsica (I) = Corse **13** CDbc
Corso, Capo– (I) = Corse,
  Cap– **13** Db
Corte [Fr.] **13** CDb
Cortina d'Ampezzo [It.] **33** BCb
Čortkov [Ucr.] **51** Ba
Cortona [It.] **31** BCb
Coruche [Port.] **21** Bab
Corvo **21** ins.a
Cosenza [It.] **25** Ca
Cosne–Cours–sur–Loire [Fr.]
  9 CDb
Costanza (I) = Constanţa
  [Rom.] **49** Ca
Costanza, Lago di– (I) =
  Bodensee **33** Bb
Costeşti [Rom.] **49** Ba
Couhé [Fr.] **9** Cb
Courmayeur [It.] **13** Ca
Courtrai / Kortrijk [Bel.] **7** Cb
Coutances [Fr.] **9** Ba
Covadonga **19** Ca
Coventry [RU] **5** Cb
Covilhã [Port.] **19** Bb
Cozia **51** Bb
Cozia, Mănăstirea– **51** Bb
Cracovia (I) = Kraków [Pol.]
  35 Db
Craignure [RU] **1** Cb
Crail [RU] **1** Db
Craiova [Rom.] **49** Aa
Crans [Svizz.] **11** Cb
Crato [Port.] **21** Ba
Crawley [RU] **5** Cbc
Creil [Fr.] **9** Ca
Crema [It.] **31** Ba
Cremona [It.] **31** Bab
Cres [Cro.] **31** Cb
Cres [Cro.] **31** Cab
Crest [Fr.] **13** Bb
Creta (I) = Kríti **45** Bc
Creta, Mar di– (I) = Kritikón
  Pélagos **45** Bc
Creus, Cabo de– **17** Da
Creuse **9** Cb
Crewe [RU] **5** Cb
Crianlarich [RU] **1** Cb
Crieff [RU] **1** Cb
Crikvenica [Cro.] **31** Ca
Crissolo [It.] **13** Cb
Crişul Alb **39** Cb
Crişul Negru **39** Cb
Crişul Repede **39** Cb
Črna gora **41** Cb
Crni Drim **43** Ab
Cromer [RU] **5** Db

Cross Fell **3** Da
Crotone [It.] **25** Cab
Crvenka [Iug.] **41** Ca
Csorna [Ung.] **39** Ab
Cudillero [Sp.] **19** BCa
Čudovo [Russia] **61** Bb
Čudskoje ozero = Ciudi, Lago
  dei– (I) **59** Eb
Cuéllar [Sp.] **19** Ca
Cuenca [Sp.] **23** Ba
Cuera / Chur [Svizz.] **33** Bb
Cúil Raithin / Coleraine [RU]
  3 Ba
Cullera [Sp.] **23** Ba
Cumnock [RU] **3** Ca
Cuneo [It.] **31** Ab
Cuorgné [It.] **31** Aa
Čupa [Russia] **63** Ba
Curtea de Argeş [Rom.] **51** Bb
Cuxhaven [D] **35** Bab
Čvylevo [Russia] **61** BCb
Czaplinek [Pol.] **37** Ab
Czarnków [Pol.] **37** Ab
Czersk [Pol.] **37** ABb
Częstochowa [Pol.] **37** Bc
Człopa [Pol.] **37** Ab
Człuchów [Pol.] **37** Ab

D

Dabas [Ung.] **39** Bb
Dąbrowa Górnicza [Pol.] **37** Bc
Dachau [D] **33** Ba
Daimiel [Sp.] **21** Ca
Dale [Norv.] **73** Aa
Dalmacija = Dalmazia (I) **41** Bb
Dalmally [RU] **1** Cb
Dalmazia (I) = Dalmacija **41** Bb
Dalvík [Isl.] **77** Cab
Danilov [Russia] **61** Eb
Danilovgrad [Iug.] **41** Cb
Danilovo [Russia] **63** Ba
Dannenberg (Elbe) [D] **35** Cb
Danubio (I) = Donau **51** Cb
Danubio (I) = Duna **51** Cb
Danubio (I) = Dunaj **51** Cb
Danubio (I) = Dunărea **51** Cb
Danubio (I) = Dunav **51** Cb
Danubio, Delta del– (I) =
  Dunării, Delta– **49** Ca
Danzica (I) = Gdańsk [Pol.]
  57 Bb
Danzica, Golfo di– (I) =
  Gdańska, Zatoka– **57** Bb
Darabani [Rom.] **51** Bab
Darbėnai / Darbenaj [Lit.]
  57 Bcb
Darbenaj / Darbėnai [Lit.]
  57 Bcb
Dardanelli (I) = Çanakkale
  bogazı **47** BCb
Darfo Boario Terme [It.] **31** Ba
Darlington [RU] **3** Da
Darłowo [Pol.] **37** Aa
Darmstadt [D] **33** Aa
Daroca [Sp.] **17** Bb
Dartmoor **5** Bc
Daruvar [Cro.] **41** Ba
Daugava = Dvina Occidentale (I)
  57 Db
Daugavpils [Lett.] **57** Db
Davos / Tavau [Svizz.] **33** Bb
Dax [Fr.] **15** Bb
Deauville [Fr.] **9** BCa
Debar [Maced.] **43** Ab
Dębica [Pol.] **39** Ca
De Biesbosch **7** Ca
Dęblin [Pol.] **37** Bb

Debrecen [Ung.] **39** Cb
Decazeville [Fr.] **15** Cb
Děčín [Rep.Ceca] **35** Dc
Degerfors [Svezia] **73** Db
Deggendorf [D] **33** Ca
Dej [Rom.] **39** CDb
Delčevo [Maced.] **43** Bab
Delémont / Delsberg [Svizz.]
  11 Cb
Delfi (I) = Dhelfoí **45** Ab
Delft [P.B.] **7** Ca
Delfzijl [P.B.] **7** Da
Deljatin [Ucr.] **51** Ba
Delmenhorst [D] **35** Bb
Delnice [Cro.] **31** Ca
Delsberg / Delémont [Svizz.]
  11 Cb
Delsbo [Svezia] **59** Aa
Demirci [Tur.] **47** Cbc
Demjansk [Russia] **61** Bb
Demmin [D] **35** Db
Den Bosch / 's Hertogenbosch
  [P.B.] **7** Ca
Den Haag / 's–Gravenhage
  [P.B.] = L'Aia (I) **7** Ca
Den Helder [P.B.] **7** Ca
Dénia / Denia [Sp.] **23** BCab
Denia / Dénia [Sp.] **23** BCab
Denizli [Tur.] **47** Cc
Derby [RU] **5** Cb
Đerdap **41** Db
Dereköy [Tur.] **47** Cab
Derg, Lough– **3** Bb
Derventa [Bos.Erz.] **41** BCab
Desertas, Ilhas– **21** ins.a
Desna **53** Ca
Dessau [D] **35** Db
Deta [Rom.] **41** Da
Detmold [D] **35** BCb
Deva [Rom.] **41** Db
Deventer [P.B.] **7** Ca
Devin [Bulg.] **47** Bb
Dhelfoí = Delfi (I) **45** Ab
Dhidhimótikhon [Grecia] **47** Bb
Dhílos [Grecia] **45** Bb
Dhodhekánisos = Dodecaneso (I)
  45 BCb
Dhomokós [Grecia] **43** Bb
Dhonoúsa **45** Bb
Diamante [It.] **25** Ca
Didima **45** Cb
Die [Fr.] **13** Bb
Dieburg [D] **33** ABa
Diekirch [Luss.] **11** Ca
Diepholz [D] **35** Bb
Dieppe [Fr.] **5** Dc
Digione (I) = Dijon [Fr.] **11** Bb
Digne–les–Bains [Fr.] **13** Cb
Digoin [Fr.] **11** Bb
Dijon [Fr.] = Digione (I) **11** Bb
Dikanäs [Svezia] **71** Db
Dilek Yarımadası **45** Cb
Dimitrovgrad [Bulg.] **49** Bab
Dimitrovgrad [Iug.] **49** Aa
Dinan [Fr.] **9** Ba
Dinant [Bel.] **7** Cb
Dinard [Fr.] **9** Ba
Dingle / An Daingean [Eire]
  3 Ab
Dingwall [RU] **1** Ca
Djatkovo [Russia] **55** Dc
Djatlovo [R.B.] **53** Aa
Djemila **23** Db
Djúpi vogur [Isl.] **77** Eb
Djurö **73** Db
Dmitrov [Russia] **55** Db
Dnepr **51** Cb
Dneprovski liman **51** Db
Dnestr **51** Cb
Dno [Russia] **61** ABb
Dobbiaco / Toblach [It.] **33** CBb
Dobele [Lett.] **57** Cb
Dobiegniew [Pol.] **37** Ab

Doboj [Bos.Erz.] **41** BCb
Dobre Miasto [Pol.] **57** Bbc
Dobrič (Tolbuhin) [Bulg.] **49** Ca
Dobrodzień [Pol.] **37** Bc
Dobrogea = Dobrugia (I) **49** Ca
Dobrugia (I) = Dobrogea **49** Ca
Docksta [Svezia] **71** Eb
Dodecaneso (I) = Dhodhekánisos **45** BCb
Doire / Londonderry [RU] **3** Ba
Dokka [Norv.] **73** Ca
Dol–de–Bretagne [Fr.] **9** Ba
Dole [Fr.] **11** Bb
Dolgellau [RU] **5** Bb
Dolianova [It.] **29** ABa
Dolina [Ucr.] **51** ABa
Dolní Dvořiště [Rep.Ceca] **33** Ca
Dolný Kubín [Slovac.] **39** Ba
Dolomiti **33** BCb
Dolomiti Bellunesi **31** BCa
Domažlice [Rep.Ceca] **33** Ca
Dombås [Norv.] **73** BCa
Dombóvár [Ung.] **39** ABb
Dôme, Puy de– **15** Ca
Domfront [Fr.] **9** Ba
Domodedovo [Russia] **55** Eb
Domodossola [It.] **31** Aa
Domogled–Valea Cernei **41** Db
Doñana **21** Bb
Donau = Danubio (I) **51** Cb
Donauwörth [D] **33** Ba
Don Benito [Sp.] **21** BCab
Doncaster [RU] **5** Cb
Donegal [Eire] **3** Ba
Donji Miholjac [Cro.] **41** BCa
Donji Vakuf [Bos.Erz.] **41** Bb
Dønna **71** Cab
Donostia / San Sebastián [Sp.] **17** Ba
Doornik / Tournai [Bel.] **7** Cb
Dorada, Costa– **17** Cb
Dorchester [RU] **5** Cc
Dordogna (I) = Dordogne **15** Cb
Dordogne = Dordogna (I) **15** Cb
Dordrecht [P.B.] **7** Ca
Dorgali [It.] **29** Bb
Dornoch [RU] **1** Ca
Dorogobuž [Russia] **55** Db
Dorohoi [Rom.] **51** Bab
Dorotea [Svezia] **71** Db
Dospat [Bulg.] **47** ABb
Douai [Fr.] **7** BCb
Douarnenez [Fr.] **9** Aab
Doubs **11** Bb
Douglas [RU] **3** Cab
Doullens [Fr.] **7** Bb
Douro **19** Bb
Dover [RU] **5** Dbc
Dover, Strait of– = Dover, Stretto di– (I) **5** Dbc
Dover, Stretto di– (I) = Dover, Strait of– **5** Dbc
Dovrefjell [Norv.] **73** Ca
Dovrefjell [Norv.] **73** Ca
Dovsk [R.B.] **53** Ca
Downpatrick / Dún Pádraig [RU] **3** Ca
Drabov [Ucr.] **53** Cb
Drac, Cuevas del– **23** Da
Drăgășani [Rom.] **49** Ba
Dragør [Dan.] **75** Ca
Draguignan [Fr.] **13** Cb
Dráma [Grecia] **47** ABb
Drammen [Norv.] **73** Bb
Drangedal [Norv.] **73** BCb
Drau = Drava (I) **41** Ba
Dráva = Drava (I) **41** Ba
Drava (I) = Drau **41** Ba
Drava (I) = Dráva **41** Ba

Dravograd [Slo.] **33** CDb
Drawa **37** Ab
Dresda (I) = Dresden [D] **35** Dbc
Dresden [D] = Dresda (I) **35** Dbc
Dreux [Fr.] **9** Ca
Drin (I) = Drini **43** Ab
Drina **41** Cb
Drini = Drin (I) **43** Ab
Drniš [Cro.] **41** Bb
Drobeta–Turnu Severin [Rom.] **41** Db
Drogheda / Droichead Átha [Eire] **3** Bb
Drogobyč [Ucr.] **39** Ca
Droichead Átha / Drogheda [Eire] **3** Bb
Drummore [RU] **3** Ca
Druskininkai / Druskininkaj [Lit.] **57** CDbc
Druskininkaj / Druskininkai [Lit.] **57** CDbc
Drut **55** Bc
Drvar [Bos.Erz.] **41** Bb
Dubăsari [Mold.] **51** Cb
Dublin / Baile Átha Cliath [Eire] = Dublino (I) **3** Bb
Dublino (I) = Baile Átha Cliath / Dublin [RU] **3** Bb
Dublino (I) = Dublin / Baile Átha Cliath [Eire] **3** Bb
Dubna [Russia] **55** Db
Dubno [Ucr.] **53** Ab
Dubrovica [Ucr.] **53** Ab
Dubrovnik [Cro.] = Ragusa (I) **41** BCb
Duero **31** CDb
Dugi Otok **31** CDb
Duhovščina [Russia] **55** Cb
Duisburg [D] **7** Da
Dukielska, Przełęcz– **39** Ca
Dukla [Pol.] **39** Ca
Dülmen [D] **7** Da
Dulovo [Bulg.] **49** BCa
Dumbarton [RU] **1** Cb
Dumfries [RU] **3** Ca
Duna = Danubio (I) **51** Cb
Dunaföldvár [Ung.] **39** Bb
Dunaharaszti [Ung.] **39** Bb
Dunaj = Danubio (I) **51** Cb
Dunajevcy [Ucr.] **51** BCa
Dunărea = Danubio (I) **51** Cb
Dunării, Delta– = Danubio, Delta del– (I) **49** Ca
Dunaújváros [Ung.] **39** Bb
Dunav = Danubio (I) **51** Cb
Duncansby Head **1** CDa
Dundalk / Dún Dealgan [Eire] **3** Bab
Dún Dealgan / Dundalk [Eire] **3** Bab
Dundee [RU] **1** CDb
Dún Garbhán / Dungarvan [Eire] **3** Bb
Dungarvan / Dún Garbhán [Eire] **3** Bb
Dunkerque [Fr.] **7** Bab
Dún Laoghaire [Eire] **3** BCb
Dunnet Head **1** Ca
Dunoon [RU] **1** Cb
Dún Pádraig / Downpatrick [RU] **3** Ca
Dunvegan [RU] **1** Ba
Dupnica [Bulg.] **49** Aa
Durance **13** BCb
Đurđevac [Cro.] **41** Ba
Düren [D] **7** Db
Durham [RU] **3** Da
Durmitor [Iug.] **41** Cb
Durmitor [Iug.] **41** Cb
Durness [RU] **1** Ca
Dürnstein [Aus.] **33** Ca

Durrës Enver Hoxha [Alb.] **43** Ab
Dursunbey [Tur.] **47** Cb
Düsseldorf [D] **7** Da
Dvina, Baia della– (I) = Dvinskaja guba **63** DEb
Dvina Occidentale (I) = Daugava **57** Db
Dvina Occidentale (I) = Zapadnaja Dvina **57** Eb
Dvina Settentrionale (I) = Severnaja Dvina **63** Eb
Dvinskaja guba = Dvina, Baia della– (I) **63** DEb
Dzeržinsk [R.B.] **55** Bc
Działdowo [Pol.] **37** Bb
Dzierżoniów [Pol.] **37** Ac
Dżúkija **57** Dbc
Džurin [Ucr.] **51** Ca

E

Eastbourne [RU] **5** Dc
Ebeltoft [Dan.] **75** Bb
Eberswalde–Finow [D] **35** Db
Eboli [It.] **27** Cb
Ebridi, Mare delle– (I) = Hebrides, Sea of the– **1** Bab
Ebridi Esterne (I) = Outer Hebrides **1** Ba
Ebridi Interne (I) = Inner Hebrides **1** Bab
Ebro **17** Cb
Eceabat [Tur.] **47** Bb
Echternach [Luss.] **11** Ca
Écija [Sp.] **21** Cb
Eckernförde [D] **35** Ca
Eckerö **59** Ba
Écrins **13** Cab
Ede [P.B.] **7** Ca
Édhessa [Grecia] **43** Bb
Edimburgo (I) = Edinburgh [RU] **1** Cb
Edinburgh [RU] = Edimburgo (I) **1** Cb
Ediniţa [Mold.] **51** Cab
Edirne [Tur.] **47** Bb
Edolo [It.] **31** Ba
Edremit [Tur.] **47** BCb
Edsbyn [Svezia] **73** Ea
Eferding [Aus.] **33** Ca
Efes = Efeso (I) **45** Cb
Efeso = Efes **45** Cb
Eforie [Rom.] **49** Ca
Égadi, Isole– **25** Bb
Ege Denizi = Egeo, Mar– (I) **45** Bb
Egeo, Mar– = Aiyaíon Pélagos **47** Bb
Egeo, Mar– (I) = Ege Denizi **45** Bb
Eger [Ung.] **39** Bab
Egersund [Norv.] **75** Aa
Eggenfelden [D] **33** Ca
Egilsstadhir [Isl.] **77** Eb
Egina (I) = Aíyina **45** Ab
Ehingen (Donau) [D] **33** Ba
Ehrwald [Aus.] **33** Bb
Eichstätt [D] **33** Ba
Eidfjord [Norv.] **73** Ba
Eidsvåg [Norv.] **73** Ba
Eidsvoll [Norv.] **73** Ca
Eigg **1** Bab
Einbeck [D] **35** Db
Eindhoven [P.B.] **7** Ca
Einsiedeln [Svizz.] **33** Ab
Eiríksjökull **77** Cb
Eisenach [D] **35** Cbc
Eisenerz [Aus.] **33** Cab
Eisenhüttenstadt [D] **35** Db
Eisenstadt [Aus.] **39** Aab

Eisfeld [D] **35** Cc
Eišiškés / Eišiškes [Lit.] **57** Dbc
Ejea de los Caballeros [Sp.] **17** Bab
Ejšiškes / Eišiškés [Lit.] **57** Dbc
Ekenäs / Tammisaari [Finl.] **59** Da
Eksjö [Svezia] **75** CDa
Elafónisos **45** Ab
Elassón [Grecia] **43** Bb
Elba **29** Ba
Elba (I) = Elbe **35** Cb
Elba (I) = Labe **33** Da
El Barco de Ávila [Sp.] **19** Cb
El Barco de Valdeorras [Sp.] **19** Ba
Elbasani [Alb.] **43** Ab
Elbe = Elba (I) **35** Cb
Elblag [Pol.] **57** Bbc
El Burgo de Osma [Sp.] **19** Cb
Elche / Elx [Sp.] **23** Bb
Elche de la Sierra [Sp.] **23** Bb
Elda [Sp.] **23** Bb
Eleja / Elēja [Lett.] **57** Cb
Elēja / Eleja [Lett.] **57** Cb
Elektrénai / Elektrenaj [Lit.] **57** Db
Elektrenaj / Elektrénai [Lit.] **57** Db
Elena [Bulg.] **49** Ba
Elevsís [Grecia] **45** Ab
Eleftheroúpolis [Grecia] **47** Bb
El Ferrol [Sp.] **19** Ba
Elgå [Norv.] **73** CDa
Elgin [RU] **1** Ca
Elhovo [Bulg.] **49** Ba
Ełk [Pol.] **57** Cc
Elmalı [Tur.] **45** Cb
Elmshorn [D] **35** Cb
Elmus [Russia] **63** Cc
El Oasis [Sp.] **23** ins.a
El Puerto de Santa María [Sp.] **21** Bb
Elster / Herzberg [D] **35** Db
Elsterwerda [D] **35** Db
Elva [Est.] **59** Db
Elvas [Port.] **21** Bab
Elvekrok [Norv.] **73** Ba
Elverum [Norv.] **73** Ca
Elx / Elche [Sp.] **23** Bb
Ely [RU] **5** Db
Emån **75** Da
Emden [D] **7** Da
Emet [Tur.] **47** Cb
Emmaboda [Svezia] **75** Db
Emmaste [Est.] **59** Cb
Emmen [P.B.] **7** Da
Emmerloord [P.B.] **7** Ca
Empoli [It.] **31** Bb
Ems **7** Da
Encs [Ung.] **39** BCa
Enez [Tur.] **47** Bb
Engadin **33** Bb
Engerdal [Norv.] **73** CDa
England = Inghilterra (I) **5** Cb
English Channel = Manica, La– (I) **5** Db
Engozero, ozero– **63** Cb
Enkhuizen [P.B.] **7** Ca
Enköping [Svezia] **59** Ab
Enna [It.] **25** Bb
Ennis / Inis [Eire] **3** ABb
Enniscorthy / Inis Córthaidh [Eire] **3** Bb
Enniskillen / Inis Ceithleann [RU] **3** Ab
Ennistymon / Inis Diomáin [Eire] **3** Ab
Enns [Aus.] **33** Ca
Enns [Aus.] **33** Ca
Eno [Finl.] **63** Bc

Enontekiö [Finl.] **67** Bb
Enschede [P.B.] **7** Da
Eolie o Lipari, Isole– **25** BCb
Épernay [Fr.] **11** Ba
Epidauro (I) = Epídhavros **45** Ab
Epídhavros = Epidauro (I) **45** Ab
Épinal [Fr.] **11** Ca
Epiro (I) = Ípiros **43** ABb
Érd [Ung.] **39** Bb
Eressós [Grecia] **47** Bb
Erétria [Grecia] **45** Ab
Erfurt [D] **35** Cbc
Ergene **47** Bb
Ergli / Ērgļi [Lett.] **57** Dab
Ērgļi / Ergli [Lett.] **57** Dab
Erice [It.] **25** Bb
Erlangen [D] **33** Ba
Ermoúpolis [Grecia] **45** Bb
Erne **3** Ba
Erne, Lower Lough– **3** Ba
Erne, Upper Lough– **3** Ba
Erris Head **3** Aa
Erseka [Alb.] **43** Ab
Eršy [Russia] **55** Db
Erzgebirge = Metalliferi, Monti– (I) **35** Dc
Esbjerg [Dan.] **75** Bb
Esbo / Espoo [Finl.] **59** Da
Escudo, Puerto del– **19** Ca
Eskifjördur [Isl.] **77** Eb
Eskilstuna [Svezia] **59** Ab
Esla **19** Ca
Es Mercadal / Mercadal [Sp.] **23** Da
Espalion [Fr.] **15** Cb
Espichel, Cabo– **21** Ab
Espinho [Port.] **19** Bb
Espoo / Esbo [Finl.] **59** Da
Esposende [Port.] **19** Bb
Essen [D] **7** Da
Esslingen am Neckar [D] **33** Ba
Estaca de Bares, Punta de la– **19** Ba
Este [It.] **31** Ba
Estella [Sp.] **17** Ba
Estepa [Sp.] **21** Cb
Estepona [Sp.] **21** Cb
Estoril [Port.] **21** Ab
Estrêla, Serra da– **19** Bb
Estremadura (I) = Extremadura **21** BCab
Estremoz [Port.] **21** Bab
Esztergom [Ung.] **39** Bb
Étain [Fr.] **11** Ba
Étampes [Fr.] **9** Ca
Etna **25** BCb
Étretat [Fr.] **9** Ca
Eubea (I) = Évvoia **45** Bb
Eugmo **65** Cb
Eura [Finl.] **59** Ca
Eure **9** Ca
Europa, Picos de– **19** Ca
Europoort **7** Ca
Euskirchen [D] **7** Db
Eutin [D] **35** Cab
Évian–les–Bains [Fr.] **11** Cb
Evje [Norv.] **75** Aa
Évora [Port.] **21** Bb
Évreux [Fr.] **9** Ca
Évros **47** Bb
Évvoia = Eubea (I) **45** Bb
Evzonoi [Grecia] **43** Bb
Exeter [RU] **5** Bc
Exmoor **5** Bb
Exmouth [RU] **5** Bc
Extremadura = Estremadura (I) **21** BCab
Eyjafjördur **77** Cab
Eymoutiers [Fr.] **15** Ba
Eyrarbakki [Isl.] **77** BCb
Ezine [Tur.] **47** Bb

F

Fåborg [Dan.] **75** Bb
Fabriano [It.] **31** Cb
Faenza [It.] **31** BCb
Fær Øer (I) = Færøerne / Föroyar **75** ins.a
Fær Øer (I) = Föroyar / Færøerne **75** ins.a
Færøerne / Föroyar = Fær Øer (I) **75** ins.a
Fågåraş [Rom.] **51** Bb
Fagernes [Norv.] **73** Ca
Fagersta [Svezia] **73** Eab
Fagurhólsmýri [Isl.] **77** Db
Faial **21** ins.a
Fair Isle **1** ins.a
Faistós **45** Bc
Falaise [Fr.] **9** Ba
Falcone, Capo del– **29** Ab
Falkenberg [Svezia] **75** Cab
Falkensee [D] **35** Db
Falkirk [RU] **1** Cb
Falköping [Svezia] **75** Ca
Falmouth [RU] **5** Bc
Falset [Sp.] **17** Cb
Falster **35** CDa
Falsterbo [Svezia] **75** Cb
Fälticeni [Rom.] **51** Bb
Falun [Svezia] **73** Ea
Fanø **75** Ab
Fano [It.] **31** Ba
Farángi Samariás **45** ABc
Fårö **57** Ba
Faro [Port.] **21** Bb
Fårösund [Svezia] **57** Ba
Fársala [Grecia] **43** Bb
Farsund [Norv.] **75** Aa
Fatima [Port.] **19** Bb
Fauske [Norv.] **69** Ba
Favignana **25** Bb
Faxaflói **77** Bb
Fécamp [Fr.] **9** Ca
Fehmarn **35** Ca
Fehmarnbelt **35** Ca
Feldbach [Aus.] **39** Ab
Feldberg **33** Aab
Feldkirch [Aus.] **33** Bb
Felixstowe [RU] **5** Db
Feltre [It.] **31** BCa
Femer Bælt **35** Ca
Femund **73** Ca
Férai [Grecia] **47** Bb
Ferentino [It.] **29** Cb
Fermo [It.] **29** Ca
Fermoselle [Sp.] **19** Bb
Fermoy / Mainistir Fhear Maí [Eire] **3** Bb
Ferrandina [It.] **27** Cb
Ferrara [It.] **31** Bb
Ferreira do Alentejo [Port.] **21** Bb
Ferro (I) = Hierro **23** ins.a
Fethiye [Tur.] **45** Cb
Feuchtwangen [D] **33** Ba
Feurs [Fr.] **13** Ba
Fidenza [It.] **31** Bab
Fiesole [It.] **31** Bb
Figeac [Fr.] **15** Cb
Figueira da Foz [Port.] **19** ABb
Figueras / Figueres [Sp.] **17** CDa
Figueres / Figueras [Sp.] **17** CDa
Filiaşi [Rom.] **49** Aa
Filicudi **25** Bb
Filippiás [Grecia] **43** ABb
Filipstad [Svezia] **73** Db
Finale Emilia [It.] **31** Bb
Finale Ligure [It.] **31** Ab
Finike [Tur.] **45** ins.a
Finisterre, Cabo– **19** Aa

Finlandia, Golfo di– (I) = Finski zaliv **59** DEab
Finlandia, Golfo di– (I) = Soomenlaht **59** DEab
Finlandia, Golfo di– (I) = Suomenlahti **59** DEab
Finnmark **69** Ea
Finnsnes [Norv.] **69** BCa
Finski zaliv = Finlandia, Golfo di– (I) **59** DEab
Finspång [Svezia] **75** Da
Fionia (I) = Fyn **75** Bb
Firenze [It.] **31** Bb
Firminy [Fr.] **13** Ba
Fishguard [RU] **5** Bb
Fiskárdhon [Grecia] **43** Ac
Fiskebøl [Norv.] **69** Ab
Fiuggi [It.] **29** Cb
Fiume (I) = Rijeka [Cro.] **31** Ca
Fjerritslev [Dan.] **75** Bab
Fjöllum, Jökulsá á– **77** Dab
Flannan Isles **1** Ba
Fläsjön **71** Db
Flatey **77** Bb
Flekkefjord [Norv.] **75** Aa
Flen [Svezia] **59** Ac
Flensburg [D] **35** Ca
Flevoland **7** Ca
Flims [Svizz.] **33** Bb
Florac [Fr.] **13** Bb
Florenville [Bel.] **11** Ba
Flores **21** ins.a
Floreşti [Mold.] **51** Cb
Flórina [Grecia] **43** Bb
Florø [Norv.] **73** Aa
Foča [Bos.Erz.] **41** Cb
Focşani [Rom.] **51** Cb
Foggia [It.] **27** Cb
Föhr **35** Ba
Foix [Fr.] **17** Ca
Foldereid [Norv.] **71** Cb
Folégandros **45** Bb
Foligno [It.] **29** Ca
Folkestone [RU] **5** Dbc
Folldals verk [Norv.] **73** Ca
Föllinge [Svezia] **71** Cb
Follonica [It.] **29** Ba
Fonsagrada [Sp.] **19** Ba
Fontainebleau [Fr.] **9** Ca
Fontenay–le–Comte [Fr.] **9** Bb
Fontur **77** Ea
Foppolo [It.] **31** Ba
Forbach [Fr.] **11** Ca
Forchheim [D] **33** Ba
Førde [Norv.] **73** ABa
Foreste Casentinesi–Monte Falterona–Campigna **31** Bb
Forfar [RU] **1** CDb
Forlì [It.] **31** BCb
Formentera **23** Cb
Formentor, Cabo de– **23** Da
Formia [It.] **29** Cb
Fornæs **75** Bb
Fornovo di Taro [It.] **31** Bb
Föroyar / Færøerne = Fær Øer (I) **75** ins.a
Forssa [Finl.] **59** Ca
Fort Augustus [RU] **1** Cab
Forte dei Marmi [It.] **31** Bb
Forth, Firth of– **1** CDb
Fort William [RU] **1** Cb
Forvik [Norv.] **71** Cb
Fossombrone [It.] **31** Cb
Fougères [Fr.] **9** Ba
Foula **1** ins.a
Foyle, Lough– **3** Ba
Fraga [Sp.] **17** Cb
Francavilla Fontana [It.] **27** Cb
Francoforte sul Meno (I) = Frankfurt am Main [D] **33** Aa
Frankenberg (Eder) [D] **35** BCbc

Frankfurt / Oder [D] **35** Db
Frankfurt am Main [D] = Francoforte sul Meno (I) **33** Aa
Františkovy Lázně [Rep.Ceca] **33** Ca
Frascati [It.] **29** Cb
Fraserburgh [RU] **1** Da
Fredericia [Dan.] **75** Bb
Frederikshavn [Dan.] **75** Ba
Frederikssund [Dan.] **75** BCb
Frederiksværk [Dan.] **75** BCb
Fredrika [Svezia] **71** Eb
Fredriksberg [Svezia] **73** Da
Fredrikshamn / Hamina [Finl.] **59** Ea
Fredrikstad [Norv.] **73** Cb
Fregenal de la Sierra [Sp.] **21** Bb
Freiberg [D] **35** Dbc
Freiburg / Fribourg [Svizz.] **11** Cb
Freiburg im Breisgau [D] = Friburgo in Brisgovia (I) **33** Aab
Freising [D] **33** Ba
Freistadt [Aus.] **33** Ca
Fréjus [Fr.] **13** Cb
Freudenstadt [D] **33** Aa
Fribourg / Freiburg [Svizz.] **11** Cb
Friburgo in Brisgovia (I) = Freiburg im Breisgau [D] **33** Aab
Friedrichshafen [D] **33** Bb
Friesach [Aus.] **33** Cb
Friesische Inseln / Waddeneilanden = Frisone, Isole– (I) **35** ABab
Frisone, Isole– (I) = Friesische Inseln / Waddeneilanden **35** ABab
Frisone, Isole– (I) = Waddeneilanden / Friesische Inseln **35** ABab
Fritzlar [D] **35** Cbc
Frombork [Pol.] **57** Bb
Fronteira [Port.] **21** Bab
Frontera [Sp.] **23** ins.a
Frosinone [It.] **29** Cb
Frøya **71** Ab
Fruška Gora **41** Ca
Frýdek Místek [Rep.Ceca] **39** Ba
Fuengirola [Sp.] **21** Cb
Fuerteventura **23** ins.a
Fulda [D] **35** Cc
Fulda [D] **35** Cc
Funäsdalen [Svezia] **73** Ca
Funchal [Port.] **21** ins.a
Fundão [Port.] **19** Bb
Fürstenfeld [Aus.] **39** Ab
Fürstenfeldbruck [D] **33** Ba
Fürth [D] **33** Ba
Furudal [Svezia] **73** DEa
Füssen [D] **33** Bb
Futa, Passo della– **31** Bb
Füzesabony [Ung.] **39** Bb
Fyn = Fionia (I) **75** Bb
Fyresdal [Norv.] **73** Bb

G

Gabrovo [Bulg.] **49** Ba
Gacko [Bos.Erz.] **41** Cb
Gäddede [Svezia] **71** Cb
Gadebush [D] **35** Cb
Gadjač [Ucr.] **53** Db
Gäeşti [Rom.] **49** Ba
Gaeta [It.] **29** Cb

Gagarin [Russia] **55** Db
Gaillac [Fr.] **15** Cb
Gaillimh / Galway [RU] **3** ABb
Galanta [Slovac.] **39** Aa
Galaroza [Sp.] **21** Bb
Galashiels [RU] **1** Db
Galaţi [Rom.] **51** Cb
Galatina [It.] **27** CDb
Gáldar [Sp.] **23** ins.a
Galicia = Galizia (I) **19** Ba
Galičic **43** Ab
Galizia (I) = Galicia **19** Ba
Galles (I) = Wales **5** Bb
Gallipoli [It.] **27** CDb
Gällivare [Svezia] **69** Cb
Gallo, Capo– (I) = Akrítas, Ákra– **45** Ab
Galloway, Mull of– **3** Ca
Galway / Gaillimh [Eire] **3** ABb
Gammelstad [Svezia] **65** Cb
Gamvik [Norv.] **69** Fa
Gand / Gent [Bel.] **7** Cab
Gandesa [Sp.] **17** Cb
Gandía / Gandia [Sp.] **23** Bab
Gandia / Gandía [Sp.] **23** Bab
Ganges [Fr.] **13** Bb
Gankovo [Russia] **61** Cab
Gannat [Fr.] **11** ABb
Gap [Fr.] **13** BCb
Gara Dragoman [Bulg.] **49** Aa
Garajonay **23** ins.a
Garda, Lago di– **31** Ba
Gardelegen [D] **35** Cb
Gardone Riviera [It.] **31** Ba
Gargaliánoi [Grecia] **45** Ab
Gargano [It.] **27** Cab
Gargano [It.] **27** Cb
Garmisch–Partenkirchen [D] **33** Bb
Garonna (I) = Garonne **15** Cb
Garonne = Garonna (I) **15** Cb
Garwolin [Pol.] **37** Cb
Gascogne = Guascogna (I) **17** BCa
Gascogne, Golfe de– = Guascogna, Golfo di– (I) **15** Bb
Gata, Cabo de– **23** Bb
Gatčina [Russia] **61** Bb
Gauja [Lett.] **57** Da
Gauja [Lett.] **57** Da
Gavarnie, Cirque de– **17** BCa
Gávdhos **45** ABc
Gävle [Svezia] **59** Aa
Gavri [Russia] **55** Bb
Gdańsk [Pol.] = Danzica (I) **57** Bb
Gdańska, Zatoka– = Danzica, Golfo di– (I) **57** Bb
Gdov [Russia] **61** Ab
Gdynia [Pol.] **57** Bb
Gebze [Tur.] **47** Cb
Gediz [Tur.] **47** Cbc
Gediz [Tur.] **45** Cb
Gedser [Dan.] **35** CDa
Gedser Odde **35** CDa
Geilo [Norv.] **73** Ba
Geiranger [Norv.] **73** Ba
Gela [It.] **25** Bb
Geldern [D] **7** Da
Gelibolu [Tur.] **47** Bb
Gelibolu Yarımadası **47** Bb
Gelsenkirchen [D] **7** Ca
Gelting [D] **35** Ca
Gemlik [Tur.] **47** Cb
Gemona del Friuli [It.] **31** Ca
General–Toševo [Bulg.] **49** Ca
Genève [Svizz.] = Ginevra (I) **11** BCb
Genil **21** Cb
Gennargentu **29** Bb
Genova [It.] **31** ABb
Genova, Golfo di– **31** ABb

Gent / Gand [Bel.] **7** Cab
Gera [D] **35** CDbc
Gérardmer [Fr.] **11** Cab
Gérgal [Sp.] **23** Bb
Gernika–Lumo / Guernica y Luno [Sp.] **17** Ba
Gerona / Girona [Sp.] **17** Cab
Getafe [Sp.] **19** Cb
Gevgelija [Maced.] **43** Bb
Geysir **77** Cb
Ghawdex / Gozo **25** Bbc
Gheorghieni [Rom.] **51** Bb
Giannina (I) = Ioánnina [Grecia] **43** Ab
Giannutri **29** Ba
Giant's Causeway **3** Ba
Giarre [It.] **25** Cb
Gibilterra (I) = Gibraltar [RU] **21** Cbc
Gibilterra, Stretto di– (I) = Gibraltar, Estrecho de– **21** Cbc
Gibraltar [RU] = Gibilterra (I) **21** Cbc
Gibraltar, Estrecho de– = Gibilterra, Stretto di– (I) **21** Cbc
Gien [Fr.] **9** Cb
Gießen [D] **35** Bc
Gifhorn [D] **35** Cb
Giglio **29** Ba
Gijón [Sp.] **19** Ca
Gimolskoje, ozero– **63** Bc
Ginevra (I) = Genève [Svizz.] **11** BCb
Ginevra, Lago di– (I) = Léman, Lac– **11** Cb
Ginzo de Límia [Sp.] **19** Bab
Gioia del Colle [It.] **27** Cb
Gioia Tauro [It.] **25** Cb
Giovi, Passo dei– **31** ABb
Girona / Gerona [Sp.] **17** Cab
Gironda (I) = Gironde **15** Ba
Gironde = Gironda (I) **15** Ba
Girvan [RU] **3** Ca
Gislaved [Svezia] **75** Ca
Gisors [Fr.] **9** Ca
Giulianova [It.] **29** Ca
Giura (I) = Jura [Eur.] **11** Cb
Giurgiu [Rom.] **49** Ba
Givet [Fr.] **7** Cb
Gižycko [Pol.] **57** Cbc
Gjirokastra [Alb.] **43** Abb
Gjøvik [Norv.] **73** Ca
Gjuhës, Kep i– **43** Ab
Gláma **73** Cb
Glarus [Svizz.] **33** ABb
Glasgow [RU] **1** Cb
Glendalough **3** Bb
Glenrothes [RU] **1** CDb
Glenveag **3** Ba
Glífádha [Grecia] **45** Ab
Glina [Cro.] **41** Ba
Gliwice [Pol.] **39** Ab
Głogów [Pol.] **37** Ab
Glomfjord [Norv.] **69** Ab
Glommersträsk [Svezia] **71** Eb
Gloucester [RU] **5** Cb
Głowno [Pol.] **37** Bb
Głubczyce [Pol.] **39** Aa
Głubokoje [R.B.] **55** Bb
Głuchołazy [Pol.] **39** Ab
Gluhov [Ucr.] **53** Da
Gmünd [Aus.] **33** CDa
Gmünd [Aus.] **33** Cb
Gmunden [Aus.] **33** Cab
Gnarp [Svezia] **59** Aa
Gniew [Pol.] **57** Bbc
Gniezno [Pol.] **37** Ab
Gnjilane [Iug.] **41** Db
Goce Delčev [Bulg.] **43** Bb
Goch [D] **7** Da
Godafoss **77** Db

Gödöllő [Ung.] **39** Bb
Goes [P.B.] **7** Ca
Gogland, ostrov– **59** DEab
Gökçeada **47** Bb
Gol [Norv.] **73** BCa
Golaja Pristan [Ucr.] **51** Db
Gölcük [Tur.] **47** Cb
Gołdap [Pol.] **57** Cb
Goldberg [D] **35** CDb
Goleniów [Pol.] **35** Db
Golfo Aranci [It.] **29** Bb
Golija **41** Cb
Goljam Perelik **47** Bb
Goloby [Ucr.] **53** Aab
Gomel [R.B.] **53** Ca
Gomera **23** ins.a
Gondomar [Port.] **19** Bb
Gönen [Tur.] **47** Cb
Göppingen [D] **33** Ba
Góra Kalwaria [Pol.] **37** Cb
Goražde [Bos.Erz.] **41** Cb
Gorce **39** Ba
Gorgona **31** Bb
Gorizia [It.] **31** Ca
Gorki [R.B.] **55** Cb
Gorlice [Pol.] **39** BCa
Görlitz [D] **35** DEbc
Gorna Orjahovica [Bulg.] **49** Ba
Gornji Vakuf [Bos.Erz.] **41** Bb
Gorodišče [Ucr.] **53** Ab
Gorodok [R.B.] **55** BCb
Gorodok [Ucr.] **39** Ca
Goryn **53** ABa
Gorzów Wielkopolski [Pol.]
      37 Ab
Gošča [Ucr.] **53** Ab
Goslar [D] **35** Cb
Gospić [Cro.] **41** Bb
Gosport [RU] **5** Cc
Gostivar [Maced.] **43** ABb
Gostyń [Pol.] **37** Ab
Gostynin [Pol.] **37** Bb
Gota älv **75** BCa
Götaland **75** CDa
Göteborg [Svezia] **75** BCa
Gotha [D] **35** Cbc
Gotland **57** Ba
Gotska Sandön [Svezia] **59** Bb
Gotska Sandön [Svezia] **59** Bb
Göttingen [D] **35** Cb
Gouda [P.B.] **7** Ca
Gournay–en–Bray [Fr.] **9** Ca
Gozo / Għawdex **25** Bbc
Gračac [Cro.] **41** Bb
Gračanica [Bos.Erz.] **41** Cb
Graciosa [Azz.–Port.] **21** ins.a
Graciosa [Can.–Sp.] **23** ins.a
Gradizsk [Ucr.] **53** CDb
Grado [It.] **31** Ca
Grajewo [Pol.] **57** Cc
Grampiani, Monti– (I) =
      Grampian Mountains **1** Cb
Grampian Mountains =
      Grampiani, Monti– (I) **1** Cb
Granada [Sp.] **21** Cb
Granadilla de Abona [Sp.]
      23 ins.a
Gran Canaria **23** ins.a
Grand Ballon **11** Cab
Grande, Val– **31** Aa
Grande Belt (I) = Store Bælt
      75 Bb
Grândola [Port.] **21** Bb
Gränna [Svezia] **75** Ca
Granön [Svezia] **71** Eb
Gran Paradiso **13** Ca
Gran San Bernardo, Colle del–
      13 Ca
Gran Sasso d'Italia **29** Ca
Gran Sasso e Monti della Laga
      29 Ca
Gran Tarajal [Sp.] **23** ins.a
Grantham [RU] **5** Cb

Granville [Fr.] **9** Ba
Gräsö **59** Ba
Grasse [Fr.] **13** Cb
Graus [Sp.] **17** Ca
Gravina in Puglia [It.] **27** Cb
Gray [Fr.] **11** Bb
Graz [Aus.] **33** Db
Great Malvern [RU] **5** Cb
Great Yarmouth [RU] **5** Db
Gredos, Sierra de– **19** Cb
Greenock [RU] **1** Cb
Greifswald [D] **35** Dab
Grein [Aus.] **33** Ca
Greiz [D] **35** Dc
Grenå [Dan.] **75** Bb
Grenen **75** Ba
Grenoble [Fr.] **13** Ba
Grense–Jakobselv [Norv.]
      67 Ea
Gressåmoen **71** Cb
Grevená [Grecia] **43** Bb
Grimmen [D] **35** Dab
Grimsby [RU] **5** CDb
Grimsey **77** CDa
Grímsstadir [Isl.] **77** Db
Grimstad [Norv.] **75** Aa
Grímsvöth **77** Db
Grindaheim [Norv.] **73** Ba
Grindavík [Isl.] **77** Bb
Grindelwald [Svizz.] **33** Ab
Grindsted [Dan.] **75** ABb
Gris–Nez, Cap– **5** Dbc
Grobiņa / Grobiņa [Lett.]
      57 BCb
Grobinja / Grobiņa [Lett.]
      57 BCb
Grodków [Pol.] **37** Ac
Grodno [R.B.] **57** CDc
Groix, Ile de– **9** Ab
Grójec [Pol.] **37** BCb
Gronau (Westfalen) [D] **7** Da
Grong [Norv.] **71** Cb
Grönhögen [Svezia] **75** Db
Groninga (I) = Groningen [P.B.]
      7 Da
Groningen [P.B.] = Groninga (I)
      7 Da
Großer Arber **33** Ca
Grosseto [It.] **29** Ba
Großglockner **33** Cb
Grudovo [Bulg.] **49** BCa
Grudziądz [Pol.] **37** Bb
Grums [Svezia] **73** Db
Grybów [Pol.] **39** BCa
Gryfice [Pol.] **37** Aab
Gstaad [Svizz.] **11** Cb
Guadalajara [Sp.] **19** CDb
Guadalquivir **21** Bb
Guadalupe [Sp.] **21** Bb
Guadiana **21** Bb
Guadix [Sp.] **21** CDb
Gualdo Tadino [It.] **29** Ca
Guarda [Port.] **19** Bb
Guardo [Sp.] **19** Ca
Guascogna (I) = Gascogne
      17 BCa
Guascogna, Golfo di– (I) =
      Gascogne, Golfe de– **15** Bb
Guastalla [It.] **31** Bab
Gubbio [It.] **31** Cb
Guben [D] **35** Db
Gubin [Pol.] **35** Db
Gudvangen [Norv.] **73** Ba
Guéret [Fr.] **9** Cb
Guernica y Luno / Gernika–
      Lumo [Sp.] **17** Ba
Guernsey **9** Ba
Guía de Isora [Sp.] **23** ins.a
Guijuelo [Sp.] **19** Cb
Guildford [RU] **5** Cb
Guillestre [Fr.] **13** Cb
Guimarães [Port.] **19** Bb
Guingamp [Fr.] **9** ABa

Guitiriz [Sp.] **19** Ba
Gulbene [Lett.] **57** Dab
Gullfoss **77** Cb
Gullspång [Svezia] **73** Db
Gunnarn [Svezia] **71** Db
Gurk [Aus.] **33** Cb
Gurskøy **73** Aa
Gusev [Russia] **57** Cb
Guspini [It.] **29** Ab
Güstrow [D] **35** CDb
Gutulia **73** Da
Gyöngyös [Ung.] **39** Bb
Győr [Ung.] **39** Ab
Gyula [Ung.] **39** Cb

H

Haapajärvi [Finl.] **65** Db
Haapamäki [Finl.] **65** Dc
Haapsalu [Est.] **59** Cb
Haarlem [P.B.] **7** Ca
Hackås [Svezia] **73** Da
Haderslev [Dan.] **75** Bb
Hadrian's Wall = Adriano, Vallo
      di– (I) **3** Da
Hadsund [Dan.] **75** Bb
Hagfors [Svezia] **73** Dab
Häggenås [Svezia] **71** CDb
Hague, Cap de la– **9** Ba
Haguenau [Fr.] **33** Aa
Hailuoto [Finl.] **65** Db
Hailuoto [Finl.] **65** Db
Hajdúböszörmény [Ung.]
      39 Cb
Hajdúszoboszló [Ung.] **39** Cb
Hajnówka [Pol.] **37** Cb
Hakkas [Svezia] **67** Bb
Hal / Halle [Bel.] **7** Cb
Halberstadt [D] **35** Cb
Halden [Norv.] **73** Cb
Halifax [RU] **5** Cb
Halle / Hal [Bel.] **7** Cb
Halle / Saale [D] **35** CDb
Hallein [Aus.] **33** Cb
Hallstatt [Aus.] **33** Cb
Hallstavik [Svezia] **59** Bab
Halmstad [Svezia] **75** Cb
Hals [Dan.] **75** Bab
Haltdålen [Norv.] **73** Ca
Hamar [Norv.] **73** Ca
Hamburg [D] = Amburgo (I)
      35 Cb
Hamburgisches Wattenmeer
      35 Bab
Hämeenlinna / Tavastehus
      [Finl.] **59** Da
Hameln [D] **35** Cb
Hamina / Fredrikshamn [Finl.]
      59 Ea
Hamm [D] **35** Bb
Ḥammâm al Anf [Tun.] **25** Ab
Ḥammâmât [Tun.] **25** Ab
Ḥammâmât, Khalīj– **25** Abc
Hammarstrand [Svezia] **71** Dbc
Hammerdal [Svezia] **71** Db
Hammerfest [Norv.] **69** Da
Hanau [D] **33** ABa
Hangö / Hanko [Finl.] **59** Db
Hanko / Hangö [Finl.] **59** Cb
Hannover [D] **35** Cb
Hanstholm [Dan.] **75** Aab
Haparanda [Svezia] **65** Dab
Hardangerfjorden **73** ABa
Hardangervidda [Norv.] **73** Ba
Hardangervidda [Norv.] **73** Ba
Harderwijk [P.B.] **7** Ca
Hareidlandet **73** ABa
Haría [Sp.] **23** ins.a
Harjavalta [Finl.] **59** Ca
Harlingen [P.B.] **7** Ca

Harmanli [Bulg.] **47** Bab
Härnösand [Svezia] **71** Dc
Haro [Sp.] **17** ABa
Harrogate [RU] **5** Cab
Harstad [Norv.] **69** Bb
Hartlepool [RU] **3** Da
Hartola [Finl.] **59** Da
Harwich [RU] **5** Db
Haskovo [Bulg.] **47** Bab
Haslach [D] **33** Aa
Hassela [Svezia] **59** Aa
Hasselt [Bel.] **7** Cab
Hässleholm [Svezia] **75** Cb
Hastings [RU] **5** Dbc
Hasvik [Norv.] **69** Da
Ḥaṭeg [Rom.] **41** Da
Hatfield [RU] **5** CDb
Hattfjelldal [Norv.] **71** Cb
Hatvan [Ung.] **39** Bb
Haugesund [Norv.] **73** Ab
Haukeligrend [Norv.] **73** Bb
Haukivesi **61** Ba
Havel **35** Db
Havel / Brandenburg [D] **35** Db
Havelberg [D] **35** CDb
Haverfordwest [RU] **5** Bb
Havírov [Rep.Ceca] **39** Ba
Havlíčkův Brod [Rep.Ceca]
      33 Da
Havneby [Dan.] **75** Ab
Hawick [RU] **3** Ca
Hayrabolu [Tur.] **47** Bcb
Hebrides, Sea of the– = Ebridi,
      Mare delle– (I) **1** Bab
Heddal [Norv.] **73** BCb
Hede [Svezia] **73** Da
Hedemora [Svezia] **73** Ea
Hedenäset [Svezia] **65** Ca
Heerenveen [P.B.] **7** CDa
Heide [D] **35** Bab
Heidelberg [D] **33** Aa
Heidenheim an der Brenz [D]
      33 Ba
Heidenreichstein [Aus.]
      33 CDa
Heilbronn [D] **33** Ba
Heiligenblut [Aus.] **33** Cb
Heimaey **77** Cb
Heinola [Finl.] **59** Da
Hel [Pol.] **57** Bb
Helgoland **35** Ba
Hella [Isl.] **77** Cb
Hellín [Sp.] **23** Bb
Helmond [P.B.] **7** Ca
Helsingborg [Svezia] **75** Cb
Helsingfors / Helsinki [Finl.]
      59 Da
Helsingør [Dan.] **75** Cb
Helsinki / Helsingfors [Finl.]
      59 Da
Helvetinjärvi **59** Ca
Hemnesberget [Norv.] **71** Ca
Hengelo [P.B.] **7** Da
Hennebont [Fr.] **9** Ab
Hercegnovi [Jug.] **41** Cb
Herdubreid **77** Db
Hereford [RU] **5** Cb
Herford [D] **35** Bb
Herma Ness **1** ins.a
Hermansverk [Norv.] **73** Ba
Herning [Dan.] **75** ABb
Herrera del Duque [Sp.] **21** Ca
Herrera de Pisuerga [Sp.]
      19 Ca
Herson [Ucr.] **51** Db
Herzberg / Elster [D] **35** Db
Herzberg am Harz [D] **35** Cb
Hesdin [Fr.] **5** Db
Hessen = Assia (I) **35** Cc
Hetolambina [Russia] **67** EFc
Heves [Ung.] **39** Bb
Hexham [RU] **3** Da
Heysham [RU] **3** CDab

Hibiny **67** Fb
Hidenportti **63** Ab
Hierro = Ferro (I) **23** ins.a
Hiitola [Russia] **61** Aa
Hiiumaa **59** Cb
Híjar [Sp.] **17** Bb
Hildesheim [D] **35** Cb
Hillerød [Dan.] **75** Cb
Hilversum [P.B.] **7** Ca
Himanka [Finl.] **65** Cb
Hinojosa del Duque [Sp.]
      21 Cb
Hirson [Fr.] **7** Cb
Hîrşova [Rom.] **49** Ca
Hirtshals [Dan.] **75** Ba
Histria **49** Ca
Hitra **71** Ab
Hjälmaren **73** Eb
Hjelmelandsvågen [Norv.]
      73 ABb
Hjørring [Dan.] **75** Ba
Hmelnicki [Ucr.] **53** ABb
Hobro [Dan.] **75** Bb
Hochharz **35** Cb
Hochtor **33** Cb
Hódmezóvásárhely [Ung.]
      39 Bb
Hodna, Chott el– **23** Dc
Hodonín [Rep.Ceca] **39** Aa
Hodorov [Ucr.] **39** Ca
Hoei / Huy [Bel.] **7** Cb
Hoek van Holland, Rotterdam–
      [P.B.] **7** Ca
Hof [D] **35** Db
Höfdakaupstadur [Isl.] **77** Bb
Höfn [Isl.] **77** Db
Hofors [Svezia] **73** Ea
Höganäs [Svezia] **75** Cb
Högfors / Karkkila [Finl.] **59** Da
Högsby [Svezia] **75** Da
Hohe Tauern **33** Cb
Højer [Dan.] **75** Ab
Holbæk [Dan.] **75** Bb
Hollabrunn [Aus.] **39** Aa
Holm [Norv.] **71** BCb
Holm [Russia] **55** Ca
Hólmavík [Isl.] **77** Bb
Holmsund [Svezia] **71** Eb
Holstebro [Dan.] **75** Ab
Holyhead [RU] **5** Bb
Homburg [D] **11** Ca
Hønefoss [Norv.] **73** Ca
Honfleur [Fr.] **9** Ca
Honiton [RU] **5** Bc
Honningsvåg [Norv.] **69** Ea
Honrubia [Sp.] **23** Ba
Hoogeveen [P.B.] **7** Da
Hooge Veluwe, De– **7** Ca
Hoorn [P.B.] **7** Ca
Hörby [Svezia] **75** Cb
Horgoš [Iug.] **41** Cb
Horn [Aus.] **39** Aa
Horn [Isl.] **77** Ba
Hornavan **71** Ca
Horncastle [RU] **5** CDb
Horol [Ucr.] **53** Db
Horsens [Dan.] **75** Bb
Horta [Port.] **21** ins.a
Horten [Norv.] **73** Cb
Hortorágy **39** BCb
Høtagen [Svezia] **71** Cb
Hotin [Ucr.] **53** Bb
Höting [Svezia] **71** Db
Houeillès [Fr.] **15** BCb
Howard, Castle– **3** Dab
Höxter [D] **35** Cb
Hoy **1** Ca
Høyanger [Norv.] **73** ABa
Hoyerswerda / Wojerecy [D]
      35 Db
Hradec Králové [Rep.Ceca]
      39 Aa

Hranice [Rep.Ceca] 39 Aa
Hron 39 Bab
Hrubieszów [Pol.] 37 CDc
Huddersfield [RU] 5 Cb
Hudiksvall [Svezia] 59 Aa
Huedin [Rom.] 39 Cb
Huelma [Sp.] 21 Cb
Huelva [Sp.] 21 Bb
Huércal-Overa [Sp.] 23 Bb
Huesca [Sp.] 17 Bab
Huéscar [Sp.] 23 Bb
Huete [Sp.] 23 Ba
Huittinen [Finl.] 59 Ca
Humber 5 CDb
Humenné [Slovac.] 39 Ca
Húnaflói 77 BCb
Hundested [Dan.] 75 BCb
Hunedoara [Rom.] 41 Da
Hünfeld [D] 35 Cc
Huntingdon [RU] 5 CDb
Huntly [RU] 1 Da
Hurez, Mănăstirea– 51 Abc
Húsavík [Isl.] 77 Dab
Huşi [Rom.] 51 Cb
Hust [Ucr.] 39 Cab
Husum [D] 35 BCa
Huy / Hoei [Bel.] 7 Cb
Hvammstangi [Isl.] 77 BCb
Hvannadalshnúkur 77 Db
Hvar [Cro.] 27 Ca
Hvar [Cro.] 27 Ca
Hveragerdi [Isl.] 77 Bb
Hveravellir [Isl.] 77 Cb
Hvítá 77 Bb
Hvolsvöllur [Isl.] 77 Cb
Hyères [Fr.] 13 BCb
Hyères, Iles d'– 13 Cb
Hyrynsalmi [Finl.] 65 Eb
Hyvinge / Hyvinkää [Finl.]
  59 Da
Hyvinkää / Hyvinge [Finl.]
  59 Da

I

Ialomiţa 49 Ca
Iaşi [Rom.] 51 Ca
Ibañeta, Puerto de– =
  Roncisvalle, Passo di– (I)
  17 Ba
Ibar 41 Cb
Ibiza 23 Cab
Ibiza / La Vila d'Eivissa [Sp.]
  23 Cab
Icod de los Vinos [Sp.]
  23 ins.a
Idar-Oberstein [D] 11 Ca
Ídhra [Grecia] 45 Ab
Ídhra = Idra (I) 45 Ab
Idra (I) = Ídhra 45 Ab
Idre [Svezia] 73 Da
Idrija [Slo.] 31 Ca
Ieper / Ypres [Bel.] 7 BCab
Ierápetra [Grecia] 45 Bc
Ifjord [Norv.] 69 EFa
Iglesias [It.] 29 Ab
Ignatovo [Russia] 61 Da
Ignatpol [Ucr.] 53 Bab
Igñeada [Tur.] 47 Cab
Igoumenitsa [Grecia] 43 Ab
Igualada [Sp.] 17 Cb
Ihtiman [Bulg.] 49 Aa
Iijoki 65 Db
Iisalmi [Finl.] 65 Eb
IJssel 7 Da
IJssel, Lago d'– (I) =
  IJsselmeer 7 Ca
IJsselmeer = IJssel, Lago
  d'– (I) 7 Ca
Ikaalinen [Finl.] 59 Ca
Ikaría 45 Bb

Iława [Pol.] 57 Bc
Ilfracombe [RU] 5 Bb
Ilia [Rom.] 41 Da
Iličevsk [Ucr.] 51 Db
Ilirska Bistrica [Slo.] 31 Ca
Illescas [Sp.] 19 Cb
Ilmajoki [Finl.] 65 Cc
Ilmen, ozero– 61 Bb
Ilmenau [D] 35 Cc
Ilomantsi [Finl.] 63 Bc
Ilūkste / Ilukste [Lett.] 57 Db
Ilukste / Ilūkste [Lett.] 57 Db
Imandra, ozero– 67 EFb
Imatra [Finl.] 61 Aa
Immenstadt im Allgäu [D]
  33 Bb
Imola [It.] 31 Bb
Imotski [Cro.] 41 Bb
Imperia [It.] 31 Ab
Imroz [Tur.] 47 Bb
Inari [Finl.] 67 CDab
Inari, Lago– (I) = Inarijärvi
  67 Dab
Inarijärvi = Inari, Lago– (I)
  67 Dab
Inca [Sp.] 23 CDa
Indalsälven 71 Dc
Indija [Iug.] 41 Cab
Indre 9 Cb
İnegöl [Tur.] 47 Cb
Infiesto [Sp.] 19 Ca
Ingenio [Sp.] 23 ins.a
Inghilterra (I) = England 5 Cb
Ingolstadt [D] 33 Ba
Ingul 51 Db
Inis / Ennis [Eire] 3 ABb
Inis Ceithleann / Enniskillen
  [RU] 3 Bab
Inis Córthaidh / Enniscorthy
  [Eire] 3 Bb
Inis Diomáin / Ennistymon
  [Eire] 3 Ab
Inn 33 Ca
Inner Hebrides =Ebridi Interne (I)
  1 Bab
Innhavet [Norv.] 69 Bb
Innsbruck [Aus.] 33 Bb
Inowrocław [Pol.] 37 Bb
Insurăţei [Rom.] 49 Ca
Interlaken [Svizz.] 33 Ab
Inveraray [RU] 1 Bb
Inverness [RU] 1 Ca
Ioánnina [Grecia] = Giannina (I)
  43 Ab
Iona 1 Bb
Ionava / Jonava [Lit.] 57 Db
Ionie, Isole– (I) = Iónioi Nísoi
  43 Abc
Ionio, Mar– 25 Cb
Ionio, Mar– (I) = Iónion
  Pélagos 43 Ac
Iónioi Nísoi = Ionie, Isole– (I)
  43 Abc
Iónion Pélagos = Ionio, Mar– (I)
  43 Ac
Ioniškis / Joniškis [Lit.] 57 Cb
Ios 45 Bb
Ipiros = Epiro (I) 43 ABb
Ipsala [Tur.] 47 Bb
Ipswich [RU] 5 Db
Iráklion [Grecia] 45 Bc
Irish Sea = Irlanda, Mar d'– (I)
  5 Bb
Irlanda, Mar d'– (I) = Irish Sea
  5 Bb
Iroise 9 Aa
Irún [Sp.] 17 Ba
Irurzun [Sp.] 17 Ba
Irvine [RU] 1 Cb
Isaccea [Rom.] 51 Cb
Isafjardardjúp 77 Ba
Ísafjörður [Isl.] 77 Bab
Isbister [RU] 1 ins.a

Ischia 29 Cb
Iseo [It.] 31 Ba
Iseo, Lago d'– 31 Ba
Isère 13 Ca
Isernia [It.] 29 Cb
Iskär 49 Aa
Islay 1 Bb
Isojärvi 59 Da
Issoire [Fr.] 13 Ba
Issoudun [Fr.] 9 Cb
İstanbul boğazı = Bosforo (I)
  47 Cb
İstanbul [Tur.] 47 Cb
Istiaía [Grecia] 45 Aab
Istra = Istria (I) 31 Ca
Istria [Rom.] 49 Ca
Istria (I) = Istra 31 Ca
Itaca (I) = Itháki 43 Ac
Itäisen Suomenlahti 59 DEa
Itämeri = Baltico, Mar– (I)
  59 BCb
Itéa [Grecia] 45 Ab
Itháki = Itaca (I) 43 Ac
Itzehoe [D] 35 Cb
Ivajlovgrad [Bulg.] 47 Bb
Ivalo [Finl.] 67 Db
Ivangorod [Russia] 61 Ab
Ivangrad [Iug.] 41 Cb
Ivanjica [Iug.] 41 Cb
Ivanjska [Bos.Erz.] 41 Bab
Ivano–Frankovsk [Ucr.] 51 Ba
Ivanovo [R.B.] 53 Aa
Ivje [R.B.] 57 Dbc
Ivrea [It.] 31 Aa
Izmail [Ucr.] 51 Cb
İzmir [Tur.] 47 Bb
İzmit [Tur.] 47 Cb
İznik [Tur.] 47 Cb
İznik Gölü 47 Cb

J

Jablanac [Cro.] 31 CDb
Jablanica [Bos.Erz.] 41 Bb
Jablanica [Bulg.] 49 ABa
Jablonec nad Nisou [Rep.Ceca]
  37 Ac
Jablonica, Passo di– (I) =
  Jablonicki, pereval– 51 Ba
Jablonicki, pereval– =
  Jablonica, Passo di– (I)
  51 Ba
Jaca [Sp.] 17 Ba
Jadransko More = Adriatico,
  Mar– (I) 27 BCa
Jaén [Sp.] 21 Cb
Jagotin [Ucr.] 53 Cb
Jaice [Bos.Erz.] 41 Bb
Jäkkvik [Svezia] 71 Da
Jakobstad / Pietarsaari [Finl.]
  65 Cb
Jalasjärvi [Finl.] 65 Cc
Jalpug, ozero– 51 Cb
Jambol [Bulg.] 49 Ba
Jamm [Russia] 61 Ab
Jampol [Ucr.] 51 Ca
Jampol [Ucr.] 53 Ab
Jämsä [Finl.] 59 Da
Janisjarvi, ozero– 61 Ba
Janiskoski [Russia] 67 Dab
Jánoshalma [Ung.] 41 Ca
Janów Lubelski [Pol.] 37 Cc
Jantra 49 Ba
Jarandilla [Sp.] 19 Cb
Jarcevo [Russia] 55 Cb
Jarlshof 1 ins.a
Jarmen [D] 35 Dab
Jarmolincy [Ucr.] 53 ABb
Jarocin [Pol.] 37 Bb
Jaroslavl [Russia] 61 Eb
Jarosław [Pol.] 39 Ca

Järvenpää [Finl.] 59 Da
Jaščera [Russia] 61 ABb
Jaselda 53 Aa
Jasło [Pol.] 39 Ca
Jasmund 35 Da
Jastrowie [Pol.] 37 Ab
Jászberény [Ung.] 39 Bb
Játiva / Xàtiva [Sp.] 23 Bab
Jawor [Pol.] 37 Abc
Jędrzejów [Pol.] 37 Bc
Jēkabpils / Jekabpils [Lett.]
  57 Db
Jekabpils / Jēkabpils [Lett.]
  57 Db
Jelcy [Russia] 55 Db
Jelenia Góra [Pol.] 37 Abc
Jelgava [Lett.] 57 Cb
Jelling [Dan.] 75 Bb
Jelnja [Russia] 55 Db
Jena [D] 35 Cbc
Jerez de la Frontera [Sp.]
  21 BCb
Jerez de los Caballeros [Sp.]
  21 Bb
Jersey 9 Bb
Jeseník [Rep.Ceca] 39 Aa
Jesi [It.] 31 Cb
Jezerišče [R.B.] 55 BCb
Jičín [Rep.Ceca] 37 Ac
Jiesjjavrre 69 Ea
Jihlava [Rep.Ceca] 33 Da
Jijel [Alg.] 23 Da
Jijona / Xixona [Sp.] 23 Bb
Jimbolia [Rom.] 41 Ca
Jindřichův Hradec [Rep.Ceca]
  33 CDa
Jiu 49 Aa
Jódar [Sp.] 21 Cb
Joensuu [Finl.] 63 Ac
Jõgeva / Jygeva [Est.] 59 Db
John o' Groat's [RU] 1 CDa
Joigny [Fr.] 11 Bab
Joinville [Fr.] 11 Ba
Jokkmokk [Svezia] 69 Bb
Jökulsá 77 Dab
Jonava / Ionava [Lit.] 57 Db
Joniškis / Ioniškis [Lit.] 57 Cb
Jönköping [Svezia] 75 Ca
Jörn [Svezia] 71 Eb
Jostedalsbreen 73 Ba
Jotunheimen [Norv.] 73 Ba
Jotunheimen [Norv.] 73 Ba
Joutsa [Finl.] 59 Da
Joutsijärvi [Finl.] 67 Db
Júcar 23 Ba
Judenburg [Aus.] 33 Cb
Juelsminde [Dan.] 75 Bb
Juhnov [Russia] 55 Db
Jukkasjärvi [Svezia] 69 Cb
Jumilla [Sp.] 23 Bb
Jungfrau 33 Ab
Junosuando [Svezia] 67 Bb
Junsele [Svezia] 71 Db
Juntusranta [Finl.] 63 Ab
Juorkuna [Finl.] 65 DEb
Jura [Eur.] = Giura (I) 11 Cb
Jura [RU] 1 BCb
Jura, Sound of– 1 Cb
Jūrmala / Jurmala [Lett.]
  57 Cab
Jurmala / Jūrmala [Lett.]
  57 Cab
Juškozero [Russia] 63 Bb
Jüterbog [D] 35 Db
Jutland (I) = Jylland 75 Bb
Juuka [Finl.] 63 Ab
Juva [Finl.] 59 Ea
Južna Morava 41 Db
Južny Bug = Bug Meridionale (I)
  51 Db
Jygeva / Jõgeva [Est.] 59 Db
Jylland = Jutland (I) 75 Bb
Jyväskylä [Finl.] 65 Dc

K

Kaamanen [Finl.] 69 Fab
Kaaresuvanto [Finl.] 67 Bb
Kābdalis [Svezia] 71 Ea
Kabylie 23 Db
Kafirévs, Ákra– 45 Bb
Kåfjord [Norv.] 69 Ea
Kagarlyk [Ucr.] 53 Cb
Kaiserslautern [D] 33 Aa
Kajaani [Finl.] 65 Eb
Kalabáka [Grecia] 43 Bb
Kalajoki [Finl.] 65 CDb
Kalámai [Grecia] 45 Ab
Kälarne [Svezia] 73 Ea
Kalavárdha [Grecia] 45 Cb
Kálavrita [Grecia] 45 Ab
Kalevala [Russia] 63 Bb
Kaliakra, Nos– 49 Cb
Kálimnos [Grecia] 45 BCb
Kálimnos [Grecia] 45 BCb
Kalinin → Tver [Russia]
  55 DEb
Kaliningrad [Russia] 57 Bb
Kalinkoviči [R.B.] 53 Cb
Kalinovka [Ucr.] 53 Bb
Kalisz [Pol.] 37 ABb
Kalisz Pomorski [Pol.] 37 Ab
Kalix [Svezia] 65 Cab
Kalixälven 65 Cb
Kalkan [Tur.] 45 ins.a
Kall [Svezia] 71 Cb
Kallavesi 65 Ebc
Kallsjön 71 Cb
Kalmar [Svezia] 75 Db
Kalmarsund 75 Db
Kalocsa [Ung.] 39 Bb
Kalofer [Bulg.] 49 Ba
Kalpáklon [Grecia] 43 Ba
Kaluga [Russia] 55 Eb
Kalundborg [Dan.] 75 Bb
Kaluš [Ucr.] 51 Ba
Kalvåg [Norv.] 73 Aa
Kamenec–Podolski [Ucr.]
  51 Ba
Kamenjak, Rt– = Promontore,
  Capo– (I) 31 Cb
Kamenka [Ucr.] 53 Cb
Kamienna Góra [Pol.] 37 Ac
Kamień Pomorski [Pol.]
  35 Dab
Kamnik [Slo.] 31 Ca
Kampen [P.B.] 7 CDa
Kampinos 37 Bb
Kandalaksa [Russia] 67 Eb
Kandalakša, Golfo di– =
  Kandalakšski zaliv 67 EFb
Kandalakšski zaliv =
  Kandalakša, Golfo di– (I)
  67 EFb
Kangasniemi [Finl.] 59 Da
Kankaanpää [Finl.] 59 Ca
Kannus [Finl.] 65 CDb
Kapellskär [Svezia] 59 Bb
Kaposvár [Ung.] 39 Ab
Kappeln [D] 35 Ca
Kapsukas → Marijampolė [Lit.]
  57 Cb
Kapustoje [Russia] 67 Fb
Kapuvár [Ung.] 39 Ab
Karabiga [Tur.] 47 Bb
Karaburun [Tur.] 45 Bb
Karacabey [Tur.] 47 Cb
Karadeniz = Nero, Mar– (I)
  49 CDb
Karamürsel [Tur.] 47 Cb
Karasjok [Norv.] 69 Ea
Kárbole [Svezia] 73 Ea
Karcag [Ung.] 39 BCb
Kardeljevo [Cro.] 27 Ca
Kardhítsa [Grecia] 43 Bb
Kärdla / Kjardla [Est.] 59 Cb

Kärdžali [Bulg.] **47** Bb
Karelija = Carelia (I) **63** BCb
Kargopol [Russia] **61** Da
Kariaí [Grecia] **47** Bb
Karigasniemi [Finl.] **69** Ea
Karis / Karjaa [Finl.] **59** Cab
Káristos [Grecia] **45** Bb
Karjaa / Karis [Finl.] **59** Cab
Karkkila / Högfors [Finl.] **59** Da
Karkonosze **37** Ac
Karlino [Pol.] **37** Aab
Karlobag [Cro.] **41** ABb
Karlovac [Cro.] **41** Ba
Karlovo [Bulg.] **49** Ba
Karlovy Vary [Rep.Ceca] **33** Ca
Karlsborg [Svezia] **75** Ca
Karlshamn [Svezia] **75** CDb
Karlskoga [Svezia] **73** Db
Karlskrona [Svezia] **75** Db
Karlsruhe [D] **33** Aa
Karlstad [Svezia] **73** Db
Karlštejn [Rep.Ceca] **33** Ca
Karmøy **73** Ab
Karnobat [Bulg.] **49** BCa
Kärnten = Carinzia (I) **33** Cb
Karow / Mecklenburg–
  Vorpommern [D] **35** Db
Kárpathos [Grecia] **45** Cc
Kárpathos [Grecia] =
  Scarpanto (I) **45** BCc
Karpaty [Eur.] = Carpazi
  Occidentali (I) **39** BCa
Karpaty [Ucr.] **51** Ba
Karpenísion [Grecia] **43** Bbc
Kärsämäki [Finl.] **65** Db
Kärsava / Karsava [Lett.] **55** Bb
Karsava / Kärsava [Lett.] **55** Bb
Karşıyka [Tur.] **45** BCb
Kartal [Tur.] **47** Cb
Kartuzy [Pol.] **37** Bb
Karungi [Svezia] **65** CDab
Karunki [Finl.] **65** CDab
Kaş [Tur.] **45** ins.a
Kašin [Russia] **55** Ea
Kaskinen / Kaskö [Finl.] **65** Cc
Kaskö / Kaskinen [Finl.] **65** Cc
Kásos = Caso (I) **45** BCc
Kassándra = Cassandra (I)
  43 Bb
Kassel [D] **35** Cb
Kastéllion [Grecia] **45** Ac
Kastoría [Grecia] **43** Bb
Katerini [Grecia] **43** Bb
Kätkäsuvanto [Svezia] **67** Bb
Káto Akhaía [Grecia] **43** Bc
Katowice [Pol.] **39** Ba
Katrineholm [Svezia] **73** Eb
Kattavía [Grecia] **45** Cbc
Kattegat **75** Bb
Kaufbeuren [D] **33** Bab
Kauhaneva–Pohjankangas
  65 Cc
Kauhava [Finl.] **65** Cbc
Kaukonen [Finl.] **67** Cb
Kaunas [Lit.] **57** CDb
Kaustinen [Finl.] **65** Cb
Kautokeino [Norv.] **69** CDa
Kavála [Grecia] **47** Bb
Kavarna [Bulg.] **49** Cb
Kávos [Grecia] **43** Ab
Kazanlăk [Bulg.] **49** Ba
Kazimierz Dolny [Pol.] **37** Cb
Kazincbarcika [Ung.] **39** Ba
Kéa **45** Bb
Kebnekaise **69** Cb
Kecel [Ung.] **39** Bb
Kecskemét [Ung.] **39** Bb
Kédainiai / Kedajnjaj [Lit.]
  57 CDb
Kedajnjaj / Kédainiai [Lit.]
  57 CDb
Kedrozero [Russia] **63** Cc
Kędzierzyn–Koźle [Pol.] **37** ABc

Kefallinía = Cefalonia (I) **43** Ac
Keflavík [Isl.] **77** Bb
Keitele **65** Dbc
Keith [RU] **1** CDa
Kelmè / Kelme [Lit.] **57** Cb
Kelme / Kelmè [Lit.] **57** Cb
Kelso [RU] **1** Db
Kem [Russia] **63** Cb
Kemi [Finl.] **65** Db
Kemi, Lago– (I) = Kemijärvi
  [Finl.] **67** Db
Kemijärvi [Finl.] **67** Db
Kemijärvi [Finl.] = Kemi,
  Lago– (I) **67** Db
Kemijoki **65** Da
Kemiö / Kimito [Finl.] **59** Ca
Kempten / Allgäu [D] **33** Bb
Kendal [RU] **3** Da
Kenmare / Neidín [Eire] **3** Ab
Kennacraig [RU] **1** Cb
Kent **5** Db
Kepe [Russia] **63** Bb
Kępno [Pol.] **37** ABb
Kerava [Finl.] **59** Da
Keret, ozero– **63** Bab
Kérkira [Grecia] **43** Ab
Kérkira [Grecia] = Corfú (I)
  43 Ab
Keşan [Tur.] **47** Bb
Kestenga [Russia] **63** Bab
Keswick [RU] **3** CDa
Keszthely [Ung.] **39** Ab
Ketama [Mar.] **21** Cc
Kętrzyn [Pol.] **57** Cbc
Kettering [RU] **5** Cb
Keuruu [Finl.] **65** Dc
Kežmarok [Slovac.] **39** Ba
Khálki = Calcide (I) **45** Cb
Khalkís [Grecia] **45** Ab
Khánia [Grecia] **45** ABc
Khíos [Grecia] **45** Bb
Khíos [Grecia] = Chio (I) **45** Bb
Khóra Sfakíon [Grecia] **45** ABc
Kiantajärvi **63** Bb
Kiappeselga [Russia] **63** Cc
Kibartai / Kybartai [Lit.] **57** Cb
Kičevo [Maced.] **43** ABb
Kiel [D] **35** Ca
Kielce [Pol.] **37** Bbc
Kihelkonna [Est.] **59** Cb
Kijev [Ucr.] **53** Cb
Kijev, Bacino di– (I) =
  Kijevskoje vodohranilišče
  53 Cab
Kijevskoje vodohranilišče =
  Kijev, Bacino di– (I) **53** Cab
Kikinda [Iug.] **41** Ca
Kikládhes = Cicladi (I) **45** Bb
Kil [Svezia] **73** Db
Kildare / Cill Dara [Eire] **3** Bb
Kildin, ostrov– **67** Fa
Kilija [Ucr.] **51** Cb
Kilingi–Nõmme / Kilingi–
  Nymme [Est.] **59** Db
Kilingi–Nymme / Kilingi–
  Nõmme [Est.] **59** Db
Kilkee / Cill Chaoi [Eire] **3** Ab
Kilkenny / Cill Chainnigh [Eire]
  3 Bb
Kilkís [Grecia] **43** Bb
Killarney **3** Ab
Killarney / Cill Airne [Eire]
  3 Ab
Killíni [Grecia] **43** ABc
Kilmarnock [RU] **1** Cb
Kilpisjärvi [Finl.] **69** CDa
Kilyos [Tur.] **47** Cb
Kími [Grecia] **45** ABb
Kimito **59** Ca
Kimito / Kemiö [Finl.] **59** Ca
Kímolos **45** Bb
Kimry [Russia] **55** Eab
Kingisepp [Russia] **61** Ab

King's Lynn [RU] **5** Db
Kingston–upon–Hull (Hull)
  [RU] **5** Cb
Kingussie [RU] **1** Cab
Kinna [Svezia] **75** Ca
Kinross [RU] **1** Cb
Kinsale / Cionn tSáile [Eire]
  3 Bb
Kinsarvik [Norv.] **73** Ba
Kiparíssia [Grecia] **45** Ab
Kipiná [Finl.] **65** Db
Kirillov [Russia] **61** Dab
Kirkağaç [Tur.] **47** Cbc
Kirkcaldy [RU] **1** CDb
Kirkenær [Norv.] **73** CDa
Kirkenes [Norv.] **69** Fa
Kirkjubæjarklaustur [Isl.]
  77 CDb
Kirklareli [Tur.] **47** Cb
Kirkudbright [RU] **3** Ca
Kirkwall [RU] **1** CDb
Kirov [Russia] **55** CDc
Kirovograd [Ucr.] **51** Da
Kirovsk [R.B.] **53** Ba
Kirovsk [Russia] **61** Bb
Kirovsk [Russia] **67** Fb
Kiruna [Svezia] **69** Cb
Kisa [Svezia] **73** Db
Kiskőrös [Ung.] **39** Bb
Kiskunfélegyháza [Ung.] **39** Bb
Kiskunhalas [Ung.] **39** Bb
Kiskunmajsa [Ung.] **39** Bb
Kiskunság **39** Bb
Kisújszállás [Ung.] **39** Bb
Kisvárda [Ung.] **39** Ba
Kíthira [Grecia] **45** Abc
Kíthira [Grecia] = Cerigo (I)
  45 Ab
Kíthnos **45** Bb
Kittilä [Finl.] **67** Cb
Kitzbühel [Aus.] **33** Cb
Kitzingen [D] **33** Ba
Kiuruvesi [Finl.] **65** Db
Kjardla / Kärdla [Est.] **59** Cb
Kjøllefjord [Norv.] **69** Fa
Kjustendil [Bulg.] **41** Db
Kladanj [Bos.Erz.] **41** Bb
Kladno [Rep.Ceca] **33** Ca
Kladovo [Iug.] **41** Db
Klagenfurt [Aus.] **33** Cb
Klaipeda / Klaipėda [Lit.]
  57 BCb
Klaipėda / Klaipeda [Lit.]
  57 BCb
Klarälven **73** Da
Klatovy [Rep.Ceca] **33** Ca
Kleve [D] **7** CDa
Klimpfjäll [Svezia] **71** CDb
Klin [Russia] **55** Eb
Klincy [Russia] **53** Ca
Klínovec **35** Dc
Klintehamn [Svezia] **57** Ba
Ključ [Bos.Erz.] **41** Bb
Kłodzko [Pol.] **37** Ac
Kløfta [Norv.] **73** CDab
Klosterneuburg [Aus.] **39** Aa
Kluczbork [Pol.] **37** Bbc
Kneža [Bulg.] **49** ABa
Knin [Cro.] **41** Bb
Knittelfeld [Aus.] **33** Cb
Knjaževac [Iug.] **41** Db
Knokke–Heist [Bel.] **7** Ca
Knosós = Cnosso (I) **45** Bc
København [Dan.] =
  Copenaghen (I) **75** Cb
Koblenz [D] **33** Ba
Kobrin [R.B.] **37** Db
Kočani [Maced.] **43** Bab
Kočevje [Slo.] **31** CDa
Kock [Pol.] **37** Cb
Kočkoma [Russia] **63** Cb
Köflach [Aus.] **33** CDb
Køge [Dan.] **75** Cb

Kohtla–Jarve / Kohtla–järve
  [Est.] **59** Eb
Kohtla–järve / Kohtla–Jarve
  [Est.] **59** Eb
Koitere **63** Bbc
Kökar **59** BCab
Kokkola [Finl.] **65** Cb
Kola [Russia] **67** EFab
Kola [Russia] **67** EFab
Kola, Penisola di– (I) = Kolski
  poluostrov **67** Fb
Kolari [Finl.] **67** Bb
Kolatselga [Russia] **61** Ba
Kolding [Dan.] **75** Bb
Kolezma [Russia] **63** CDb
Koli [Finl.] **63** Abc
Koli [Finl.] **63** Abc
Kolín [Rep.Ceca] **33** Da
Kolka [Lett.] **59** Cb
Kolkasrags **59** Cb
Köln [D] = Colonia (I) **7** Dab
Kołobrzeg [Pol.] **37** Aa
Kolomyja [Ucr.] **51** Ba
Kolpino [Russia] **61** Bb
Kolski poluostrov = Kola,
  Penisola di– (I) **67** Fb
Komárno [Slovac.] **39** ABb
Komárom [Ung.] **39** ABb
Komló [Ung.] **41** Ca
Komotini [Grecia] **47** Bb
Kondopoga [Russia] **63** Cc
Kongsberg [Norv.] **73** Cb
Kongsvinger [Norv.] **73** CDa
Koniecpol [Pol.] **37** Bc
Konin [Pol.] **37** Bb
Kónitsa [Grecia] **43** Ab
Konjic [Bos.Erz.] **41** BCb
Konoša [Russia] **61** Ea
Konotop [Ucr.] **53** CDa
Końskie [Pol.] **37** Bb
Konstanz [D] **33** Bb
Kontiomäki [Finl.] **65** Eb
Köpasker [Isl.] **77** Da
Koper [Slo.] **31** Ca
Köping [Svezia] **73** Eb
Koppang [Norv.] **73** Ca
Kopparberg [Svezia] **73** DEab
Koprivnica [Cro.] **41** Ba
Korça [Alb.] **43** Ab
Korčula [Cro.] **27** Ca
Korčula [Cro.] **27** Ca
Korgen [Norv.] **71** Cab
Korinthiakós Kólpos = Corinto,
  Golfo di– (I) **45** Ab
Kórinthos [Grecia] **45** Ab
Korisía [Grecia] **45** Bb
Körmend [Ung.] **39** Ab
Kornati [Cro.] **41** Bb
Kornati [Cro.] **41** Bb
Korneuburg [Aus.] **39** Aa
Kórnik [Pol.] **37** Ab
Kóroni [Grecia] **45** Ab
Körös **39** Bb
Korosten [Ucr.] **53** Bab
Korostyšev [Ucr.] **53** Bb
Korpilombolo [Svezia] **67** Bb
Korpo / Korppoo [Finl.] **59** Cab
Korppoo / Korpo [Finl.] **59** Cab
Korsnäs [Finl.] **65** Cc
Korsør [Dan.] **75** Bb
Korsun–Ševčenkovski [Ucr.]
  53 Cb
Kortrijk / Courtrai [Bel.] **7** Cb
Kos [Grecia] **45** Cb
Kos [Grecia] **45** BCb
Kościan [Pol.] **37** Ab
Kościerzyna [Pol.] **37** ABab
Košice [Slovac.] **39** Ca
Koski [Finl.] **59** Ca
Koskolovo [Russia] **61** Ab
Kostajnica [Cro.] **41** Ba

Kostenec [Bulg.] **49** ABa
Kostomukša [Russia] **63** Bb
Kostopol [Ucr.] **53** Aab
Koszalin [Pol.] **37** Aa
Kőszeg [Ung.] **39** Ab
Kotala [Finl.] **67** Db
Kotel [Bulg.] **49** Ba
Köthen / Anhalt [D] **35** CDb
Kotka [Finl.] **59** DEa
Kotlenski prohod **49** Ba
Kotor [Iug.] **41** Bb
Kotor Varoš [Bos.Erz.] **41** Bb
Kotovsk [Ucr.] **51** Cb
Kötschach–Mauthen [Aus.]
  33 Cb
Kouvola [Finl.] **59** Da
Kovačica [Iug.] **41** Cab
Kovdozero, ozero– **67** Cb
Kovel [Ucr.] **37** Db
Köycegiz [Tur.] **45** Cb
Kozáni [Grecia] **43** Bb
Kozara **41** Bab
Kozienice [Pol.] **37** Cb
Kragerø [Norv.] **73** Cb
Kragujevac [Iug.] **41** CDb
Kraídhion [Grecia] **45** Ab
Kraków [Pol.] **39** Ba
Kraków [Pol.] = Cracovia (I)
  35 Db
Králíky [Rep.Ceca] **39** Aa
Kraljevo [Iug.] **41** Cb
Kramfors [Svezia] **71** Dc
Kranj [Slo.] **31** Ca
Kranjska Gora [Slo.] **33** Cb
Krapkowice [Pol.] **37** Ab
Kraslava / Krāslava [Lett.]
  55 ABb
Krāslava / Kraslava [Lett.]
  55 ABb
Kraśnik [Pol.] **37** Cbc
Krasnoje Selo [Russia] **61** Bb
Krasny Holm [Russia] **61** Db
Krasnystaw [Pol.] **37** Cbc
Krefeld [D] **7** Da
Kremenčug [Ucr.] **53** Cb
Kremenčug, Bacino di– (I) =
  Kremenčugskoje
  vodohranilišče **53** Cb
Kremenčugskoje vodohranilišče
  = Kremenčug, Bacino di– (I)
  53 Cb
Kremenec [Ucr.] **53** Ab
Kremnica [Slovac.] **39** Ba
Krems an der Donau [Aus.]
  33 Da
Krestcy [Russia] **61** Bb
Kričev [R.B.] **55** Cc
Kriós, Ákra– **45** Ac
Kristiansand [Norv.] **75** Aa
Kristianstad [Svezia] **75** Cb
Kristiansund [Norv.] **71** Abc
Kristiinankaupunki /
  Kristinestad [Finl.] **65** Cc
Kristinehamn [Svezia] **73** Db
Kristinestad /
  Kristiinankaupunki [Finl.]
  65 Cc
Kríti = Creta (I) **45** Bc
Kritikón Pélagos = Creta, Mar
  di– (I) **45** Bc
Kriva Palanka [Maced.] **41** Db
Križevci [Cro.] **41** Ba
Krk [Cro.] **31** Cab
Krk [Cro.] **31** Cab
Krka **41** Bb
Krkonoše **37** Ac
Krnov [Rep.Ceca] **39** Aa
Krokom [Svezia] **71** Db
Kroměříž [Rep.Ceca] **39** Aa
Kronach [D] **33** Ba
Kronštadt [Russia] **61** Aab
Krośniewice [Pol.] **37** Bb
Krosno [Pol.] **39** Ca

Krosno Odrzańskie [Pol.]
37 Ab
Krotoszyn [Pol.] **37** Ab
Kruja [Alb.] **43** Ab
Krumovgrad [Bulg.] **47** Bb
Kruševac [Iug.] **41** Db
Krušné Hory = Metalliferi,
Monti– (I) **35** Dc
Krynica [Pol.] **39** BCa
Ksar el Kebir [Mar.] **21** BCc
Kubenskoje, ozero– **61** Eb
Kuçukçekmece [Tur.] **47** Cb
Kudova–Zdrój [Pol.] **37** Ac
Kufstein [Aus.] **33** BCb
Kuhmo [Finl.] **63** Ab
Kuhmoinen [Finl.] **59** Da
Kuivaniemi [Finl.] **65** Db
Kuivastu [Est.] **59** Cb
Kukësi [Alb.] **41** Cbc
Kukuj [Russia] **61** Bb
Kula [Bulg.] **41** Db
Kula [Tur.] **45** Cb
Kuldiga / Kuldīga [Lett.]
57 Cab
Kuldīga / Kuldiga [Lett.]
57 Cab
Kulmbach [D] **33** Ba
Kumanovo [Maced.] **41** Db
Kumla [Svezia] **73** DEb
Kungsbacka [Svezia] **75** BCa
Kuolismaa [Russia] **63** Bc
Kuopio [Finl.] **65** Ec
Kuortane [Finl.] **65** Cc
Kupa **41** Ba
Kupiškis [Lit.] **57** Db
Kuressaare [Est.] **59** Cb
Kurikka [Finl.] **65** Cc
Kurów [Pol.] **37** Cb
Kuršėnai / Kuršėnaj [Lit.]
57 Cb
Kuršėnaj / Kuršėnai [Lit.]
57 Cb
Kurski zaliv **57** BCb
Kuršumlija [Iug.] **41** Db
Kuşadası [Tur.] **45** Cb
Kuş Cenneti **47** Cb
Kuş Gölü **47** Cb
Kutina [Cro.] **41** Ba
Kutná Hora [Rep.Ceca] **33** Da
Kutno [Pol.] **37** Bb
Kuusamo [Finl.] **63** Aab
Kuusankoski [Finl.] **59** Da
Kuvšinovo [Russia] **55** Dab
Kvænangen **69** Ca
Kvaløy **69** Ca
Kvaløya **69** DEa
Kvalsund [Norv.] **69** DEa
Kvam [Norv.] **73** Ca
Kvanndal [Norv.] **73** Ba
Kvikkjokk [Svezia] **69** Bb
Kvinesdal [Norv.] **75** Aa
Kwidzyn [Pol.] **57** Bc
Kybartai / Kibartaj [Lit.] **57** Cb
Kyle of Lochalsh [RU] **1** Ca
Kyrksæterora [Norv.] **71** ABb
Kyyjärvi [Finl.] **65** Dbc

L

La Alberca [Sp.] **19** BCa
La Almunia de Doña Godina
[Sp.] **17** Bb
La Bañeza [Sp.] **19** BCa
La Baule–Escoublac [Fr.] **9** Bb
Labe = Elba (I) **33** Da
Labin [Cro.] **31** Cab
Lača, ozero– **61** Ba
Lacanau–Océan, Lacanau– [Fr.]
15 Bab
La Carolina [Sp.] **21** Cb
Lacaune [Fr.] **15** Cb
La Charité–sur–Loire [Fr.]
11 ABb
La Châtre [Fr.] **9** Cb
La Chaux–de–Fonds [Svizz.]
11 Cb
La Ciotat [Fr.] **13** Bb
La Ciutat de Mallorca / Palma
[Sp.] **23** Ca
Laconi [It.] **29** ABb
La Coruña / A Coruña [Sp.]
19 Ba
Ladoga, Lago– (I) = Ladožskoje
ozero **61** Ba
Ladožskoje ozero = Ladoga,
Lago– (I) **61** Ba
Lærdalsøyri [Norv.] **73** Ba
La Escala / l'Escala [Sp.]
17 CDab
Læsø **75** Ba
La Ferté–Bernard [Fr.] **9** Ca
La Ferté–sous–Jouarre [Fr.]
11 ABa
La Flèche [Fr.] **9** BCb
Lågen **73** Ca
Lagoa [Port.] **21** Bb
Lagonegro [It.] **25** Ca
Lágos [Grecia] **47** Bb
Lagos [Port.] **21** Bb
La Guardia [Sp.] **19** ABab
La Gudiña [Sp.] **19** Bab
Lahdenpohja [Russia] **61** ABa
Lahemaa **59** Db
Laholm [Svezia] **75** Cb
Lahti [Finl.] **59** Da
L'Aia (I) = Den Haag / 's–
Gravenhage [P.B.] **7** Ca
L'Aia (I) = 's Gravenhage / Den
Haag [P.B.] **7** Ca
Laihia [Finl.] **65** Cbc
Lairg [RU] **1** Ca
Laitila [Finl.] **59** Ca
Lajes do Pico [Port.] **21** ins.a
Lajosmizse [Ung.] **39** Bb
Lake District **3** Ca
Laksefjorden **69** EFa
Lakselv [Norv.] **69** Ea
La Laguna [Sp.] **23** ins.a
Lalín [Sp.] **19** Ba
La Línea [Sp.] **21** Cb
La Mancha **23** ABab
Lamastre [Fr.] **13** Bab
Lamballe [Fr.] **9** Ba
Lamego [Port.] **19** Bb
Lamía [Grecia] **45** Ab
Lamotte–Beuvron [Fr.] **9** Cb
Lampedusa **25** Bc
Lampione **25** Bc
La Mure [Fr.] **13** Bab
Lanark [RU] **1** Cb
Lancaster [RU] **3** Dab
Landau an der Isar [D] **33** Ca
Landau in der Pfalz [D] **33** Aa
Landeck [Aus.] **33** Bb
Landerneau [Fr.] **9** Aa
Landsberg am Lech [D] **33** Bab
Land's End **5** Bc
Landshut [D] **33** BCa
Landskrona [Svezia] **75** Cb
Langádhia [Grecia] **45** Ab
Langeland **75** Bb
Langholm [RU] **3** CDa
Langjökull **77** Cb
Langogne [Fr.] **13** Bb
Langon [Fr.] **15** Bb
Langreo [Sp.] **19** Ca
Langres [Fr.] **11** Bab
Långtrask [Svezia] **71** Eb
Languedoc = Linguadoca (I)
13 Bb

Lannemezan [Fr.] **17** Ca
Lannion [Fr.] **9** Aa
Lanusei [It.] **29** Bb
Lanzarote **23** ins.a
Lanzo Torinese [It.] **31** Aa
Laon [Fr.] **11** Ba
la Orotava [Sp.] **23** ins.a
Lapalisse [Fr.] **11** Bb
La Palma **23** ins.a
La Palma del Condado [Sp.]
21 Bb
Lappajärvi **65** Cbc
Lappeenranta / Villmanstrand
[Finl.] **61** Aa
Lappi = Lapponia (I) **67** CDb
Lappland = Lapponia (I)
71 DEa
Lappo / Lapua [Finl.] **65** Cbc
Lapponia (I) = Lappi **67** CDb
Lapponia (I) = Lappland
71 DEa
Lâpseki [Tur.] **47** Bb
Lapua / Lappo [Finl.] **65** Cbc
L'Aquila [It.] **29** Ca
Larache [Mar.] **21** BCc
L' Arbresle [Fr.] **13** Ba
Larche, Col de– = Maddalena,
Colle della– (I) **13** Cb
Laredo [Sp.] **19** Ca
Larino [It.] **29** CDb
Lario → Como, Lago di–
31 Ba
Lárisa [Grecia] = Larissa (I)
43 Bb
Larissa (I) = Lárisa [Grecia]
43 Bb
Larne / Latharna [RU] **3** BCa
La Robla [Sp.] **19** Ca
La Roche–en–Ardenne [Bel.]
7 Cb
La Rochefoucauld [Fr.] **15** Ca
La Rochelle [Fr.] **9** Bb
La Roche–sur–Yon [Fr.] **9** Bb
La Roda [Sp.] **23** Ba
Larvik [Norv.] **73** Cab
la Seu d'Urgell / Seo de Urgel
[Sp.] **17** Ca
La Souterraine [Fr.] **9** Cb
Las Palmas de Gran Canaria
[Sp.] **23** ins.a
La Spezia [It.] **31** Bb
Lastovo [Cro.] **27** Ca
Lastovo [Cro.] **27** Ca
Latharna / Larne [RU] **3** BCa
Latina [It.] **29** Cb
La Tour–du–Pin [Fr.] **13** Ba
Lauhanvuori **59** Ca
Launceston [RU] **5** Bc
La Unión [Sp.] **23** Bb
Lausanne / Losanna (I) =
Lausanne [Svizz.] **11** Cb
Lausitzer Neiße **35** Db
Laval [Fr.] **9** Bab
Lavangen [Norv.] **69** Bb
La Vila d'Eivissa / Ibiza [Sp.]
23 Cab
La Vila Joiosa / Villajoyosa
[Sp.] **23** Bb
Lávrion [Grecia] **45** ABb
Lazarevac [Iug.] **41** Cb
Łeba [Pol.] **37** Aa
Lebesby [Norv.] **69** EFa
Le Blanc [Fr.] **9** Cb
Lębork [Pol.] **37** Aa
Le Bourg–d'Oisans [Fr.]
13 BCab
Lecce [It.] **27** Db
Lecco [It.] **31** Ba
Le Creusot [Fr.] **11** Bb
Le Croisic [Fr.] **9** Bb
Lectoure [Fr.] **15** Cb
Łęczyca [Pol.] **37** Bb
Ledmozero [Russia] **63** Bb

Le Dorat [Fr.] **9** Cb
Leeds [RU] **5** Cb
Leeuwarden [P.B.] **7** Ca
Legionowo [Pol.] **37** BCb
Legnago [It.] **31** Ba
Legnica [Pol.] **37** Ab
Le Havre [Fr.] **9** BCa
Leibnitz [Aus.] **33** Db
Leicester [RU] **5** Cb
Leiden [P.B.] **7** Ca
Leie **7** Cab
Leipzig [D] = Lipsia (I) **35** Db
Leiria [Port.] **19** Bb
Leirvik [Norv.] **73** Ab
Leksand [Svezia] **73** DEa
Leksozero, ozero– **63** Bb
Leksvik [Norv.] **71** Bb
Le Lavandou [Fr.] **13** Cb
Léman, Lac– = Ginevra, Lago
di– (I) **11** Cb
Le Mans [Fr.] **9** Cab
Lemdiyya [Alg.] **23** Cb
Lemmenjoki **67** Cb
Lemno = Límnos **47** Bb
Lempäälä [Finl.] **59** Ca
Lemvig [Dan.] **75** Ab
Lendava [Slo.] **39** Ab
Lendery [Russia] **63** Bb
Lenhovda [Svezia] **75** Dab
Lenin [R.B.] **53** Ba
Lens [Fr.] **7** Bb
Lentiira [Finl.] **63** ABb
Lentini [It.] **25** BCb
Leoben [Aus.] **33** CDb
Leominster [RU] **5** Cb
León [Sp.] **19** Ca
Leone, Golfo del– (I) = Lion,
Golfe du– **13** Bb
Leonídhion [Grecia] **45** Ab
Le Palais [Fr.] **9** Bb
Lepel [R.B.] **55** Bb
Leppäniemi [Russia] **61** Ba
Le Puy–en–Velay [Fr.] **13** Bab
Lercara Friddi [It.] **25** Bb
Lérida / Lleida [Sp.] **17** Cb
Lerma [Sp.] **19** Cab
Léros [Grecia] **45** Bb
Lerum [Svezia] **75** Ca
Lerwick [RU] **1** ins.a
Les Andelys [Fr.] **9** Ca
Les Baux–de–Provence [Fr.]
13 Bb
Lesbo (I) = Lésvos **47** Bb
l'Escala / La Escala [Sp.]
17 CDab
Les Eyzies–de–Tayac [Fr.]
15 Cab
Lesja [Norv.] **73** Ba
Lesko [Pol.] **39** Ca
Leskovac [Iug.] **41** Db
Leskoviku [Alb.] **43** Bb
Les Sables–d'Olonne [Fr.]
9 Bb
Lésvos = Lesbo (I) **47** Bb
Leszno [Pol.] **37** Ab
Letenye [Ung.] **39** Ab
Letičev [Ucr.] **53** Bb
Le Touquet–Paris–Plage [Fr.]
5 Dc
Le Tréport [Fr.] **5** Dc
Letterkenny [Eire] **3** Ba
Leucade (I) = Levkás [Grecia]
43 Ac
Leuven / Louvain [Bel.] **7** Cab
Levádhia [Grecia] **45** Ab
Levanger [Norv.] **71** Bb
Le Verdon–sur–Mer [Fr.] **15** Ba
Leverkusen [D] **7** Dab
Levice [Slovac.] **39** Ba
Levkás [Grecia] **43** Ac

Levkás [Grecia] = Leucade (I)
43 Ac
Levoča [Slovac.] **39** Ba
Levski [Bulg.] **49** Ba
Lewis, Butt of– **1** Ba
Lewis, Isle of– **1** Ba
Ležajsk [Pol.] **39** Ca
Lezha [Alb.] **43** Ab
Liberec [Rep.Ceca] **37** Ac
Libourne [Fr.] **15** Bab
Librazhdi [Alb.] **43** Ab
Licata [It.] **25** Bb
Lichtenfels [D] **33** Ba
Licosa, Punta– **29** Cb
Lida [R.B.] **57** Dbc
Lidköping [Svezia] **75** Da
Lido di Jesolo [It.] **31** Ca
Lido di Metaponto [It.] **27** Cab
Lido di Ostia [It.] **29** Cb
Lidzbark Warmiński [Pol.]
57 Bbc
Liège / Luik [Bel.] = Liegi (I)
7 Cb
Liegi (I) = Liège / Luik [Bel.]
7 Cb
Liegi (I) = Luik / Liège [Bel.]
7 Cb
Lieksa [Finl.] **63** ABb
Lielupė **57** Cb
Lienz [Aus.] **33** Cb
Liepāja / Liepaja [Lett.] **57** Bb
Liepaja / Liepāja [Lett.] **57** Bb
Lier / Lierre [Bel.] **7** Cab
Lierre / Lier [Bel.] **7** Cab
Liesjärvi **59** CDa
Liezen [Aus.] **33** Cb
Lignano Sabbiadoro [It.] **31** Ca
Ligure, Mar– **31** ABb
Lihula [Est.] **59** Cb
Liinahamari [Russia] **67** Ca
L' Ile Rousse [Fr.] **13** CDb
Lilienfeld [Aus.] **39** Aab
Lilla (I) = Lille **7** BCb
Lille (Fr.) = Lilla (I) **7** BCb
Lille Bælt = Piccolo Belt (I)
75 Bb
Lillehammer [Norv.] **73** Ca
Lillestrøm [Norv.] **73** Cab
Lillhärdal [Svezia] **73** Da
Lim **41** Cb
Lima [Svezia] **73** Da
Limburg an der Lahn [D] **35** Bc
Limerick / Luimneach [Eire]
3 Bb
Limfjorden **75** ABab
Limingen **71** Cb
Liminka [Finl.] **65** Db
Límnos = Lemno (I) **47** Bb
Limoges [Fr.] **15** Ca
Limone Piemonte [It.] **31** Ab
Limoux [Fr.] **17** Ca
Linares [Sp.] **21** Cb
Lincoln [RU] **5** Cb
Lindau (Bodensee) [D] **33** Cb
Lindesberg [Svezia] **73** Eb
Lindesnes **75** Aa
Líndhos [Grecia] **45** Cbc
Lingen (Ems) [D] **7** Da
Linguadoca (I) = Languedoc
13 Bb
Linköping [Svezia] **75** Da
Linnansaari **61** Aa
Linosa **25** Bbc
Linsell [Svezia] **73** Da
Linz [Aus.] **33** Ca
Lion, Golfe du– = Leone, Golfo
del– (I) **13** Bb
Lione (I) = Lyon [Fr.] **13** Ba
Lios na gCearrbhach / Lisburn
[RU] **3** BCa
Liozno [R.B.] **55** Cb
Lipari [It.] **25** BCb

Lipari [It.] **25** BCb
Lipcani [Mold.] **51** Ba
Lipno [Pol.] **37** Bb
Lipova [Rom.] **41** Da
Lippstadt [D] **35** Bb
Lipsia (I) = Leipzig [D] **35** Db
Liptovský Mikuláš [Slovac.]
39 Ba
Liria / Llíria [Sp.] **23** Ba
Lisboa [Port.] = Lisbona (I)
21 Ab
Lisbona (I) = Lisboa [Port.]
21 Ab
Lisburn / Lios na gCearrbhach
[RU] **3** BCa
Lisieux [Fr.] **9** Ca
Líthinon, Ákra– **45** Bc
Litókhoron [Grecia] **43** Bb
Litoměřice [Rep.Ceca] **35** Dc
Livádhi [Grecia] **45** Bb
Līvāni / Livany [Lett.] **57** Db
Livany / Līvāni [Lett.] **57** Db
Liverpool [RU] **5** BCb
Liverpool Bay **5** Bb
Livno [Bos.Erz.] **41** Bb
Livorno [It.] **31** Bb
Lizard [RU] **5** Bc
Lizard Point **5** Bc
Līžespasts [Lett.] **57** Da
Ljady [Russia] **61** Ab
Ljaskelja [Russia] **61** Ba
Ljubar [Ucr.] **53** Bb
Ljubljana [Slo.] = Lubiana (I)
31 Ca
Ljubovija [Iug.] **41** Cb
Ljubuški [Bos.Erz.] **27** Ca
Ljubytino [Russia] **61** Cb
Ljudinovo [Russia] **55** Dbc
Ljugarn [Svezia] **57** Ba
Ljungan **71** Cc
Ljungby [Svezia] **75** Cb
Ljungdalen [Svezia] **73** Da
Ljusdal [Svezia] **73** Ea
Ljusnan **59** Aa
Llandovery [RU] **5** Bb
Llandrindod Wells [RU] **5** Bb
Llandudno [RU] **5** Bb
Llanelli [RU] **5** Bb
Llanes [Sp.] **19** Ca
Lleida / Lérida [Sp.] **17** Cb
Llerena [Sp.] **21** BCb
Llíria / Liria [Sp.] **23** Ba
Llucena / Lucena del Cid [Sp.]
23 Ba
Löbau / Lubij [D] **35** Dbc
Locarno [Svizz.] **31** Aa
Lochaline [RU] **1** Ba
Lochboisdale [RU] **1** Ba
Loches [Fr.] **9** Ca
Loch Garman / Wexford [Eire]
3 Bb
Lochgilphead [RU] **1** Cb
Lochinver [RU] **1** Ca
Lochmaddy [RU] **1** Ba
Lochranza [RU] **1** Cb
Locminé [Fr.] **9** Bab
Locri [It.] **25** Cb
Lodejnoje Pole [Russia] **61** Ca
Lodève [It.] **13** Bb
Lodi [It.] **31** Ba
Lødingen [Norv.] **69** Bb
Łódź [Pol.] **37** Bb
Lofoten **69** Ab
Logojsk [R.B.] **55** Bb
Logroño [Sp.] **17** Ba
Logrosán [Sp.] **21** Ca
Løgstør [Dan.] **75** Bab
Lohiniva [Finl.] **67** Db
Lohja / Lojo [Finl.] **59** CDa
Lohusuu [Est.] **59** DEb
Lohvica [Ucr.] **53** Db
Loimaa [Finl.] **59** Ca
Loir **9** Cb

Loira (I) = Loire **9** Bb
Loire = Loira (I) **9** Bb
Loja [Sp.] **21** Cb
Lojo / Lohja [Finl.] **59** CDa
Lokantekojärvi **67** Dab
Lokka [Finl.] **67** Db
Løkken [Dan.] **75** Ba
Loknja [Russia] **55** BCb
Lokot [Russia] **53** Da
Lolland **35** Ca
Lom [Bulg.] **49** Aa
Lom [Norv.] **73** Bba
Łomża [Pol.] **37** Cb
London [RU] = Londra (I)
5 CDb
Londonderry / Doire [RU] **3** Ba
Londra (I) = London [RU]
5 CDb
Longford / An Longfort [Eire]
3 Bb
Longuyon [Fr.] **11** Ba
Longwy [Fr.] **11** Ba
Lønsdal [Norv.] **69** Ab
Lons–le–Saunier [Fr.] **11** Bb
Loop Head **3** Ab
Lopphavet **69** CEa
Lora del Río [Sp.] **21** Cb
Lorca [Sp.] **23** Bb
Loreto [It.] **31** Cb
Lorient [Fr.] **9** Ab
Lorn, Firth of– **1** Cb
Losanna (I) = Lausanne [Svizz.]
11 Cb
Los Cristianos [Sp.] **23** ins.a
Lošinj **31** Cb
Los Llanos de Aridane [Sp.]
23 ins.a
Los Navalmorales [Sp.]
19 Cb
Lot **15** Cb
Lotta **67** DEb
Loudéac [Fr.] **9** Ba
Loudun [Fr.] **9** BCb
Loughborough [RU] **5** Cb
Louhi [Russia] **63** BCab
Loulé [Port.] **21** Bb
Louny [Rep.Ceca] **35** Dc
Lourdes [Fr.] **17** BCa
Louth [RU] **5** CDb
Loutrá Aidhipsoú [Grecia]
45 Aab
Louvain / Leuven [Bel.] **7** Cab
Louviers [Fr.] **9** Ca
Lövånger [Svezia] **65** Cb
Lovat **55** Ca
Lövberga [Svezia] **71** Db
Lovćen **41** Cb
Loveč [Bulg.] **49** Bb
Lovere [It.] **31** Ba
Loviisa / Lovisa [Finl.] **59** Cb
Lovisa / Loviisa [Finl.] **59** Cb
Lovozero [Russia] **67** Fb
Lovozero, ozero– **71** Db
Lowestoft [RU] **5** Db
Łowicz [Pol.] **37** Bb
Lozère, Mont– **13** Bb
Loznica [Iug.] **41** Cb
Luarca [Sp.] **19** Ba
Lubań [Pol.] **37** Abc
Lubartów [Pol.] **37** Cb
Lubawa [Pol.] **37** Bb
Lübben (Spreewald) / Lubin [D]
35 Db
Lubecca (I) = Lübeck [D]
35 Cab
Lübeck [D] = Lubecca (I)
35 Cab
Lubenec [Rep.Ceca] **33** Ca
Lubiana (I) = Ljubljana [Slo.]
31 Ca
Lubij / Löbau [D] **35** Dbc
Lubin [Pol.] **37** Ab

Lubin / Lübben (Spreewald) [D]
35 Db
Lublin [Pol.] = Lublino (I)
37 Cb
Lubliniec [Pol.] **37** Bc
Lublino (I) = Lublin [Pol.]
37 Cb
Lubny [Ucr.] **53** CDb
Lubsko [Pol.] **35** DEb
Lucca [It.] **31** Bb
Lucena [Sp.] **21** Cb
Lucena del Cid / Llucena [Sp.]
23 Ba
Lučenec [Slovac.] **39** Ba
Lucera [It.] **27** Cb
Luck [Ucr.] **53** Ab
Luckau [D] **35** Db
Luckenwalde [D] **35** Db
Luçon [Fr.] **9** Bb
Ludlow [RU] **5** Cb
Ludvika [Svezia] **73** Eab
Ludwigsburg [D] **33** Ba
Ludwigshafen am Rhein [D]
33 Aa
Ludwigslust [D] **35** Cb
Ludza [Lett.] **55** Bb
Luga [Russia] **61** ABb
Lugano [Svizz.] **31** ABa
Lugo [Sp.] **19** Ba
Lugoj [Rom.] **41** Da
Luik / Liège [Bel.] = Liegi (I)
7 Cb
Luimneach / Limerick [Eire]
3 Bb
Lukovit [Bulg.] **49** ABa
Łuków [Pol.] **37** Cb
Luleå [Svezia] **65** Cb
Luleälven **65** Ca
Lüleburgaz [Tur.] **47** Cb
Lumparland [Finl.] **59** Bab
Lund [Svezia] **75** Cb
Lundy Island **5** Bb
Lüneburg [D] **35** Cb
Lünen [D] **35** Bb
Lunéville [Fr.] **11** Bb
Luninec [R.B.] **53** Aa
Lupeni [Rom.] **41** Da
Lure [Fr.] **11** Cb
Lushnja [Alb.] **43** Ab
Lussemburgo (I) = Luxembourg /
Luxemburg [Luss.] **11** Ca
Lussemburgo (I) = Luxemburg /
Luxembourg [Luss.] **11** Ca
Luton [RU] **5** Cb
Luxembourg / Luxemburg
[Luss.] = Lussemburgo (I)
11 Ca
Luxembourg / Luxemburg
[Luss.] = Lussemburgo (I)
11 Ca
Luxeuil–les–Bains [Fr.] **11** Cb
Luz, Costa de la– **21** Bb
Luzern [Svizz.] **33** Aa
Lvov [Ucr.] **39** CDa
Lwówek Śląski [Pol.] **37** Abc
Lychsele [Svezia] **71** Eb
Lyngdal [Norv.] **75** Aa
Lyngen **69** Ca
Lyngseidet [Norv.] **69** Ca
Lyon [Fr.] = Lione (I) **13** Ba
Lys **7** Bb
Lysekil [Svezia] **75** Ba

M

Maanselkä **67** Db
Maarianhamina / Mariehamn
[Finl.] **59** Bab
Maas = Mosa (I) **7** Ca
Maastricht [P.B.] **7** Cab
Määttälänvaara [Finl.] **63** Aab

Macdhui, Ben– **1** Cab
Macedonia (I) = Makedhonía
43 Bb
Macerata [It.] **31** Cb
Machaire Rátha / Maghera [RU]
3 Ba
Machico [Port.] **21** ins.a
Macocha **39** Aa
Macomer [It.] **29** Aa
Mâcon [Fr.] **11** Bb
Macugnaga [It.] **31** Aa
Madalena [Port.] **21** ins.a
Madara [Bulg.] **49** BCa
Maddalena **29** Bb
Maddalena, Arcipelago della–
29 Bb
Maddalena, Colle della– **13** Cb
Maddalena, Colle della– (I) =
Larche, Col de– **13** Cb
Madeira **21** ins.a
Madeira, Arcipelago di– (I) =
Madeira, Arquipélago da–
21 ins.a
Madeira, Arquipélago da– =
Madeira, Arcipelago di– (I)
21 ins.a
Madesimo [It.] **33** Bb
Madona [Lett.] **57** Bb
Madonna di Campiglio [It.]
31 Ba
Madrid [Sp.] **19** Cb
Madridejos [Sp.] **21** Cb
Mafra [Port.] **21** Aab
Magdeburg [D] =
Magdeburgo (I) **35** Cb
Magdeburgo (I) = Magdeburg
[D] **35** Cb
Magerøya **69** Ea
Maggiore, Lago– **31** Aa
Maghera / Machaire Rátha [RU]
3 Ba
Maglaj [Bos.Erz.] **41** BCb
Maglie [It.] **27** Db
Magnor [Norv.] **73** Dab
Magura **41** Bb
Mahón / Maó [Sp.] **23** Da
Maîche [Fr.] **11** Cb
Maidstone [RU] **5** Db
Maiella, La– [It.] **29** Cab
Maiella, La– [It.] **29** Cab
Main = Meno (I) **33** Ba
Mainistir Fhear Maí / Fermoy
[Eire] **3** Bb
Mainistir na Búille / Boyle
[Eire] **3** Bab
Mainland [RU] **1** Ca
Mainland [RU] **1** Ca
Mainz [D] **33** Aa
Maiorca (I) = Mallorca **23** CDa
Majáz al Bāb [Tun.] **25** Ab
Majdanpek [Iug.] **41** Db
Makarska [Cro.] **41** Bb
Makedhonía = Macedonia (I)
43 Bb
Makljen **41** Bb
Makó [Ung.] **41** Ca
Malá [Svezia] **71** Eb
Mala / Mallow [Eire] **3** Bb
Malacky [Slovac.] **39** Aa
Malá Fatra **39** Ba
Málaga [Sp.] **21** Cb
Malagón [Sp.] **21** Ca
Malaja Višera [Russia] **61** Bb
Mälaren **59** Ab
Malbork [Pol.] **37** Bbc
Maléas, Ákra– = Malía, Capo– (I)
45 Ab
Mália [Grecia] **45** Bc
Malía, Capo– (I) = Maléas,
Ákra– **45** Ab
Mali Lošinj [Cro.] **31** Cb
Malines / Mechelen [Bel.]
7 Cab

Malin Head **3** Ba
Malin More [Eire] **3** Ba
Malkara [Tur.] **47** BCb
Malles Venosta [It.] **33** Bb
Mallorca = Maiorca (I) **23** CDa
Mallow / Mala [Eire] **3** Bb
Malm [Norv.] **71** Bb
Malmberget [Svezia] **69** Cb
Malmö [Svezia] **75** Cb
Malorita [R.B.] **37** Db
Måløy [Norv.] **73** Aa
Malta [Lett.] **55** Bb
Malta [Malta] **25** Bc
Malung [Svezia] **73** Da
Mamaia [Rom.] **49** Ca
Mamonovo [Russia] **57** Bb
Mamry, Jezioro– **57** Cbc
Ma'mūrah, Ra's al– **25** Ab
Man, Isle of– **3** Cab
Manacor [Sp.] **23** Da
Manasija, Manastir– **41** Db
Manche, La– = Manica, La– (I)
5 BCb
Manchester [RU] **5** Cb
Mandal [Norv.] **75** Aa
Mandoúdhion [Grecia] **45** Ab
Manduria [It.] **27** Db
Manfredonia [It.] **27** Cb
Mangalia [Rom.] **49** Ca
Maniago [It.] **31** Ca
Manica, La– (I) = English
Channel **5** BCb
Manica, La– (I) = Manche, La–
5 BCb
Manisa [Tur.] **45** Cb
Mannheim [D] **33** Aa
Manosque [Fr.] **13** Bb
Manresa [Sp.] **17** Cb
Mansfield [RU] **5** Cb
Mantes–la–Jolie [Fr.] **9** Ca
Mantova [It.] **31** Bab
Mänttä [Finl.] **59** Da
Mänttälä [Finl.] **59** Da
Manzanares [Sp.] **21** Ca
Manzil Tamīm [Tun.] **25** Ab
Maó / Mahón [Sp.] **23** Da
Maramureş **39** Ea
Maratea [It.] **25** Ca
Marbella [Sp.] **21** Cb
Marburg [D] **35** Bc
Marby [Svezia] **71** Cb
March **39** Aa
Marche–en–Famenne [Bel.]
7 Cb
Maréttimo **25** ABb
Margate [RU] **5** Db
Mariánské Lázně [Rep.Ceca]
33 Ca
Mariazell [Aus.] **33** Db
Maribo [Dan.] **35** Ca
Maribor [Slo.] **39** Ab
Marica **47** Bb
Mariefred [Svezia] **59** Ab
Mariehamn / Maarianhamina
[Finl.] **59** Bab
Mariestad [Svezia] **75** Ca
Marijampole [Lit.] **57** Cb
Marina di Leuca [It.] **27** Db
Marinha Grande [Port.] **19** ABb
Marina Gorka [R.B.] **53** Ba
Märjamaa / Marjamaa [Est.]
59 Db
Marjamaa / Märjamaa [Est.]
59 Db
Markaryd [Svezia] **75** Cb
Marktredwitz [D] **33** BCa
Marmande [Fr.] **15** BCb
Marmara, Mar di– =
Marmara Denizi **47** Cb
Marmara Denizi = Marmara,
Mar di– (I) **47** Cb

Marmaris [Tur.] **45** Cb
Marmolada **33** BCb
Marna (I) = Marne **11** Ba
Marne = Marna (I) **11** Ba
Maros **41** Ca
Marroquí, Punta– **21** Cbc
Marrti [Finl.] **67** Db
Marsala [It.] **25** Bb
Marseille [Fr.] = Marsiglia (I)
   13 Bb
Marsiglia (I) = Marseille [Fr.]
   13 Bb
Marstal [Dan.] **35** Ca
Martigny [Svizz.] **11** Cb
Martigues [Fr.] **13** Bb
Martin [Slovac.] **39** Ba
Martina Franca [It.] **27** Cb
Masäkin [Tun.] **25** Ac
Masi [Norv.] **69** Da
Mask, Lough– **3** Ab
Massa [It.] **31** Bb
Massa Marittima [It.] **29** Ba
Matapán, Capo– (I) = Taínaron,
   Ákra– **45** Ab
Mataró [Sp.] **17** Cb
Matera [It.] **27** Cb
Mátészalka [Ung.] **39** Cab
Mâţir [Tun.] **25** Ab
Matosinhos [Port.] **19** Bb
Mátra **39** Bb
Matrei in Osttirol [Aus.]
   33 Cb
Mattighofen [Aus.] **33** Cab
Maubeuge [Fr.] **7** Cb
Mauriac [Fr.] **15** Ca
Mavrovo **43** Ab
Mayen [D] **7** Db
Mayenne [Fr.] **9** Ba
Mayenne [Fr.] **9** Ba
Mayrhofen [Aus.] **33** BCb
Mazamet [Fr.] **17** Ca
Mazara del Vallo [It.] **25** Bb
Mažeikiai / Mažejkjaj [Lit.]
   57 Cb
Mažejkjaj / Mažeikiai [Lit.]
   57 Cb
Mazirbe [Lett.] **59** Cb
Mazurskie, Pojezierze– **57** BCc
Mealhada [Port.] **19** Bb
Meaux [Fr.] **9** CDa
Mechelen / Malines [Bel.]
   7 Cab
Mecklenburg = Meclemburgo (I)
   35 CDb
Mecklenburger Bucht **35** Ca
Mecklenburg-Vorpommern /
   Karow [D] **35** Db
Meclemburgo (I) =
   Mecklenburg **35** CDb
Medgidia [Rom.] **49** Ca
Mediaş [Rom.] **51** Bb
Medinaceli [Sp.] **17** Bb
Medina del Campo [Sp.]
   19 Cb
Medina de Rioseco [Sp.]
   19 Cab
Medina–Sidonia [Sp.] **21** BCb
Medininkai / Medininkaj [Lit.]
   57 Db
Medininkaj / Medininkai [Lit.]
   57 Db
Mediterranée, Mer– =
   Mediterraneo, Mar– (I)
   13 BCbc
Mediterraneo, Mar– **25** BCb
Mediterráneo, Mar– (I) =
   Mediterraneo, Mar– (I)
   23 CDb
Mediterraneo, Mar– (I) =
   Mediterranée, Mer–
   13 BCbc
Mediterraneo, Mar– (I) =
   Mediterráneo, Mar– **23** CDb

Mediterraneo, Mar– (I) =
   Mesoyéios Thálassa **45** Ac
Medvežjegorsk [Russia]
   63 Cbc
Megalópolis [Grecia] **45** Ab
Mégara [Grecia] **45** Ab
Megève [Fr.] **13** Ca
Mehadia [Rom.] **41** Db
Meiningen [D] **35** Cc
Meißen [D] **35** Dbc
Melbu [Norv.] **69** Ab
Melfi [It.] **27** Cb
Melilla [Sp.] **21** CDc
Melito di Porto Salvo [It.]
   25 Cb
Melk [Aus.] **33** Da
Mellerud [Svezia] **75** Ca
Mělník [Rep.Ceca] **35** Dc
Meltaus [Finl.] **67** Cb
Melun [Fr.] **9** Ca
Memmingen [D] **33** Bab
Mena [Ucr.] **53** Ca
Mende [Fr.] **13** Bb
Menemen [Tur.] **45** BCb
Meno (I) = Main **33** Ba
Menorca (I) = Minorca (I) **23** Da
Menton [Fr.] **31** Ab
Meppel [P.B.] **7** Da
Meppen [D] **7** Da
Mequinenza, Embalse de–
   17 BCb
Meráker [Norv.] **71** Bb
Meran / Merano [It.] **33** Bb
Merano / Meran [It.] **33** Bb
Mercadal / Es Mercadal [Sp.]
   23 Da
Mercantour **13** Cb
Meriç **47** Bb
Mérida [Sp.] **21** Bab
Mérihas [Grecia] **45** Bb
Merikarvia [Finl.] **59** Ca
Merkinė / Merkine [Lit.]
   57 Dbc
Merkine / Merkinė [Lit.]
   57 Dbc
Merrick **3** Ca
Merseburg / Saale [D] **35** CDb
Mērsrags / Mērsrags [Lett.]
   57 Ca
Mērsrags / Mersrags [Lett.]
   57 Ca
Merthyr Tydfil [RU] **5** Bb
Mértola [Port.] **21** Bb
Meschede [D] **35** Bb
Mesolóngion [Grecia] **43** Bc
Mesoyéios Thálassa =
   Mediterraneo, Mar– (I)
   45 Ac
Messina [It.] **25** Cb
Messina, Stretto di– **25** Cb
Messíni [Grecia] **45** Ab
Metalliferi, Monti– (I) =
   Erzgebirge **35** Dc
Metalliferi, Monti– (I) = Krušné
   Hory **35** Dc
Metéora **43** Bb
Methóni [Grecia] **45** Ab
Metlika [Slo.] **41** Ba
Métsovon [Grecia] **43** ABb
Metz [Fr.] **11** BCa
Meuse = Mosa (I) **7** Ca
Meyísti **45** ins.a
Meža **55** Cb
Mezdra [Bulg.] **49** Aa
Mežgorje [Ucr.] **39** Ca
Mezőberény [Ung.] **39** Ca
Mezőkövesd [Ung.] **39** Bb
Mezőtúr [Ung.] **39** Bb
Miajadas [Sp.] **21** BCab
Miastko [Pol.] **37** Aa
Micene (I) = Mikínai **45** Ab
Michalovce [Slovac.] **39** Ca
Michelstadt [D] **33** ABa

Mičurin [Bulg.] **49** Cab
Midar [Mar.] **21** Cc
Middelburg [P.B.] **7** Ca
Middlesbrough [RU] **3** Da
Midžor **41** Db
Miechów [Pol.] **37** Bc
Międzylesie [Pol.] **39** Aa
Mielec [Pol.] **39** Ca
Miercurea Ciuc [Rom.] **51** Bb
Mieres [Sp.] **19** Ca
Mihajlovgrad [Bulg.] **49** Aa
Mikínai = Micene (I) **45** Ab
Mikkeli / Sankt Michel [Finl.]
   59 Ea
Míkonos [Grecia] **45** Bb
Míkonos [Grecia] **45** Bb
Mikulov [Rep.Ceca] **39** Aa
Milano [It.] **31** Ba
Milàs [Tur.] **45** Cb
Milazzo [It.] **25** Cb
Milet = Mileto (I) **45** Cb
Mileto (I) = Milet **45** Cb
Milford Haven [RU] **5** Bb
Milicz [Pol.] **37** Ab
Millau [Fr.] **13** ABb
Millstatt [Aus.] **33** Cb
Milo (I) = Mílos [Grecia] **45** Bb
Mílos [Grecia] **45** Bb
Mílos [Grecia] = Milo (I) **45** Bb
Milton Keynes [RU] **5** Cb
Mimizan [Fr.] **15** Bb
Minden [D] **35** Bcb
Minehead [RU] **5** Bb
Minglanilla [Sp.] **23** Ba
Minho **19** Ba
Miño **19** Ba
Minorca (I) = Menorca **23** Da
Minsk [R.B.] **55** Bbc
Mińsk Mazowiecki [Pol.] **37** Cb
Mira [Port.] **19** Bb
Mirambeau [Fr.] **15** Ba
Miranda de Corvo [Port.]
   19 Bb
Miranda de Ebro [Sp.] **17** Ba
Miranda do Douro [Port.]
   19 Bb
Mirande [Fr.] **17** Ca
Mirandela [Port.] **19** Ba
Mirandola [It.] **31** Ba
Miravete, Puerto de– **19** Cb
Mirecourt [Fr.] **11** BCa
Mírina [Grecia] **47** Bb
Mironovka [Ucr.] **53** Ca
Mirtóon Pélagos **45** ABb
Miskolc [Ung.] **39** Bab
Misso [Est.] **55** Ba
Mistelbach [Aus.] **39** Aa
Mistrás **45** Ab
Mistretta [It.] **25** Bb
Míthimna [Grecia] **47** Bb
Mitilíni [Grecia] **47** Bbc
Mizen Head **3** Ab
Mizil [Rom.] **51** Bbc
Mjölby [Svezia] **75** CDa
Mjøsa **73** Ca
Mladá Boleslav [Rep.Ceca]
   35 DEc
Mladenovac [Iug.] **41** Cb
Mława [Pol.] **37** Bb
Mljet [Cro.] **27** Ca
Mljet [Cro.] **27** Ca
Modane [Fr.] **13** Ca
Modena [It.] **31** Bb
Modica [It.] **25** Bb
Modriča [Bos.Erz.] **41** Cab
Moffat [RU] **3** Ca
Mogadouro [Port.] **19** Bb
Mogilev [R.B.] **55** Cbc
Mogilev–Podolski [Ucr.] **51** Ca
Mohács [Ung.] **41** Ca
Mohammadia [Alg.] **23** BCc
Mohelnice [Rep.Ceca] **39** Aa
Mo i Rana [Norv.] **71** Ca

Moissac [Fr.] **15** Cb
Mojkovac [Iug.] **41** Cb
Moláoi [Grecia] **45** Ab
Moldava (I) = Vltava **33** Ca
Moldavia (I) = Moldova
   51 BCb
Molde [Norv.] **73** Ba
Moldova = Moldavia (I)
   51 BCb
Moldova Nouă [Rom.] **41** Db
Moldoveanu, Vîrful– **51** Bb
Moldoviţa, Mănăstirea– **51** Bb
Molfetta [It.] **27** Cb
Molina de Aragón [Sp.] **17** Bb
Mölln [D] **35** Cb
Molodečno [R.B.] **57** DEb
Mologa **61** Cb
Momčilgrad [Bulg.] **47** Bb
Monaco (I) = München [D]
   33 Ba
Monaghan [Eire] **3** Ba
Monastir [It.] **29** ABb
Monção [Port.] **19** Bab
Mončegorsk [Russia] **67** Bcb
Moncenisio, Colle del– (I) =
   Mont Cenis, Col du– **13** Ca
Mönchengladbach [D] **7** Da
Monchique [Port.] **21** Bb
Mondego **19** ABb
Mondego, Cabo– **19** ABb
Mondoñedo [Sp.] **19** Ba
Mondoví [It.] **31** Ab
Monemvasía [Grecia] **45** Ab
Monfalcone [It.] **31** Ca
Monforte [Port.] **21** Bab
Monforte de Lemos [Sp.]
   19 Ba
Monginevro, Colle del– (I) =
   Montgenèvre, Col de–
   13 Cab
Mondólithos [Grecia] **45** Cbc
Monopoli [It.] **27** Cb
Monor [Ung.] **39** Bb
Monreal del Campo [Sp.]
   17 Bb
Monreale [It.] **25** Bb
Mons / Bergen [Bel.] **7** Cb
Monselice [It.] **31** Ba
Montagnana [It.] **31** Ba
Montalbán [Sp.] **17** Bb
Montargis [Fr.] **9** Cab
Montauban [Fr.] **9** Ba
Montauban [Fr.] **15** Ca
Montbard [Fr.] **11** Bb
Montbéliard [Fr.] **11** Cb
Montblanc [Sp.] **17** Cb
Montceau–les–Mines [Fr.]
   11 Bb
Mont Cenis, Col du– =
   Moncenisio, Colle del– (I)
   13 Ca
Mont–de–Marsan [Fr.] **15** Bb
Monte, Castel del– **27** Cb
Monte–Carlo [PMC] **13** Cb
Montecassino **29** Cb
Montecatini Terme [It.] **31** Bb
Montecristo **29** Ba
Montefalco [It.] **29** Ca
Montefiascone [It.] **29** BCa
Montélimar [Fr.] **13** Bb
Montemor–o–Novo [Port.]
   21 Bb
Montepulciano [It.] **29** Ba
Montereau–faut–Yonne [Fr.]
   9 CDa
Monte Sant'Angelo [It.] **27** Cb
Montgenèvre, Col de– =
   Monginevro, Colle del– (I)
   13 Cab
Montijo [Port.] **21** ABb
Mont–Louis [Fr.] **17** Ca
Montluçon [Fr.] **9** Cb

Montmarault [Fr.] **9** CDb
Montmédy [Fr.] **11** Ba
Montmirail [Fr.] **11** Ba
Montpellier [Fr.] **13** Bb
Montreuil [Fr.] **5** Dc
Montreux [Svizz.] **11** Cb
Montrose [RU] **1** Db
Montserrat, Monasterio de–
   17 Cb
Monza [It.] **31** Ba
Monzón [Sp.] **17** Cab
Mór [Ung.] **39** Bb
Mora [Port.] **21** Bab
Mora [Svezia] **73** Ba
Morąg [Pol.] **57** Bbc
Morava [Eur.] **39** Aa
Morava [Rep.Ceca] = Moravia (I)
   39 Aa
Moravia (I) = Morava
   [Rep.Ceca] **39** Aa
Moravské Budějovice
   [Rep.Ceca] **39** Aa
Moray Firth **1** Ca
Morella [Sp.] **17** BCb
Morena, Sierra– **21** Cb
Morgat [Fr.] **9** Aa
Morjärv [Svezia] **65** Cda
Morlaix [Fr.] **9** Aa
Morón de la Frontera [Sp.]
   21 Cb
Morpeth [RU] **3** Da
Mors **75** Aab
Mörsil [Svezia] **71** Cb
Mortagne–au–Perche [Fr.] **9** Ca
Morteau [Fr.] **11** Cb
Moržovec, ostrov– **63** Fa
Mosa (I) = Maas **7** Ca
Mosa (I) = Meuse **7** Ca
Mosbach [D] **33** Ba
Mosca (I) = Moskva [Russia]
   55 Eb
Moščny, ostrov– **59** Eab
Mosel = Mosella (I) **11** Cb
Mosella (I) = Mosel **11** Ca
Mosella (I) = Moselle **11** Ca
Moselle = Mosella (I) **11** Ca
Mosjøen [Norv.] **71** Cab
Moskenesøy **69** Ab
Moskosel [Svezia] **71** Eab
Moskva [Russia] = Mosca (I)
   55 Eb
Mosonmagyaróvár [Ung.]
   39 Aab
Moss [Norv.] **73** Ba
Most [Rep.Ceca] **35** Dc
Mostar [Bos.Erz.] **41** Bb
Mota del Cuervo [Sp.] **23** Ba
Mota del Marqués [Sp.] **19** Cba
Motala [Svezia] **75** CDa
Motherwell [RU] **1** Cb
Motilla del Palancar [Sp.]
   23 Ba
Motovski zaliv **67** Ea
Motril [Sp.] **23** Cb
Mouaskar [Alg.] **23** BCc
Moúdhros [Grecia] **47** Bb
Moulins [Fr.] **11** Bb
Moura [Port.] **21** Bb
Mourão [Port.] **21** Bb
Moûtiers [Fr.] **13** Ca
Možajsk [Russia] **55** DEb
Mozyr [R.B.] **53** Ba
Mrągowo [Pol.] **57** Cbc
Mrkonjić Grad [Bos.Erz.] **41** Bb
M'Sila [Alg.] **23** Dc
Msta **61** Bb
Mstislavl [R.B.] **55** Cbc
Much Wenlock [RU] **5** Cb
Mudanya [Tur.] **47** Cb
Muddus **69** Cb
Muğla [Tur.] **45** Cb
Mühlhausen / Thüringen [D]
   35 Cb

Muhos [Finl.] **65** Db
Mukačevo [Ucr.] **39** Ca
Mula [Sp.] **23** Bb
Mulhacén **21** Cb
Mulhouse [Fr.] **11** Cb
Mull, Island of– **1** BCb
Müllheim [D] **33** Ab
Mullingar / An Muileann
gCearr [Eire] **3** Bb
Münchberg [D] **33** Ba
München [D] = Monaco (I)
33 Ba
Münden [D] **35** Cb
Munera [Sp.] **23** Bab
Munkedal [Svezia] **75** Ba
Munkfors [Svezia] **73** Dab
Münster [D] **35** Bb
Muodoslompolo [Svezia]
67 Bb
Muonio [Finl.] **67** Bb
Muonioälven **67** Bb
Muonionjoki **67** Bb
Mur **33** Db
Mura **33** Db
Murat [Fr.] **15** Ca
Murat Daği **47** Cbc
Murau [Aus.] **33** Cb
Muravera [It.] **29** Bb
Murcia [Sp.] **23** Bb
Mureş **41** Da
Muret [Fr.] **17** Ca
Murighiol [Rom.] **49** Ca
Müritz [D] **35** Db
Müritz [D] **35** Db
Murmansk [Russia] **67** EFab
Murmaši [Russia] **67** Eab
Muros [Sp.] **19** ABa
Murro di Porco, Capo– **25** Cb
Murska Sobota [Slo.] **39** Ab
Murten [Svizz.] **11** Cb
Murtovaara [Finl.] **63** Ab
Mürzzuschlag [Aus.] **39** Ab
Musala **49** Aa
Mustafakemalpaşa [Tur.] **47** Cb
Mustvee [Est.] **59** DEb
Muurola [Finl.] **67** Cb
Mynämäki [Finl.] **59** Ca
Myre [Norv.] **69** ABab
Mysen [Norv.] **73** Cb
Myślenice [Pol.] **39** Ba
Myślibórz [Pol.] **35** Db
Myszyniec [Pol.] **37** Cb
Mytišči [Russia] **55** Eb
Mývatn **77** Db

N

Naab **33** BCa
Naantali / Nådendal [Finl.]
59 Ca
Naas [Eire] **3** Bb
Nábul [Tun.] **25** Ab
Náchod [Rep.Ceca] **37** Ac
Nådendal / Naantali [Finl.]
59 Ca
Nădlac [Rom.] **41** Ca
Nador [Mar.] **21** CDc
Næstved [Dan.] **75** Bb
Nagyatád [Ung.] **41** Ba
Nagykanizsa [Ung.] **39** Ab
Nagykáta [Ung.] **39** Bb
Nagykőrös [Ung.] **39** Bb
Nairn [RU] **1** Ca
Nájera [Sp.] **17** Ba
Nakło nad Notecią [Pol.] **37** Ab
Nakskov [Dan.] **35** Ca
Namen / Namur [Bel.] **7** Cb
Namsos [Norv.] **71** Bb
Namsskogan [Norv.] **71** Cb
Namur / Namen [Bel.] **7** Cb
Namysłów [Pol.] **37** Abc

Nancy [Fr.] **11** Ca
Nantes [Fr.] **9** Bb
Nantua [Fr.] **11** Bb
Nao, Cabo de la– **23** Cb
Náousa [Grecia] **43** Bb
Napoli [It.] **29** Cb
Narbonne [Fr.] **17** CDa
Nardó [It.] **27** CDb
Narew **37** Cb
Narni [It.] **29** Ca
Naroč [R.B.] **57** Db
Naroč, ozero– **57** Db
Naro–Fominsk [Russia] **55** Eb
Närpes / Närpio [Finl.] **65** Cc
Närpio / Närpes [Finl.] **65** Cc
Narva [Est.] **61** Ab
Narva laht **59** Eb
Narvik [Norv.] **69** Bb
Narvski zaliv **59** Eb
Näsåker [Svezia] **71** Db
Näsåud [Rom.] **51** Bb
Našice [Cro.] **41** BCa
Näsijärvi **59** Ca
Nässjö [Svezia] **75** Ca
Nasso (I) = Náxos [Grecia]
45 Bb
Nauen [D] **35** Db
Naumburg / Saale [D] **35** Cbc
Navacerrada, Puerto de– **19** Cb
Navahermosa [Sp.] **19** Cb
Navalmoral de la Mata [Sp.]
19 Cb
Navlja [Russia] **53** Da
Návpaktos [Grecia] **43** Bc
Návplion [Grecia] **45** Ab
Náxos [Grecia] **45** Bb
Náxos [Grecia] = Nasso (I)
45 Bb
Nazaré [Port.] **19** ABb
Nazilli [Tur.] **45** Cb
Néa Artáki [Grecia] **45** Ab
Neagh, Lough– **3** Ba
Neagră, Marea– = Nero, Mar– (I)
49 CDa
Néa Moudhaniá [Grecia] **43** Bb
Neamţ, Mănăstirea– **51** Bb
Neápolis [Grecia] **45** Ab
Neápolis [Grecia] **43** Bb
Neápolis [Grecia] **45** Bc
Neckar **33** Aa
Negotin [Iug.] **41** Db
Negotino [Maced.] **43** Bb
Negru Vodă [Rom.] **49** Ca
Neiden [Norv.] **69** Fa
Neidín / Kenmare [Eire] **3** Ab
Neige, Crêt de la– **11** Bb
Neksø [Dan.] **75** Db
Nelidovo [Russia] **55** Cb
Nellim [Finl.] **67** Dab
Neman **57** Cb
Neméa [Grecia] **45** Ab
Nemirov [Ucr.] **51** Ca
Nemours [Fr.] **9** Ca
Néon Karlovásion [Grecia]
45 Bb
Nepomuk [Rep.Ceca] **33** Ca
Nérac [Fr.] **15** Ca
Neretva **27** Ca
Nero, Mar– (I) = Černoje more
51 Db
Nero, Mar– (I) = Černo More
49 Ca
Nero, Mar– (I) = Karadeniz
49 CDb
Nero, Mar– (I) = Neagră,
Marea– **49** CDa
Nes [Norv.] **73** Ca
Nesbyen [Norv.] **73** BCa
Nesebăr [Bulg.] **49** Ca
Neskaupstaður [Isl.] **77** Eb
Nesna [Norv.] **71** Ca
Ness, Loch– **1** Ca
Nesviž [R.B.] **53** Aa

Neubrandenburg [D] **35** Db
Neuchâtel / Neuenburg [Svizz.]
11 Cb
Neuchâtel, Lac de– =
Neuchâtel, Lago di– (I)
11 Cb
Neuchâtel, Lago di– (I) =
Neuchâtel, Lac de– **11** Cb
Neuenburg / Neuchâtel [Svizz.]
11 Cb
Neufchâteau [Fr.] **11** Ba
Neufchâtel–en–Bray [Fr.] **9** Ca
Neumarkt in der Oberpfalz [D]
33 Ba
Neumünster [D] **35** Cab
Neunkirchen [Aus.] **39** Ab
Neuruppin [D] **35** Db
Neusiedler See **39** Aab
Neustadt am Rübenberge [D]
35 Cb
Neustadt an der Aisch [D]
33 Ba
Neustrelitz [D] **35** Db
Neu–Ulm [D] **33** Ba
Neva **61** Bb
Nevada, Sierra– **21** CDb
Nevel [Russia] **55** BCb
Nevers [Fr.] **11** ABb
Nevesinje [Bos.Erz.] **41** BCb
Nevis, Ben– **1** Cb
Newark–on–Trent [RU] **5** Cb
Newbury [RU] **5** Cb
Newcastle / An Caisleán Nua
[RU] **3** BCa
Newcastle–upon–Tyne [RU]
3 Da
Newgrange **3** Bb
Newhaven [RU] **5** CDc
Newport [RU] **5** BCb
Newport [RU] **5** Cb
Newquay [RU] **5** Bc
Newry / an t–Iúr [RU] **3** Ba
Newton Stewart [RU] **3** Ca
Newtown [RU] **5** Bb
Nežin [Ucr.] **53** Ca
Nica / Nica [Lett.] **57** BCa
Nica / Nica [Lett.] **57** BCb
Nicastro, Lamezia Terme– [It.]
25 Cab
Nice [Fr.] = Nizza (I) **13** Cb
Nicosia [It.] **25** Bb
Nidzica [Pol.] **37** Bb
Niedersächsisches Wattenmeer
7 Da
Nienburg (Weser) [D] **35** Cb
Nigižma [Russia] **61** Da
Nihoiu [Rom.] **51** Bb
Nijmegen [P.B.] **7** CDa
Nikel [Russia] **67** DEa
Niki [Grecia] **43** Bb
Nikkaluokta [Svezia] **69** Cb
Nikolajev [Ucr.] **39** CDa
Nikolajev [Ucr.] **51** Db
Nikolajevo [Russia] **61** Ab
Nikopol [Bulg.] **49** Ba
Nikšić [Iug.] **41** Cb
Nilakka **65** Dbc
Nilsiä [Finl.] **65** Eb
Nîmes [Fr.] **11** ABb
Nin [Cro.] **41** Bb
Niort [Fr.] **9** Bb
Niš [Iug.] **41** Db
Nísiros **45** BCb
Nisko [Pol.] **37** Cc
Nistru **51** Cb
Nivala [Finl.] **65** Db
Nizke Tatry **39** Ba
Nižnjaja Zolotica [Russia]
63 Eb
Nizza (I) = Nice [Fr.] **13** Cb
Njandoma [Russia] **61** Ea
Njuk, ozero– **63** Bb

Nockberge **33** Cb
Nogent–le–Rotrou [Fr.] **9** Ca
Nogent–sur–Seine [Fr.] **11** Ba
Noia / Noya [Sp.] **19** ABa
Noirmoutier, Ile de– **9** Bb
Nokia [Finl.] **59** Ca
Noordzee = Nord, Mare del– (I)
7 Ca
Noormarkku / Norrmark [Finl.]
59 Ca
Norcia [It.] **29** Ca
Nord, Capo– (I) = Nordkapp
69 Ea
Nord, Mare del– (I) = Noordzee
7 Ca
Nord, Mare del– (I) = Nordsee
35 ABa
Nord, Mare del– (I) =
Nordsjøen **75** Aa
Nord, Mare del– (I) = North
Sea **7** Ba
Norden [D] **7** Da
Nordenham [D] **35** Bb
Norderney [D] **7** Da
Nordfjord **73** Aa
Nordfjordeid [Norv.] **73** ABa
Nordfold [Norv.] **69** ABb
Nordhausen [D] **35** Cb
Nordhorn [D] **7** Da
Nordkapp = Nord, Capo– (I)
69 Ea
Nordkinn **69** Fa
Nordkjosbotn [Norv.] **69** Ca
Nord–Kvaløy **69** Ca
Nordli [Norv.] **71** Cb
Nördlingen [D] **33** Ba
Nordmaling [Svezia] **71** Eb
Nordsee = Nord, Mare del– (I)
35 ABa
Nordsjøen = Nord, Mare del– (I)
75 Aa
Nordsøen **75** Ab
Norfolk **5** Cb
Norimberga (I) = Nürnberg [D]
33 Ba
Normandia (I) = Normandie
9 BCa
Normandie = Normandia (I)
9 BCa
Nørresundby [Dan.] **75** Bab
Norrköping [Svezia] **75** Ca
Norrland **71** DEb
Norrmark / Noormarkku [Finl.]
59 Ca
Norrtälje [Svezia] **59** Bb
Norsjö [Svezia] **71** Eb
Northampton [RU] **5** Cb
North Berwick [RU] **1** Db
North Channel **3** Ca
North Foreland **5** Db
North Minch **1** BCa
North Rona **1** Ca
North Sea = Nord, Mare del– (I)
7 Ba
North Uist **1** Ba
Northumberland **3** Da
North York Moors **3** Da
Norwich [RU] **5** Cb
Nosovka [Ucr.] **53** Cab
Noteć **37** Bb
Nótioi Sporádhes = Sporadi
Meridionali (I) **45** Bbc
Noto [It.] **25** BCb
Notodden [Norv.] **73** Cb
Nottingham [RU] **5** Cb
Nová Bystřice [Rep.Ceca]
33 CDa
Nova Gorica [Slo.] **31** Ca
Nova Gradiška [Cro.] **41** Ba
Novaja Ladoga [Russia] **61** Bab
Novara [It.] **31** Aa
Nova Varoš [Iug.] **41** Cb
Nova Zagora [Bulg.] **49** Ba

Nové Mesto nad Váhom
[Slovac.] **39** Aa
Nové Zámky [Slovac.] **39** ABab
Novgorod [Russia] **61** Bb
Novgorod–Severski [Ucr.]
53 Da
Novi Ligure [It.] **31** Ab
Novi Pazar [Bulg.] **49** BCa
Novi Pazar [Iug.] **41** Cb
Novi Sad [Iug.] **41** Ca
Novoarhangelsk [Ucr.] **51** Da
Novodvinsk [Russia] **63** Eb
Novograd–Volynski [Ucr.]
53 Bb
Novogrudok [R.B.] **57** Dc
Novo Mesto [Slo.] **41** ABa
Novoržen [Russia] **55** Cb
Novosokolniki [Russia] **55** Cb
Novoukrainka [Ucr.] **51** Da
Novozybkov [Russia] **53** Ca
Novska [Cro.] **41** Ba
Novy Bug [Ucr.] **51** Db
Novy Bykov [Ucr.] **53** Cb
Nový Jičín [Rep.Ceca]
39 ABa
Nowa Sól [Pol.] **37** Ab
Nowe [Pol.] **57** Bc
Nowe Miasto Lubawskie [Pol.]
37 Bb
Nowy Dwór Mazowiecki [Pol.]
37 Bb
Nowy Sącz [Pol.] **39** Ba
Nowy Targ [Pol.] **39** Ba
Noya / Noia [Sp.] **19** ABa
Noyon [Fr.] **9** CDa
Nozay [Fr.] **9** Bb
Nunnanen [Finl.] **67** Cb
Nuorgam [Finl.] **69** Fa
Nuoro [It.] **29** Bb
Nuova Castiglia (I) = Castilla la
Nueva **19** Cb
Nurmes [Finl.] **63** Ab
Nürnberg [D] = Norimberga (I)
33 Ba
Nybergsund [Norv.] **73** Da
Nyborg [Dan.] **75** Bb
Nybro [Svezia] **75** Db
Nyírbátor [Ung.] **39** Cb
Nyíregyháza [Ung.] **39** Cab
Nykarleby / Uusikaaelepyy
[Finl.] **65** Cb
Nykøbing [Dan.] **75** Bb
Nykøbing [Dan.] **75** ABb
Nykøbing Falster [Dan.]
35 CDa
Nyköping [Svezia] **59** Ab
Nynäshamn [Svezia] **59** ABb
Nyons [Fr.] **13** Bc
Nyrud [Norv.] **69** Fab
Nysa [Pol.] **37** Ac
Nysa Łużycka **35** Db
Nystad / Uusikaupunki [Finl.]
59 Ca

O

Oban [RU] **1** Ca
Oberstdorf [D] **33** Bb
Obervellach [Aus.] **33** Cb
Óbidos [Port.] **21** Aa
Obinsk [Russia] **55** Eb
Oborniki [Pol.] **37** Ab
Obozerski [Russia] **63** Eb
Obrenovac [Iug.] **41** Cb
Obrovac [Cro.] **41** Bb
Obzor [Bulg.] **49** Ca
Očakov [Ucr.] **51** Db
Ocaña [Sp.] **19** Cb
Ockelbo [Svezia] **59** Ab
Ocrida, Lago di– (I) = Ohridsko
jezero **43** Ab

Ocrida, Lago di– (I) = Ohrit, Liqen i– **43** Ab
Odda [Norv.] **73** Bab
Odemira [Port.] **21** Bb
Ödemiş [Tur.] **45** Cc
Odense [Dan.] **75** Bb
Oder **35** Db
Oder / Frankfurt [D] **35** Db
Ödeshög [Svezia] **75** Ca
Odessa [Ucr.] **55** Ebc
Odojev [Russia] **55** Ebc
Odorheiu Secuiesc [Rom.] **51** Bb
Odra **35** Db
Ofanto **27** Cb
Offenburg [D] **33** Aa
Oglio **31** Ba
Ogre [Lett.] **57** Db
Ogulin [Cro.] **41** Ba
Ohrid [Maced.] **43** Ab
Ohridsko jezero = Ocrida, Lago di– (I) **43** Ab
Ohrit, Liqen i– = Ocrida, Lago di– (I) **43** Ab
Oiti **45** Aab
Oituz, Pasul– **51** Bb
Ojków **39** Ba
Øksfjord [Norv.] **69** Da
Okstindan **71** Ca
Olafsfjörður [Isl.] **77** Cab
Ólafsvík [Isl.] **77** Bb
Öland **75** Db
Oława [Pol.] **37** Abc
Olbernhau [D] **35** Dc
Olbia [It.] **29** Bb
Oldenburg (Oldenburg) [D] **35** Bb
Oldenburg in Holstein [D] **35** Ca
Olderdalen [Norv.] **69** Ca
Olecko [Pol.] **57** Cbc
Ølen [Norv.] **73** Ba
Olenegorsk [Russia] **67** EFb
Olenica [Russia] **67** Fb
Oléron, Ile d'– **15** Ba
Oleśnica [Pol.] **37** Ab
Olesno [Pol.] **37** Bbc
Olevsk [Ucr.] **53** Ba
Olhão [Port.] **21** Bb
Olhava [Finl.] **65** Db
Olimbía = Olimpia (I) **43** Bc
Ólimbos **43** Bb
Ólimbos, Óros– = Olimpo, Monte– (I) **43** Bb
Olimpia (I) = Olimbía **43** Bc
Olimpo, Monte– (I) = Ólimbos, Óros– **43** Bb
Olkusz [Pol.] **39** Ba
Olmedo [Sp.] **19** Cb
Olomouc [Rep.Ceca] **39** Aa
Olonec [Russia] **61** BCa
Oloron-Sainte-Marie [Fr.] **17** Ba
Olot [Sp.] **17** Ca
Olpe [D] **35** Bbc
Olsztyn [Pol.] **57** Bc
Olsztynek [Pol.] **57** Bc
Olt **49** Ba
Olten [Svizz.] **33** Ab
Oltenia **49** Aa
Olteniţa [Rom.] **49** Ba
Olvera [Sp.] **19** Ca
Omagh / An Omaigh [RU] **3** Ba
Ombrone **29** Ba
Omiš [Cro.] **41** Bb
Oña [Sp.] **19** Ca
Ondarroa / Ondárroa [Sp.] **17** Ba
Ondárroa / Ondarroa [Sp.] **17** Ba
Ondozero [Russia] **63** BCb
Ondozero, ozero– **63** Cb
Onega [Russia] **63** Eb

Onega [Russia] **63** Db
Onega. Baia di– (I) = Onežskaja guba **63** Db
Onega, Lago– (I) = Onežskoje ozero **61** Ca
Oneşti [Rom.] **51** Bb
Onežskaja guba = Onega, Baia di– (I) **63** Db
Onežskoje ozero = Onega, Lago– (I) **61** Ca
Oostende / Ostende [Bel.] **7** BCa
Opatija [Cro.] **31** Ca
Opatów [Pol.] **37** Cc
Opava [Rep.Ceca] **39** ABa
Opočka [Russia] **55** Bb
Opoczno [Pol.] **37** Bb
Opole [Pol.] **37** ABc
Oppdal [Norv.] **73** Ca
Oradea [Rom.] **39** Cb
Oran, Grande Sebkha d'– **23** Bc
Orange [Fr.] **13** Bb
Oranienburg [D] **35** Db
Orăştie [Rom.] **41** Da
Oraviţa [Rom.] **41** Dab
Orbetello [It.] **29** Ba
Orcadi, Isole– (I) = Orkney Islands **1** CDa
Órdenes / Ordes [Sp.] **19** Ba
Ordes / Órdenes [Sp.] **19** Ba
Ordesa **17** Ba
Orduña [Sp.] **17** ABa
Orebić [Cro.] **27** Ca
Örebro [Svezia] **73** Eb
Orense / Ourense [Sp.] **19** Ba
Orestiás [Grecia] **47** Bb
Øre Sund **75** Ca
Orgaz [Sp.] **19** Cb
Orgnac, Aven d'– **13** Bb
Orhangazi [Tur.] **47** Cb
Orhei [Mold.] **51** Cb
Orihuela [Sp.] **23** Bb
Oripää [Finl.] **59** Ca
Orissare / Orissaare [Est.] **59** Cb
Orissare / Orissaare [Est.] **59** Cb
Oristano [It.] **29** Ab
Orivesi [Finl.] **59** Da
Orivesi [Finl.] **63** Ac
Orjahovo [Bulg.] **49** ABa
Ørje [Norv.] **73** Cb
Orkanger [Norv.] **71** Bb
Örkelljunga [Svezia] **75** Cb
Orkney Islands = Orcadi, Isole– (I) **1** CDa
Orlando, Capo d'– **25** Bc
Orléans [Fr.] **9** Cab
Orne **9** Ba
Ørnes [Norv.] **69** Aa
Orneta [Pol.] **57** Bbc
Örnsköldsvik [Svezia] **71** Eb
Orosei e Gennargentu, Golfo di– **29** Bb
Orosháza [Ung.] **39** Bb
Orša [R.B.] **55** Cb
Orsa [Svezia] **73** Da
Orşova [Rom.] **41** Db
Orta San Giulio [It.] **31** Aa
Orte [It.] **29** Ca
Ortegal, Cabo– = Ortegal, Capo– (I) **19** Ba
Ortegal, Capo– (I) = Ortegal, Cabo– **19** Ba
Orthez [Fr.] **17** Ba
Ortigueira [Sp.] **19** Ba
Ortisei [It.] **33** Bb
Ortler / Ortles **33** Bb
Ortles / Ortler **33** Bb
Ortona [It.] **29** Ca
Orust **75** Ba
Orvieto [It.] **29** BCa

Orzola [Sp.] **23** ins.a
Orzysz [Pol.] **57** Cc
Osäm **49** Ba
Osby [Svezia] **75** Cb
Oschatz [D] **35** Db
Oschiri [It.] **29** ABb
Osen [Norv.] **71** Bb
Osijek [Cro.] **41** Ca
Osipoviči [R.B.] **53** Ba
Oskarshamn [Svezia] **75** Da
Oslo [Norv.] **73** Cb
Ošmjany [R.B.] **57** Db
Osnabrück [D] **35** Bb
Osor [Cro.] **31** Cb
Ostaškov [Russia] **55** CDab
Ostende / Oostende [Bel.] **7** BCa
Osterburg / Altmark [D] **35** Cb
Österdalälven **73** Da
Ostermark / Teuva [Finl.] **65** Cc
Østerøa **75** ins.a
Østerøya **73** Ba
Östersjön = Baltico, Mar– (I) **75** Dab
Østersøen = Baltico, Mar– (I) **75** Dab
Östersund [Svezia] **71** Cb
Östhammar [Svezia] **59** Ba
Oštinski Pogost [Russia] **61** Ca
Ostrava [Rep.Ceca] **39** Ba
Ostróda [Pol.] **57** Bc
Ostrołęka [Pol.] **37** Cb
Ostrov [Russia] **55** Ba
Ostrowiec Świętokrzyski [Pol.] **37** Cbc
Ostrów Mazowiecka [Pol.] **37** Cb
Ostrów Wielkopolski [Pol.] **37** Ab
Ostsee = Baltico, Mar– (I) **75** Cb
Ostseebad Göhren [D] **35** Da
Ostuni [It.] **27** Cb
Otterndorf [D] **35** BCb
Ottobeuren [D] **33** Bab
Otočac [Cro.] **41** Bab
Otra **73** Bb
Otranto [It.] **27** Db
Otranto, Canale d'– **27** Db
Otranto, Canale d'– (I) = Otrantos, Kanali i– **27** Db
Otrantos, Kanali i– = Otranto, Canale d'– (I) **27** Db
Otta [Norv.] **73** Ca
Otterndorf [D] **35** BCb
Ottobeuren [D] **33** Bab
Ouahran [Alg.] **23** Bc
Oudenaarde / Audenarde [Bel.] **7** Cab
Ouessant, Ile d'– **9** Aa
Ouezzane [Mar.] **21** Cc
Oulainen [Finl.] **65** Db
Oulanka **63** Aa
Oulu / Uleåborg [Finl.] **65** Db
Oulu, Lago– (I) = Oulujärvi **65** Ba
Oulujärvi = Oulu, Lago– (I) **65** Bb
Oulujoki **65** Db
Ounasjoki **67** Cb
Ouranópolis [Grecia] **43** BCb
Ourense / Orense [Sp.] **19** Ba
Ouse [Fr.] **5** Cab
Ouse [RU] **5** CDc
Outer Hebrides = Ebridi Esterne (I) **1** Ba
Outokumpu [Finl.] **63** Ac
Ovar [Port.] **19** Bb
Overhalla [Norv.] **71** BCb
Överkalix [Svezia] **65** Ca
Övertorneå [Svezia] **67** Bb
Oviedo [It.] **19** BCa

Øvre Anarjokka **67** Cb
Øvre Årdal [Norv.] **73** Ba
Øvre Dividal **69** Cb
Øvre Pasvik **69** Fa
Övre Soppero [Svezia] **67** Bb
Ovruč [Ucr.] **53** Ba
Oxelösund [Svezia] **59** Ab
Oxford [RU] **5** Cb
Ózd [Ung.] **39** Ba
Ozieri [It.] **29** ABb

P

Paavola [Finl.] **65** Db
Pabianice [Pol.] **37** Bb
Pachino [It.] **25** BCb
Paczków [Pol.] **37** Ac
Padany [Russia] **63** Cb
Paderborn [D] **35** Bb
Padirac, Gouffre de– **15** Cab
Padjelanta **69** Bb
Padova [It.] **31** BCa
Padrón [Sp.] **19** Ba
Paestum **27** BCb
Pag [Cro.] **31** CDb
Pag [Cro.] **41** ABb
Päijänne **59** Ca
Paimpol [Fr.] **9** ABa
Pajala [Svezia] **67** Bb
Pajares, Puerto de– **19** Ca
Paklenica **41** Bb
Palafrugell [Sp.] **17** CDab
Palagruža **27** Ca
Palaiokastrítsa **43** Ab
Palamós [Sp.] **17** CDb
Palanga [Lit.] **57** BCb
Palau [It.] **29** Bb
Palazzolo Acreide [It.] **25** BCb
Paldiski [Est.] **59** CDb
Palencia [Sp.] **19** Cab
Palermo [It.] **25** Bb
Palestrina [It.] **29** Cb
Palinuro [It.] **27** Ca
Palinuro, Capo– **25** Ca
Pallas–Ounastunturi **67** BCb
Palma / La Ciutat de Mallorca [Sp.] **23** Ca
Palmanova [It.] **31** Ca
Palmi [It.] **25** Cb
Palojoensuu [Finl.] **67** Bb
Palos, Cabo de– **23** Bb
Paltamo [Finl.] **65** Eb
Pamiers [Fr.] **17** Ca
Pampilhosa de la Serra [Port.] **19** Bb
Pamplona [Sp.] **17** Ba
Pamporovo [Bulg.] **47** Bb
Panagjurište [Bulg.] **49** Ba
Panarea **25** Cb
Pančevo [Iug.] **41** Cab
Pančičev vrh **41** Cb
Panevėžis / Panevėžys [Lit.] **57** Db
Panevėžys / Panevėžis [Lit.] **57** Db
Pantelleria [It.] **25** ABb
Pantelleria [It.] **25** ABb
Paola [It.] **25** Ca
Pápa [Ung.] **39** Ab
Papenburg [D] **7** Da
Papey **77** Cb
Paracín [Iug.] **41** Db
Parainen / Pargas [Finl.] **59** Ca
Páramo de Masa, Puerto de– **19** Ca
Paranéstion [Grecia] **47** Bb
Paray-le-Monial [Fr.] **11** Bb
Pardubice [Rep.Ceca] **39** Aa
Parentis-en-Born [Fr.] **15** Bb
Párga [Grecia] **43** Ab

Pargas / Parainen [Finl.] **59** Ca
Parigi (I) = Paris [Fr.] **9** Ca
Parikkala [Finl.] **61** Aa
Paringul Mare, Vîrful– **51** Ab
Paris [Fr.] = Parigi (I) **9** Ca
Parkano [Finl.] **59** Ca
Parma [It.] **31** Bb
Parnaso (I) = Parnassós Óros **45** Ab
Parnassós **45** Ab
Parnassós Óros = Parnaso (I) **45** Ab
Párnis **45** Ab
Pärnu / Pjarnu [Est.] **59** Db
Páros [Grecia] **45** Bb
Páros [Grecia] **45** Bb
Parthenay [Fr.] **9** Bb
Partizánske [Slovac.] **39** Ba
Pärvomaj [Bulg.] **49** Bab
Paşcani [Rom.] **51** Bb
Pasewolk [D] **35** Db
Pasłęk [Pol.] **57** Bbc
Passau [D] **33** Ca
Passero, Capo– **25** BCb
Pasvalys [Lit.] **57** Db
Paternò [It.] **25** BCb
Pátmos **45** Bb
Pátrai [Grecia] = Patrasso (I) **43** Bc
Patrasso (I) = Pátrai [Grecia] **43** Bc
Patreksfjörður [Isl.] **77** ABb
Patvinsuo **63** Bbc
Pau [Fr.] **17** Ba
Pavia [It.] **31** ABa
Pavilosta / Pãvilosta [Lett.] **57** BCab
Pãvilosta / Pavilosta [Lett.] **57** BCab
Pavlikeni [Bulg.] **49** Ba
Pavullo nel Frignano [It.] **31** Bb
Paxoí **43** Ab
Pazardžik [Bulg.] **49** Ba
Pazin [Cro.] **31** Ca
Peack District **5** Cb
Peć [Iug.] **41** Cb
Pečenga [Russia] **67** Ea
Pécs [Ung.] **41** Ca
Peel [RU] **3** Ca
Peipsi järv = Ciudi, Lago dei– (I) **59** Eb
Pelagie, Isole– **25** Bc
Pélagos **47** ABb
Pelh'imov [Rep.Ceca] **33** Da
Pelister **43** ABb
Pelješac **27** Ca
Pelkosenniemi [Finl.] **67** Cb
Pello [Finl.] **67** BCb
Peloponneso (I) = Pelopónnisos **45** Ab
Pelopónnisos = Peloponneso (I) **45** Ab
Pembroke [RU] **5** Bb
Pembrokeshire Coast **5** Bb
Peñafiel [Port.] **19** Bb
Peñafiel [Sp.] **19** Cb
Penamacor [Port.] **19** Bb
Peñaranda de Bracamonte [Sp.] **19** Cb
Peñarroya–Pueblonuevo [Sp.] **21** Cb
Peñas, Cabo de– **19** BCa
Pendik [Tur.] **47** Cb
Peneda-Gerês **19** Bb
Peniche [Port.] **21** Aa
Peñíscola / Peníscola [Sp.] **17** Cb
Peníscola / Peñíscola [Sp.] **17** Cb
Penmarch, Pointe de– **9** Ab
Pennines = Pennini, Monti– (I) **3** Da

Pennini, Monti– (I) = Pennines **3** Da
Penrith [RU] **3** Da
Pentland Firth **1** Ca
Penzance [RU] **5** Bc
Perales, Puerto de– **19** Bb
Peräseinäjoki [Finl.] **65** Cc
Perast [Iug.] **41** Cb
Perdido, Monte– **17** BCa
Perejaslav–Hmelnicki [Ucr.] **53** Cb
Pergamo (I) = Pergamon **47** Cbc
Pergamon = Pergamo (I) **47** Cbc
Périgueux [Fr.] **15** Ca
Perleberg [D] **35** CDb
Përmeti [Alb.] **43** Ab
Pernik [Bulg.] **49** Aa
Perpignan [Fr.] = Perpignano (I) **17** CDa
Perpignano (I) = Perpignan [Fr.] **17** CDa
Perros–Guirec [Fr.] **9** Aa
Perth [RU] **1** Ca
Perugia [It.] **29** Ca
Pervomajsk [Ucr.] **51** Dab
Pesaro [It.] **31** Ca
Pescara [It.] **29** Ca
Pescasseroli [It.] **29** Cb
Pescatori, Penisola dei– (I) = Rybačí, poluostrov– **67** Ea
Peschici [It.] **27** Cab
Peshkopia [Alb.] **43** Ab
Peso da Régua [Port.] **19** Bb
Peštera [Bulg.] **49** Bb
Pestovo [Russia] **61** Cb
Petäjävesi [Finl.] **65** Cc
Peterborough [RU] **5** Cb
Peterhead [RU] **1** Da
Petkeljärvi **63** Bc
Petkula [Finl.] **67** Cb
Petrič [Bulg.] **43** Bb
Petrila [Rom.] **41** Da
Petrodvorek [Russia] **61** ABb
Petronell [Aus.] **39** Aab
Petroşani [Rom.] **41** Da
Petrovac [Iug.] **41** Db
Petrovski Jam [Russia] **63** Cb
Petrozavodsk [Russia] **61** Ca
Pézenas [Fr.] **13** Bc
Pfaffenhofen an der Ilm [D] **33** Ba
Pforzheim [D] **33** Aa
Philippeville [Bel.] **7** Cb
Piacenza [It.] **31** Bab
Pianosa [It.] **27** Ca
Pianosa [It.] **29** Ba
Piaski [Pol.] **37** Cbc
Piatra Neamţ [Rom.] **51** Bb
Piave **31** Ca
Piazza Armerina [It.] **25** Bb
Piccolo Belt (I) = Lille Bælt **75** Bb
Piccolo San Bernardo, Colle del– **13** Ca
Pico **21** ins.a
Piedrabuena [Sp.] **21** Cab
Piedrafita, Puerto de– **19** Ba
Piedrahíta [Sp.] **19** Cb
Pieksämäki [Finl.] **65** Ec
Pielavesi [Finl.] **65** Cb
Pielinen **63** Ab
Pieljekaise **71** Da
Pieniny **39** Ba
Pienza [It.] **29** Ba
Pieskehaure **69** Bb
Piešťany [Slovac.] **39** Aa
Pietarsaari / Jakobstad [Finl.] **65** Cb
Pieve di Cadore [It.] **33** Cb
Pihkva järv = Pskov, Lago di– (I) **61** Ab

Pihtipudas [Finl.] **65** Db
Pikalevo [Russia] **61** Cb
Piła [Pol.] **37** Ab
Pilica **37** Bb
Pílos [Grecia] **45** Ab
Pilzno [Pol.] **39** Ca
Píndhos **43** Bb
Píndhos Óros = Pindo (I) **43** Bb
Pindo (I) = Píndhos Óros **43** Bb
Pinerolo [It.] **13** Cb
Pinhel [Port.] **19** Bb
Pinoso [Sp.] **23** Bb
Pinsk [R.B.] **53** Aa
Piombino [It.] **29** Ba
Pionerski [Russia] **57** Bb
Piotrków Trybunalski [Pol.] **37** Bb
Piqueras, Puerto de– **17** Ba
Piraiévs [Grecia] = Píreo (I) **45** Ab
Piran [Slo.] **31** Ca
Pirenei (I) = Pirineos **17** BCa
Pirenei (I) = Pyrénées **17** BCa
Píreo (I) = Piraiévs [Grecia] **45** Ab
Pirgós [Grecia] **43** Bb
Pírgos [Grecia] **43** Bc
Pirin **43** Bb
Pirineos = Pirenei (I) **17** BCa
Pirjatin [Ucr.] **53** Cb
Pirmasens [D] **33** Aa
Pirna [D] **35** Dbc
Pirot [Iug.] **41** Db
Pirttikoski [Finl.] **67** CDb
Piryí [Grecia] **45** Bb
Pisa [It.] **31** Bb
Pisa [Pol.] **37** Cb
Písek [Rep.Ceca] **33** Ca
Pistoia [It.] **31** Bb
Pisuerga **19** Cb
Pisz [Pol.] **57** Cc
Piteå [Svezia] **65** Cb
Piteälven **65** Bb
Piteşti [Rom.] **49** Ba
Pithiviers [Fr.] **9** Cab
Pitigliano [It.] **29** Ba
Pitkjaranta [Russia] **61** Ba
Pitlochry [RU] **1** Cb
Pjalica [Russia] **63** Ea
Pjalma [Russia] **63** Cb
Pjaozero, ozero– **63** Bab
Pjarnu / Pärnu [Est.] **59** Db
Plasencia [Sp.] **19** BCb
Plataniá [Grecia] **43** Bbc
Plauen [D] **35** CDc
Pļaviņas / Pļavinjas [Lett.] **57** Db
Plavsk [Russia] **55** Ec
Playa Blanca [Sp.] **23** ins.a
Pleseck [Russia] **63** Ecc
Pleszew [Pol.] **37** Ab
Pleven [Bulg.] **49** Ba
Pleyben [Fr.] **9** Aa
Plitvice [Cro.] **41** Bab
Plitvička Jezera **41** Bab
Pljavinjas / Pļaviņas [Lett.] **57** Db
Pljevlja [Iug.] **41** Cb
Płock [Pol.] **37** Bb
Ploërmel [Fr.] **9** Bab
Ploieşti [Rom.] **49** Ba
Plomárion [Grecia] **45** Bab
Płońsk [Pol.] **37** Bb
Płoty [Pol.] **37** Ab
Plovdiv [Bulg.] **49** Ba
Plunge / Plungé [Lit.] **57** Cb
Plungé / Plunge [Lit.] **57** Cb
Plymouth [RU] **5** Bc
Plzeň [Rep.Ceca] **33** Ca
Pniewy [Pol.] **37** Ab
Po **31** BCab

Poarta de Fier a Transilvaniei **41** Da
Počep [Russia] **53** Da
Poděbrady [Rep.Ceca] **33** Da
Podgorica (Titograd) [Iug.] **41** Cb
Podolico, Ripiano– (I) = Podolskaja vozvyšennost **51** BCa
Podolsk [Russia] **55** Eb
Podolskaja vozvyšennost = Podolico, Ripiano– (I) **51** BCa
Podporožje [Russia] **61** Ca
Podravska Slatina [Cro.] **41** Ba
Podvyí **39** Aa
Poggibonsi [It.] **31** Bb
Pöggstall [Aus.] **33** Da
Pogradeci [Alb.] **43** Ab
Pohjanlahti = Botnia, Golfo di– (I) **65** BCbc
Pohořelice [Rep.Ceca] **39** Aa
Poiana Braşov [Rom.] **51** Bb
Poitiers [Fr.] **9** Cb
Pokka [Finl.] **67** Cc
Pola de Lena [Sp.] **19** Ca
Pola di Siero [Sp.] **19** Ca
Połczyn Zdrój [Pol.] **37** Ab
Polesia (I) = Polesje **53** ABa
Polesie **37** Cb
Polesje = Polesia (I) **53** ABa
Políaigos **45** Bb
Policoro [It.] **27** Cb
Poligny [Fr.] **11** Bb
Políyiros [Grecia] **43** Bb
Poljarnyje Zori [Russia] **67** Eb
Pöllau [Aus.] **39** Ab
Pollença [Sp.] **23** CDa
Pollino **25** Ca
Pollino, Monte– **25** Ca
Polmak [Norv.] **69** Fa
Polock [R.B.] **55** Bb
Polski Trămbeš [Bulg.] **49** Ba
Poltava [Ucr.] **53** Db
Põltsamaa / Pyltsamaa [Est.] **59** Db
Pombal [Port.] **19** Bb
Pomerania (I) = Pommern **35** Db
Pommern = Pomerania (I) **35** Db
Pomorije [Bulg.] **49** Ca
Pomorze **37** Ab
Pompei [It.] **29** Cb
Ponferrada [Sp.] **19** Ba
Ponoarele [Rom.] **49** Aa
Pons [Sp.] **17** Cab
Ponta Delgada [Port.] **21** ins.a
Pont-à-Mousson [Fr.] **11** BCa
Pontarlier [Fr.] **11** Cb
Pont-Audemer [Fr.] **9** Ca
Pontchâteau [Fr.] **9** Bb
Pont-du-Garde [Fr.] **13** Bb
Ponte de Sor [Port.] **21** Ba
Pontedeume / Puentedeume [Sp.] **19** Ba
Ponte di Legno [It.] **31** Ba
Ponte Leccia [Fr.] **13** Db
Pontevedra [Sp.] **19** Ba
Pontivy [Fr.] **9** ABab
Pont-l'Abbé [Fr.] **9** Aab
Pontremoli [It.] **31** Bb
Pontresina [Svizz.] **33** Bb
Pont-Saint-Esprit [Fr.] **13** Bb
Ponza **29** Cb
Poole [RU] **5** Cc
Popoli [It.] **29** Ca
Popovo [Bulg.] **49** Ba
Poprad [Slovac.] **39** Ba
Porcuna [Sp.] **21** Cb
Pordenone [It.] **31** Ca
Poreč [Slo.] **31** Ca
Porhov [Russia] **61** Ab

Pori / Björneborg [Finl.] **59** Ca
Porjus [Svezia] **69** Cb
Pornic [Fr.] **9** Bb
Póros [Grecia] **45** Ab
Póros [Grecia] **45** Ab
Porosozero [Russia] **63** Bc
Porrentruy [Svizz.] **11** Cb
Porretta Terme [It.] **31** Bb
Porsangen **69** Ea
Porsgrunn [Norv.] **73** Cb
Portadown / Port an Dúnáin [RU] **3** Ba
Portaferry [RU] **3** Ca
Portalegre [Port.] **21** Ba
Port an Dúnáin / Portadown [RU] **3** Ba
Port Askaig [RU] **1** BCb
Portbou / Port–Bou [Sp.] **17** CDa
Port–Bou / Portbou [Sp.] **17** CDa
Port-Cros **13** Cb
Porte di Ferro (I) = Portile de Fier **41** Db
Port Ellen [RU] **1** Ba
Porthmadog [RU] **5** Bb
Portile de Fier = Porte di Ferro (I) **41** Db
Portimão [Port.] **21** Bb
Port Láirge / Waterford [Eire] **3** Ba
Port Laoise / Portlaoise [Eire] **3** Ba
Portlaoise / Port Laoise [Eire] **3** Ba
Porto [Port.] **19** Bb
Porto Azzurro [It.] **29** Bb
Porto Cervo [It.] **29** Bb
Porto Empedocle [It.] **25** Bb
Portoferraio [It.] **29** Ba
Portofino [It.] **31** Bb
Port of Ness [RU] **1** Ba
Portogruaro [It.] **31** Ca
Porto San Giorgio [It.] **29** Ca
Porto Santo [It.] **21** ins.a
Porto Santo [Port.] **21** ins.a
Porto Santo Stefano [It.] **29** Ba
Porto Tolle [It.] **31** Cab
Porto Torres [It.] **29** Ab
Porto Vecchio [It.] **13** Dc
Portovenere [It.] **31** Bb
Portree [Eire] **1** Ba
Port Rois / Portrush [RU] **3** Ba
Portrush / Port Rois [RU] **3** Ba
Pörtschach [Aus.] **33** Cb
Portsmouth [RU] **5** Cc
Port Talbot [RU] **5** Bc
Porttipahdantekojärvi **67** Cb
Portugalete [Sp.] **19** CDa
Portumna [Eire] **3** Ba
Porvoo / Borgå [Finl.] **59** Da
Pošehonje–Volodarsk [Russia] **61** Db
Posio [Finl.] **65** Eab
Postavy [R.B.] **57** DEb
Postojna [Slo.] **31** Ca
Potenza [It.] **27** Cb
Potes [Sp.] **19** Ca
Potsdam [D] **35** Db
Považská Bystrica [Slovac.] **39** Ba
Povlja [Cro.] **41** Bb
Povoação [Port.] **21** ins.a
Póvoa de Varzim [Port.] **19** Bb
Požarevac [Iug.] **41** Db
Požega [Iug.] **41** Db
Poznań [Pol.] **37** Ab
Pozoblanco [Sp.] **21** Cb
Pozzuoli [It.] **29** Cb
Prachatice [Rep.Ceca] **33** Ca

Prades [Fr.] **17** Ca
Praga (I) = Praha [Rep.Ceca] **33** Ca
Praha [Rep.Ceca] = Praga (I) **33** Ca
Praia a Mare [It.] **25** Ca
Praia da Rocha [Port.] **21** Bb
Praia da Vitória [Port.] **21** ins.a
Prasonísion **45** Cbc
Prato [It.] **31** Bb
Predeal [Rom.] **51** Bb
Preetz [D] **35** Ca
Prekule / Priekulė [Lit.] **57** Cb
Prenaj / Prienai [Lit.] **57** CDb
Prenzlau [D] **35** Db
Přerov [Rep.Ceca] **39** Aa
Preslav [Bulg.] **49** Ba
Prešov [Slovac.] **39** Ca
Préspa **43** ABb
Prespa, Lago di– (I) = Prespansko jezero **43** ABb
Prespansko jezero = Prespa, Lago di– (I) **43** ABb
Preston [RU] **5** Cb
Préveza [Grecia] **43** Abc
Priboj [Iug.] **41** Cb
Příbram [Rep.Ceca] **33** Ca
Priego [Sp.] **17** Bb
Priekule [Lett.] **57** Cb
Priekulė / Prekule [Lit.] **57** Cb
Prienai / Prenaj [Lit.] **57** CDb
Priene **45** Cb
Prievidza [Slovac.] **39** Ba
Prijedor [Bos.Erz.] **41** Bab
Prijepolje [Iug.] **41** Cb
Prilep [Maced.] **43** Bb
Priluki [Ucr.] **53** Cb
Primorje [Russia] **57** Bb
Primorsk [Russia] **61** Aa
Primorsko [Bulg.] **49** Ca
Primošterv [Cro.] **41** Bb
Priozersk [Russia] **61** ABa
Pripjat **53** Ba
Prirečny [Russia] **67** DEab
Prislop, Pasul– **51** Bb
Priština [Iug.] **41** CDb
Pritzwalk [D] **35** Db
Privas [Fr.] **13** Bb
Prizren [Iug.] **41** Cb
Prokuplje [Iug.] **41** Db
Promontore, Capo– (I) = Kamenjak, Rt– **31** Cb
Propriano [Fr.] **13** Dc
Prostějov [Rep.Ceca] **39** Aa
Provadija [Bulg.] **49** Ca
Provence = Provenza (I) **13** BCb
Provenza (I) = Provence **13** BCb
Provins [Fr.] **11** Ba
Prudnik [Pol.] **37** Ac
Prüm [D] **7** Db
Pruszków [Pol.] **37** Bb
Prut **51** Cb
Pružany [R.B.] **57** Db
Przasnysz [Pol.] **37** BCb
Przemyśl [Pol.] **39** Ca
Przeworsk [Pol.] **39** Ca
Psará **45** Bb
Psёl **53** Db
Pskov [Russia] **61** Ab
Pskov, Lago di– (I) = Pihkva järv **61** Ab
Pskov, Lago di– (I) = Pskovskoje ozero **61** Ab
Pskovskoje ozero = Pskov, Lago di– (I) **61** Ab
Psёl **53** Ba
Ptolemaïs [Grecia] **43** Bb
Ptuj [Slo.] **31** Ca
Puck [Pol.] **57** Bb
Pudasjärvi [Finl.] **65** DEb

Pudož [Russia] **61** Da
Puebla de Don Fabrique [Sp.]
23 Bb
Puebla de Guzmán [Sp.] **21** Bb
Puebla de Sanabria [Sp.]
19 Bab
Puentedeume / Pontedeume
[Sp.] **19** Ba
Puente-Genil [Sp.] **21** Cb
Puerto de la Cruz [Sp.]
23 ins.a
Puerto de la Estaca [Sp.]
23 ins.a
Puerto del Rosario [Sp.]
23 ins.a
Puerto de Mazarrón [Sp.]
23 Bb
Puertollano [Sp.] **21** Cb
Puka [Alb.] **41** Cbc
Pula [It.] **29** ABbc
Pula (Pola) [Cro.] **31** Cab
Puławy [Pol.] **37** Db
Pulkkila [Finl.] **65** Db
Puttusk [Pol.] **37** BCb
Puolanka [Finl.] **65** Eb
Purchena [Sp.] **23** Bb
Puškin [Russia] **61** Bb
Puškino [Russia] **55** Cb
Pušnoj [Russia] **67** Fb
Püspökladány [Ung.] **39** BCb
Pustoška [Russia] **55** Bb
Putivl [Ucr.] **53** Da
Puttgarten [D] **35** Ca
Puulavesi **59** Da
Puymorens, Col de– **17** Ca
Pwllheli [RU] **5** Bb
Pyhä Häkki **65** Dbc
Pyhäjärvi [Finl.] **65** Db
Pyhäjärvi [Finl.] **65** Db
Pyhäjoki [Finl.] **65** Db
Pyhäjoki [Finl.] **65** Db
Pyhäntä [Finl.] **65** Db
Pyhätunturi **67** CDb
Pyltsamaa / Pôltsamaa [Est.]
59 Db
Pyrénées = Pirenei (I) **17** BCa
Pyrénées Occidentales **17** Ba
Pyrzyce [Pol.] **35** DEb
Pytalovo [Russia] **55** Bab

Q

Quattro Cantoni, Lago dei– (I)
= Vierwaldstätter See **33** Ab
Quedlinburg [D] **35** Cb
Quesada [Sp.] **21** Cbb
Quiberon [Fr.] **9** ABb
Quillan [Fr.] **17** Ca
Quimper [Fr.] **9** Aab
Quimperlé [Fr.] **9** Bb
Quintanar de la Orden [Sp.]
19 CDb
Qulaybîyah [Tun.] **25** Ab

R

Raab **39** Ab
Raahe / Brahestad [Finl.]
65 Db
Rab [Cro.] **31** Cb
Rab [Cro.] **31** Cb
Rába **39** Ab
Rabat / Victoria [Malta] **25** Bbc
Rabka [Pol.] **39** Ba
Rabočeostrovsk [Russia] **63** Cb
Racibórz [Pol.] **39** Ba
Rădăuţi [Rom.] **51** Bab
Radimlje [Bos.Erz.] **41** BCb
Radom [Pol.] **37** BCb

Radomsko [Pol.] **37** Bbc
Radoškoviči [R.B.] **55** Bb
Radoviš [Maced.] **43** Bb
Radstadt [Aus.] **33** Cb
Radviliškis [Lit.] **57** Cb
Radziejów [Pol.] **37** Bb
Radzyń Podlaski [Pol.] **37** Cb
Rafína [Grecia] **45** ABb
Rago **69** Bb
Ragusa [It.] **25** Bb
Ragusa (I) = Dubrovnik [Cro.]
41 BCb
Rahov [Ucr.] **51** Bab
Raisi, Punta– **25** Bb
Raja Jcoseppi [Finl.] **67** Db
Rakkestad [Norv.] **73** Ca
Rakvere [Est.] **59** Db
Rambouillet [Fr.] **9** Ca
Ramigala / Ramygala [Lit.]
57 Db
Ramsele [Svezia] **71** Db
Ramsey [RU] **3** Ca
Ramsgate [RU] **5** Db
Ramsjö [Svezia] **73** Ea
Ramygala / Ramigala [Lit.]
57 Db
Randazzo [It.] **25** BCb
Randers [Dan.] **75** Bb
Randsfjorden **73** Ca
Rantsila [Finl.] **65** Cb
Ranua [Finl.] **65** Dab
Rapallo [It.] **31** Bb
Raseiniai / Rasejnjaj [Lit.]
57 Cb
Rasejnjaj / Raseiniai [Lit.]
57 Cb
Raška [Iug.] **41** Cb
Ras–Tarf, Cap– **21** Cc
Rastatt [D] **33** Aa
Rätansbyn [Svezia] **73** Da
Rathenow [D] **35** Db
Ráth Luirc / An Ráth [Eire]
3 Bb
Ratisbona (I) = Regensburg [D]
33 BCa
Ratno [Ucr.] **37** Db
Rättvik [Svezia] **73** Ea
Ratzeburg [D] **35** Cb
Raufarhöfn [Isl.] **77** Da
Rauma / Raumo [Finl.] **59** Ca
Raumo / Rauma [Finl.] **59** Ca
Räut **51** Cb
Rava–Russkaja [Ucr.] **39** Ca
Ravenna [It.] **31** Cb
Ravensburg [D] **33** Bb
Rawa Mazowiecka [Pol.] **37** Bb
Rawicz [Pol.] **37** Ab
Raz, Pointe du– **9** Aab
Razgrad [Bulg.] **49** Ba
Razlog [Bulg.] **43** Db
Ré, Ile de– **9** Bb
Reading [RU] **5** Cb
Reboly [Russia] **63** Bb
Rečica [R.B.] **53** Ca
Recoaro Terme [It.] **31** Ba
Redon [Fr.] **9** Bb
Redondela [Sp.] **19** Ba
Redondo [Port.] **21** Bb
Ree, Lough– **3** Bb
Regen [D] **33** Ca
Regensburg [D] = Ratisbona (I)
33 BCa
Reggio di Calabria [It.] **25** Cb
Reggio nell'Emilia [It.] **31** Bb
Reghim [Rom.] **51** Bb
Reims [Fr.] **11** Ba
Reinosa [Sp.] **19** Ca
Reisa **69** Da
Relizane [Alg.] **23** Cc
Remiremont [Fr.] **11** Cab
Remscheid [D] **7** Da
Rena [Norv.] **73** Ca

Rendsburg [D] **35** Ca
Reni [Ucr.] **51** Cb
Rennes [Fr.] **9** Bab
Reno **31** Bb
Reno (I) = Rhein **11** Ca
Reno (I) = Rhin **11** Cb
Repki [Ucr.] **53** Ca
Requena [Sp.] **23** Ba
Resen [Maced.] **43** ABb
Rešetilovka [Ucr.] **53** Db
Resia, Passo di– **33** Bb
Reşiţa [Rom.] **41** Da
Retavas / Rietavas [Lit.] **57** Cb
Retezat **41** Da
Rethel [Fr.] **11** Ba
Réthimmon [Grecia] **45** Bc
Rétság [Ung.] **39** Bab
Retz [Aus.] **39** Aa
Reus [Sp.] **17** Cb
Reutlingen [D] **33** Ba
Revonlahti [Finl.] **65** Db
Reykjalíd [Isl.] **77** Db
Reykjanes **77** Bb
Reykjavík [Isl.] **77** Bb
Rezekne / Rēzekne [Lett.]
55 Bb
Rēzekne / Rezekne [Lett.]
55 Bb
Rezovo [Bulg.] **47** Cab
Rgotina [Iug.] **41** Db
Rheda–Wiedenbrück [D] **35** Bb
Rhein = Reno (I) **11** Ca
Rheinfelden (Baden) [D] **33** Ab
Rhin = Reno (I) **11** Cb
Rho [It.] **31** ABa
Rhondda [RU] **5** Bb
Rhône = Rodano (I) **13** Bb
Rhum **1** Bab
Riaño [Sp.] **19** Ca
Rías Altas **19** Ba
Rías Bajas **19** Aa
Riaza [Sp.] **19** Cb
Ribadavia [Sp.] **19** Ba
Ribadeo [Sp.] **19** Ba
Ribadesella [Sp.] **19** Ca
Ribe [Dan.] **75** Ab
Ribeira Brava [Port.] **21** ins.a
Ribeira Grande [Port.] **21** ins.a
Ribniţa [Mold.] **51** Cb
Ribnitz–Damgarten [D] **35** Ca
Riccione [It.] **31** Cb
Ried im Innkreis [Aus.] **33** Ca
Riesa [D] **35** Db
Rietavas / Retavas [Lit.] **57** Cb
Rieti [It.] **29** Ca
Rif **21** Cc
Rifstangi **77** Da
Riga / Rīga [Lett.] **57** CDab
Rīga / Riga [Lett.] **57** CDab
Rīga, Golfo di– (I) = Rīgas jūras
līcis **57** Ca
Rīga, Golfo di– (I) = Riia laht
59 Cb
Rīgas jūras līcis = Rīga, Golfo
di– (I) **57** Ca
Riia laht = Rīga, Golfo di– (I)
59 Cb
Riihimäki [Finl.] **59** Da
Riisitunturi **65** Eab
Rijeka [Cro.] = Fiume (I) **31** Ca
Riksgränsen [Svezia] **69** BCb
Rila **49** Aa
Rilski Manastir **49** Aa
Rimavská Šobota [Slovac.]
39 Ba
Rimini [It.] **31** Cb
Rîmnicu Sărat [Rom.] **51** BCb
Rîmnicu Vîlcea [Rom.] **51** Bbc
Ringebu [Norv.] **73** Ca
Ringkøbing [Dan.] **75** Ab
Ringsted [Dan.] **75** Bb
Ringvassøy **69** Ca
Riom [Fr.] **11** ABb

Rìon [Grecia] **43** Bc
Ripoll [Sp.] **17** Ca
Ripon [RU] **3** Dab
Risbäck [Svezia] **71** Db
Risnjak **31** Ca
Risør [Norv.] **75** Ba
Risøyhamn [Norv.] **69** Bab
Rissa [Norv.] **71** Bb
Risti [Est.] **59** CDb
Riva del Garda [It.] **31** Ba
Rivoli [It.] **13** Cab
Rizzuto, Capo– **25** Cab
Rjukan [Norv.] **73** Bab
Roanne [Fr.] **11** Bb
Robertsfors [Svezia] **71** EFb
Roca, Cabo da– **21** Ab
Rocamadour [Fr.] **15** Cb
Roccaraso [It.] **29** Cab
Rochefort [Bel.] **7** Cb
Rochefort [Fr.] **15** Ba
Rochester [RU] **5** Db
Rocroi [Fr.] **7** Cb
Rodano (I) = Rhône **13** Bb
Rødberg [Norv.] **73** BCa
Rødbyhavn [Dan.] **35** Ca
Rodel [RU] **1** Ba
Rodez [Fr.] **15** Ca
Ródhos [Grecia] = Rodi (I)
45 Cb
Ródhos [Grecia] = Rodi (I)
45 Cb
Rodi (I) = Ródhos [Grecia]
45 Cb
Rodi (I) = Ródhos [Grecia]
45 Cb
Rodi Garganico [It.] **27** Cab
Roeselare / Roulers [Bel.]
7 BCab
Rogačev [R.B.] **53** BCa
Rogaška Slatina [Slo.] **41** Ba
Rogatica [Bos.Erz.] **41** Cb
Rogatin [Ucr.] **39** Da
Rognan [Norv.] **69** Bb
Rogozhina [Alb.] **43** Ab
Rokiškis [Lit.] **57** Db
Rokua **65** Db
Rokycany [Rep.Ceca] **33** Ca
Roma [It.] **29** Cab
Romagna **31** Cb
Roman [Rom.] **51** BCb
Romans–sur–Isère [Fr.] **13** Bab
Romilly–sur–Seine [Fr.] **11** Ba
Romny [Ucr.] **53** Db
Rømø **75** Ab
Romorantin–Lanthenay [Fr.]
9 Cb
Roncesvalles [Sp.] **17** Ba
Roncisvalle, Passo di– (I) =
Ibañeta, Puerto de– **17** Ba
Ronda [Sp.] **21** Cb
Rondane **73** Ca
Rønne [Dan.] **75** Cb
Ronneby [Svezia] **75** Cb
Roosendaal [P.B.] **7** Ca
Roquefort [Fr.] **15** Bb
Røros [Norv.] **73** Ca
Rørvik [Norv.] **71** Bb
Ros **53** Cb
Rosa, Monte– **31** Aa
Rosal de la Frontera [Sp.]
21 Bb
Rosas / Roses [Sp.] **17** Da
Roscoff [Fr.] **9** Aa
Ros Comáin / Roscommon
[Eire] **3** Bb
Roscommon / Ros Comáin
[Eire] **3** Bb
Ros Cré / Roscrea [Eire] **3** Bb
Roscrea / Ros Cré [Eire] **3** Bb
Rosendal [Norv.] **73** ABab
Rosenheim [D] **33** BCab
Roses / Rosas [Sp.] **17** Da

Roshage **75** Aab
Roşiori de Vede [Rom.] **49** Ba
Roskilde [Dan.] **75** BCb
Ros Láir / Rosslare [Eire] **3** Bb
Roslavl [Russia] **55** Cbc
Rossano [It.] **25** Ca
Rossan Point **3** Ba
Rosslare / Ros Láir [Eire] **3** Bb
Ross–on–Wye [RU] **5** Cb
Røssvatnet **71** Cb
Rostock [D] **35** CDab
Røsvik [Norv.] **69** Bb
Rotenburg (Wümme) [D] **35** Cb
Roth [D] **33** Ba
Rothenburg ob der Tauber [D]
33 Ba
Rothesay [RU] **1** Cb
Rotterdam [P.B.] **7** Ca
Rottweil [D] **33** Aab
Roubaix [Fr.] **7** BCb
Rouen [Fr.] **9** Ca
Roulers / Roeselare [Bel.]
7 BCab
Rousay **1** CDa
Rovaniemi [Finl.] **67** Db
Rovereto [It.] **31** Ba
Rovigo [It.] **31** Bab
Rovinj [Cro.] **31** Cab
Rovno [Ucr.] **53** Ab
Royal Tunbridge Wells [RU]
5 Dbc
Royan [Fr.] **15** Ba
Rožňava [Slovac.] **39** Ba
Roztocze [Eur.] **37** Cc
Roztocze [Pol.] **37** Cc
Rozvadov [Rep.Ceca] **33** Ca
Rucava [Lett.] **57** BCb
Rudkøbing [Dan.] **35** Ca
Rudnik [Bulg.] **49** Ca
Rudnja [Russia] **55** Cb
Ruffec [Fr.] **15** Ca
Rugby [RU] **5** Cb
Rügen **35** Da
Rügen / Bergen [D] **35** Da
Ruiena / Rūjiena [Lett.] **59** Db
Rūjiena / Ruiena [Lett.] **59** Db
Ruma [Iug.] **41** Cab
Rumburk [Rep.Ceca] **35** Dbc
Ruovesi [Finl.] **59** CDa
Rupea [Rom.] **51** Bb
Ruse [Bulg.] **49** Ba
Rusenski Lom **49** Ba
Ružany [R.B.] **53** Aa
Ružomberok [Slovac.] **39** Ba
Rybači, poluostrov– =
Pescatori, Penisola dei– (I)
67 Ea
Rybinsk [Russia] **61** Db
Rybinsk, Bacino di– (I) =
Rybinskoje vodohranilišče
61 Db
Rybinskoje vodohranilišče =
Rybinsk, Bacino di– (I)
61 Db
Rybnik [Pol.] **39** Ba
Rychnov nad Kněžnou
[Rep.Ceca] **39** Aa
Ryd [Svezia] **75** Cb
Rylsk [Russia] **53** Ca
Rypin [Pol.] **37** Bb
Rzepin [Pol.] **35** Db
Rzeszów [Pol.] **39** Ca
Ržev [Russia] **55** Db

S

Saalbach [Aus.] **33** Cb
Saale **35** Cb
Saale / Bernburg [D] **35** Cb
Saale / Halle [D] **35** CDb
Saale / Merseburg [D] **35** CDb

Saale / Naumburg [D] **35** Cbc
Saale / Saalfeld [D] **35** Cc
Saalfeld / Saale [D] **35** Cc
Saalfelden am Steinernen Meer
 [Aus.] **33** Cb
Saarbrücken [D] **11** Ca
Saaremaa **59** Cb
Saarijärvi [Finl.] **65** Dc
Saaristomeri **59** Cab
Saarlouis [D] **11** Ca
Saas Fee [Svizz.] **31** Aa
Šabac [Iug.] **41** Cb
Sabadell [Sp.] **17** Cb
Sabaudia [It.] **29** Cb
Sabbioneta [It.] **31** Bab
Šabla [Bulg.] **49** Ca
Sabugal [Port.] **19** Bb
Sacedón [Sp.] **17** Bb
Sachsen = Sassonia (I) **35** Db
Sachsische Schweiz **35** Dbc
Sádaba [Sp.] **17** Ba
Sado **21** Bb
Sæby [Dan.] **75** Ba
Säffle [Svezia] **73** Db
Safonovo [Russia] **55** Db
Sagres [Port.] **21** ABb
Sagunto / Sagunt o Morvedre
 [Sp.] **23** Ba
Sagunt o Morvedre / Sagunto
 [Sp.] **23** Ba
Šahy [Slovac.] **39** Bab
Saimaa **61** Aa
Saint-Affrique [Fr.] **15** CDb
Saint Albans [RU] **5** Cb
Saint-Amand-Montrond [Fr.]
 9 Cb
Saint-André-de-Cubzac [Fr.]
 15 Bab
Saint Andrews [RU] **1** Db
Saint Austell [RU] **5** Bc
Saint-Avold [Fr.] **11** Ca
Saint-Benoît-sur-Loire [Fr.]
 9 Cb
Saint-Brieuc [Fr.] **9** Ba
Saint-Calais [Fr.] **9** Cab
Saint-Claude [Fr.] **11** Bb
Saint David's Head **5** Bb
Saint-Dié [Fr.] **11** Ca
Saint-Dizier [Fr.] **11** Ba
Saint-Éloy-les-Mines [Fr.]
 15 Ca
Sainte-Maure-de-Touraine
 [Fr.] **9** Cb
Sainte-Maxime [Fr.] **13** Cb
Sainte-Menehould [Fr.]
 11 Ba
Saintes [Fr.] **15** Ba
Saintes-Maries-de-la-Mer
 [Fr.] **13** Bb
Saint-Étienne [Fr.] **13** Ba
Saint-Florent [Fr.] **13** Ba
Saint-Flour [Fr.] **13** ABab
Saint-Gaudens [Fr.] **17** Ca
Saint George's Channel = San
 Giorgio, Canale di– (I)
 3 BCb
Saint-Germain-en-Laye [Fr.]
 9 Ca
Saint-Girons [Fr.] **17** Ca
Saint Helier [RU] **9** Ba
Saint Ives [RU] **5** Bc
Saint-Jean-d'Angély [Fr.]
 15 Ba
Saint-Jean-de-Luz [Fr.]
 17 Ba
Saint-Jean-de-Maurienne [Fr.]
 13 Ca
Saint-Jean-de-Monts [Fr.]
 9 Bb
Saint-Jean-Pied-de-Port [Fr.]
 17 Ba
Saint-Junien [Fr.] **15** Ca
Saint Kilda **1** Ba

Saint-Léonard-de-Noblat [Fr.]
 15 Ca
Saint-Lô [Fr.] **9** Ba
Saint-Maixent-l'École [Fr.]
 9 Bb
Saint-Malo [Fr.] **9** Ba
Saint-Malo, Golfe de– = Saint-
 Malo, Golfo di– (I) **9** Ba
Saint-Malo, Golfo di– (I) =
 Saint-Malo, Golfe de– **9** Ba
Saint-Mathieu, Pointe de–
 9 Aa
Saint-Nazaire [Fr.] **9** Bb
Saint-Nicolas / Sint Niklaas
 [Bel.] **7** Ca
Saint-Omer [Fr.] **7** Bb
Saint Peter Port [RU] **9** Ba
Saint Pierre–le–Moûtier [Fr.]
 11 ABb
Saint-Pol-de-Léon [Fr.] **9** Aa
Saint-Pons [Fr.] **17** Ca
Saint-Pourçain-sur-Sioule
 [Fr.] **11** Bb
Saint-Quentin [Fr.] **11** Ba
Saint-Raphaël [Fr.] **13** Cb
Saint-Trond / Sint–Truiden
 [Bel.] **7** Ca
Saint-Tropez [Fr.] **13** Cb
Saint-Valery-en-Caux [Fr.]
 9 Ca
Saint-Vincent [It.] **31** Aa
Sakskøbing [Dan.] **35** Ca
Sala [Svezia] **59** Aab
Salacgriva / Salacgrīva [Lett.]
 59 Db
Salacgrīva / Salacgriva [Lett.]
 59 Db
Sala Consilina [It.] **27** Cb
Salamajärvi **65** Db
Salamanca [Sp.] **19** Cb
Salamina (I) = Salamís [Grecia]
 45 Ab
Salamís [Grecia] **45** Ab
Salamís [Grecia] = Salamina (I)
 45 Ab
Salas de los Infantes [Sp.]
 19 Cab
Salbris [Fr.] **9** Cb
Saldus [Lett.] **57** Cb
Sälen [Svezia] **73** Da
Salerno [It.] **29** Cb
Salgótarján [Ung.] **39** Bab
Salice Terme [It.] **31** ABab
Salihli [Tur.] **45** Cb
Salina **25** Bb
Salins-les-Bains [Fr.] **11** BCb
Salisburgo (I) = Salzburg [Aus.]
 33 Cb
Salisbury [RU] **5** Cbc
Salla [Finl.] **67** Db
Salmi [Russia] **61** Ba
Salò [It.] **31** Ba
Salon-de-Provence [Fr.] **13** Bb
Salonicco (I) = Thessaloníki
 [Grecia] **43** Bb
Salonicco, Golfo di– (I) =
 Thermaïkós Kólpos **43** Bb
Salonta [Rom.] **39** Ca
Salpausselkä **59** DEa
Salses-le-Château [Fr.]
 17 CDa
Šalski [Russia] **61** CDa
Salsomaggiore Terme [It.]
 31 Bb
Saltoluokta [Svezia] **69** Cb
Saluzzo [It.] **13** Cb
Salzach **33** Cab
Salzburg [Aus.] = Salisburgo (I)
 33 Cb
Salzgitter [D] **35** Cb
Salzwedel [D] **35** Cb
Sambor [Ucr.] **39** Ca

Sámi [Grecia] **43** Ac
Saminski Pogost [Russia]
 61 Da
Samo (I) = Sámos [Grecia]
 45 Bb
Samokov [Bulg.] **49** Aa
Sámos [Grecia] **45** BCb
Sámos [Grecia] = Samo (I)
 45 Bb
Samothráki [Grecia] **47** Bb
Samothráki [Grecia] =
 Samotracia (I) **47** Bb
Samotracia (I) = Samothráki
 [Grecia] **47** Bb
Samsø **75** Ba
San **37** Cc
San Antonio Abad [Sp.]
 23 Cab
San Bartolomeo in Galdo [It.]
 27 BCb
San Benedetto del Tronto [It.]
 29 Ca
San Bernardino, Passo del–
 33 ABb
Sand [Norv.] **73** Ab
Sandane [Norv.] **73** Ba
Sandanski [Bulg.] **43** Bb
Sanday **1** Da
Sande [Norv.] **73** Cb
Sandefjord [Norv.] **73** Cb
Sandnes [Norv.] **73** Ab
Sandness [RU] **1** ins.a
Sandnessjøen [Norv.] **71** Cab
Sandø **75** ins.a
Sandomierz [Pol.] **37** Cc
Sandvig-Allinge [Dan.] **75** Cb
Sandviken [Svezia] **59** Aa
San Felice Circeo [It.] **29** Cb
San Felìu de Guíxols [Sp.]
 17 CDb
San Fernando [Sp.] **21** Bb
Sänfjället **73** Da
San Francisco Javier [Sp.]
 23 Cb
Sangerhausen [D] **35** Cb
San Gimignano [It.] **31** Bb
San Giorgio, Canale di– (I) =
 Saint George's Channel
 3 BCb
San Giovanni in Fiore [It.]
 25 Ca
San Giovanni Valdarno [It.]
 31 Bb
San Gottardo / Sankt Gothard
 Paß **33** Ab
Sangüesa [Sp.] **17** Ba
San Juan Bautista [Sp.] **23** Cab
Sankt Anton am Arlberg [Aus.]
 33 Bb
Sankt Gallen [Svizz.] **33** Bb
Sankt Gothard Paß / San
 Gottardo **33** Ab
Sankt Johann im Pongau [Aus.]
 33 Cb
Sankt Michel / Mikkeli [Finl.]
 59 Ea
Sankt Moritz [Svizz.] **33** Bb
Sankt-Peterburg (Leningrad)
 [Russia] = San Pietroburgo (I)
 61 Bab
Sankt Peter-Ording [D] **35** Ba
Sankt Pölten [Aus.] **39** Aa
Sankt Veit an der Glan [Aus.]
 33 Cb
Sankt Wendel [D] **11** Ca
Sankt Wolfgang im
 Salzkammergut [Aus.] **33** Cb
San Lorenzo de El Escorial
 [Sp.] **19** Cb
San Lorenzo de la Parrilla [Sp.]
 23 Ba
Sanlúcar de Barrameda [Sp.]
 21 Bb

Sanluri [It.] **29** ABb
San Marino [RSM] **31** Cb
San Martín de Valdeiglesias
 [Sp.] **19** Cb
San Martino di Castrozza [It.]
 31 Ba
San Mateo / Sant Mateu del
 Maestrat [Sp.] **17** Cb
San Miniato [It.] **31** Bb
San Nicolas de Tolentino [It.]
 23 ins.a
Sanok [Pol.] **39** Ca
San Pietro **29** Ab
San Pietroburgo (I) = Sankt-
 Peterburg (Leningrad)
 [Russia] **61** Bab
San Remo [It.] **31** Ab
San Roque [Sp.] **21** Cb
San Sebastián / Donostia [Sp.]
 17 Ba
San Sebastián de la Gomera
 [Sp.] **23** ins.a
Sansepolcro [It.] **31** Cb
San Severo [It.] **27** Cb
Sanski Most [Bos.Erz.] **41** Bb
Santa Clara, Barragem do–
 21 Bb
Santa Coloma de Farners [Sp.]
 17 Cab
Santa Cruz da Graciosa [Port.]
 21 ins.a
Santa Cruz das Flores [Port.]
 21 ins.a
Santa Cruz de la Palma [Sp.]
 23 ins.a
Santa Cruz de Tenerife [Sp.]
 23 ins.a
Sant'Agata di Militello [It.]
 25 Bb
Santa Lucia [Sp.] **23** ins.a
Santa Margherita di Pula [It.]
 29 ABbc
Santa Maria **21** ins.a
Santa Maria di Leuca, Capo–
 27 Cb
Santana [Port.] **21** ins.a
Santander [Sp.] **19** Ca
Sant'Antioco [It.] **29** Abc
Sant'Antioco [It.] **29** Abc
Santañy / Santanyí [Sp.]
 23 CDa
Santanyí / Santañy [Sp.]
 23 CDa
Santa Olalla del Cala [Sp.]
 21 Bb
Santa Pola [Sp.] **23** Bb
Santarém [Port.] **21** Ba
Santa Teresa Gallura [It.] **29** Bb
Santhià [It.] **31** Aa
Santiago de Compostela [Sp.]
 19 Ba
Santiago de la Ribera [Sp.]
 23 Bb
Santiago do Cacém [Port.]
 21 Bb
Santillana [Sp.] **19** Ca
Sant Mateu del Maestrat / San
 Mateo [Sp.] **17** Cb
Santo Domingo de la Calzada
 [Sp.] **17** ABa
Santo Domingo de Silos [Sp.]
 19 Cb
Santoña [Sp.] **19** Ca
Santorino (I) = Thíra [Grecia]
 45 Bb
Santo Tirso [Port.] **19** Bb
San Vicente de la Barquera
 [Sp.] **19** Ca
San Vito, Capo– **25** Bb
São João da Madeira [Port.]
 19 Bb
São Jorge **21** ins.a
São Miguel **21** ins.a

Saona (I) = Saône **13** Ba
Saône = Saona (I) **13** Ba
São Pedro do Sul [Port.] **19** Bb
Saône = Saona (I) **13** Ba
São Vicente, Cabo de– **21** ABb
Sápai [Grecia] **47** Bb
Sapiéntza **45** Ab
Sapri [It.] **25** Ca
Saragozza (I) = Zaragoza [Sp.]
 17 Bb
Sarajevo [Bos.Erz.] **41** Cb
Saranda [Alb.] **43** Ab
Sarata [Ucr.] **51** Cb
Saray [Tur.] **47** Cb
Saraykôy [Tur.] **45** Cb
Sárbogárd [Ung.] **39** Bb
Sardegna **29** Bb
Sardegna, Mar di– **29** Ab
Sardes **45** Cb
Sarek **69** Bb
Sariá **45** Cbc
Sariñena [Sp.] **17** Bb
Sarıyer [Tur.] **47** Cb
Sark **9** Ba
Şarköy [Tur.] **47** BCb
Sarlat-la-Canéda [Fr.] **15** Cab
Sarmizegetuza [Rom.] **41** Da
Särna [Svezia] **73** Da
Sarnen [Svizz.] **33** Ab
Sarny [Ucr.] **53** Ca
Sárospatak [Ung.] **39** Ca
Sarpsborg [Norv.] **73** Cb
Sarralbe [Fr.] **11** Ca
Sarrebourg [Fr.] **11** Ca
Sarreguemines [Fr.] **11** Ca
Sarria [Sp.] **19** Ba
Sartène [Fr.] **13** CDc
Sarthe **9** Bb
Saruhanlı [Tur.] **45** Cbc
Sárvár [Ung.] **39** Ab
Sarzana [It.] **31** Bb
Sassari [It.] **29** Ab
Saßnitz [D] **35** Da
Sassonia (I) = Sachsen **35** Db
Sasyk, ozero– (Kunduk) **51** Cb
Šatalovo [Russia] **55** Cb
Sátoraljaújhely [Ung.] **39** Ca
Satu Mare [Rom.] **39** Cb
Sauda [Norv.] **73** Ab
Saudárkrókur [Isl.] **77** Cb
Saulieu [Fr.] **11** Bb
Saulkrasti / Saulkrasty [Lett.]
 57 Da
Saulkrasty / Saulkrasti [Lett.]
 57 Da
Saumur [Fr.] **9** BCb
Sava **41** Cb
Saverne [Fr.] **11** Ca
Savigliano [It.] **31** Ab
Savitaipale [Finl.] **59** Ea
Šavnik [Iug.] **41** Cb
Savoia (I) = Savoie **13** Ca
Savoie = Savoia (I) **13** Ca
Savona [It.] **31** Ab
Savonlinna [Finl.] **61** Aa
Savonranta [Finl.] **63** Ac
Savukoski [Finl.] **67** Db
Sazonovo [Russia] **61** CDa
Sbruč **51** Ba
Scafell Pike **3** Ca
Scalloway [RU] **1** ins.a
Scania (I) = Skåne **75** Cb
Scarborough [RU] **3** Da
Scarpanto (I) = Kárpathos
 [Grecia] **45** BCc
Schaffhausen [Svizz.] **33** Ab
Schärding [Aus.] **33** Ca
Schelda (I) = Schelde **7** Cab
Schelde = Schelda (I) **7** Cab
Schio [It.] **31** Ba
Schladming [Aus.] **33** Cb
Schleswig [D] **35** Ca
Schleswing Holsteinisches
 Wattenmeer **35** Ba

Schlüchtern [D] **35** Cc
Schongau [D] **33** Bb
Schouwen **7** Ca
Schruns [Aus.] **33** Bb
Schuls / Scuol [Svizz.] **33** Bb
Schwäbisch Gmünd [D] **33** Ba
Schwäbisch Hall [D] **33** Ba
Schwandorf [D] **33** BCa
Schwarzwald = Selva Nera (I)
    33 Aab
Schwaz [Aus.] **33** Bb
Schwedt an der Oder [D]
    35 Db
Schweinfurt [D] **33** Ba
Schwerin [D] **35** Cb
Schwyz [Svizz.] **33** Ab
Sciacca [It.] **25** Bb
Scilly, Isles of– = Scilly,
    Isole– (I) **5** Ac
Scilly, Isole– (I) = Scilly, Isles
    of– **5** Ac
Ščors [Ucr.] **53** Ca
Scotland = Scozia (I) **1** CDab
Scozia (I) = Scotland **1** CDab
Scunthorpe [RU] **5** Db
Scuol / Schuls [Svizz.] **33** Bb
Scutari (I) = Shkodra [Alb.]
    41 Cb
Scutari, Lago di– (I) =
    Shkodrës, Liqen i– **41** Cb
Scutari, Lago di– (I) =
    Skadarsko jezero **41** Cb
Sebeş [Rom.] **51** Ab
Sebež [Russia] **55** Bb
Seckau [Aus.] **33** Cb
Sedan [Fr.] **11** Ba
Seefeld in Tirol [Aus.] **33** Bb
Seelow [D] **35** Db
Sées [Fr.] **9** BCa
Segesta **25** Bb
Segeža [Russia] **63** Cb
Seghedino (I) = Szeged [Ung.]
    41 Ca
Segorbe [Sp.] **23** Ba
Segovia [Sp.] **19** Cb
Segozero, ozero– **63** Cb
Segre **17** Cb
Segré [Fr.] **9** Bb
Segura **23** Bb
Seia [Port.] **19** Bb
Seiland **69** Da
Seinäjoki [Finl.] **65** Cc
Seine = Senna (I) **9** Ca
Seine, Baia de la– = Senna,
    Baia della– (I) **9** Ba
Seitsemisen **59** Ca
Sejm **53** Ca
Šeksna [Russia] **61** Db
Selbu [Norv.] **71** Bb
Selçuk [Tur.] **45** Cb
Sélestat [Fr.] **33** Aa
Selfoss [Isl.] **77** BCb
Selgy [Russia] **63** Cbc
Seliger, ozero– **55** Da
Selinunte **25** Bb
Seližarovo [Russia] **55** Dab
Selje [Norv.] **73** Aa
Seljord [Norv.] **73** Bb
Selva Boema (I) = Böhmerwald
    33 Ca
Selva Boema (I) = Šumava
    33 Ca
Selvagens, Ilhas– **21** ins.a
Selva Nera (I) = Schwarzwald
    33 Aab
Semani = Semeni (I) **43** Ab
Semeni (I) = Semani **43** Ab
Semmering Kurort [Aus.]
    39 Ab
Semour–en–Auxois [Fr.] **11** Bb
Senftenberg / Zły Komorow [D]
    35 Db
Senica [Slovac.] **39** Aa

Senigallia [It.] **31** Cb
Senj [Cro.] **31** CDab
Senja **69** Ba
Senlis [Fr.] **9** Ca
Senna (I) = Seine **9** Ca
Senna, Baia della– (I) = Seine,
    Baie de la– **9** Ba
Sens [Fr.] **11** Ba
Senta [Iug.] **41** Ca
Seo de Urgel / la Seu d'Urgell
    [Sp.] **17** Ca
Šepetovka [Ucr.] **53** ABb
Serbia (I) = Srbija **41** CDb
Sered' [Slovac.] **39** Aa
Seret **51** Ba
Sérifos **45** Bb
Serock [Pol.] **37** BCb
Serpa [Port.] **21** Bb
Serpuhov [Russia] **55** Eb
Sérrai [Grecia] **43** Bb
Serra San Bruno [It.] **25** Cb
Serres [Fr.] **13** Bb
Sérvia [Grecia] **43** Bb
Sesimbra [Port.] **21** ABb
Sessa Aurunca [It.] **29** Cb
Sestriere [It.] **13** Cab
Sestri Levante [It.] **31** Bb
Sestroreck [Russia] **61** ABab
Sesvete [Cro.] **41** Ba
Sète [Fr.] **13** Bb
Setermoen [Norv.] **69** Cab
Setúbal [Port.] **21** ABb
Setúbal, Baía de– **21** ABb
Severn **5** Cb
Severnaja Dvina = Dvina
    Settentrionale (I) **63** Eb
Severny [Russia] **63** Bb
Severodvinsk [Russia] **63** Eb
Severomorsk [Russia] **67** Fab
Sevettijärvi [Finl.] **69** Fa
Sevilla [Sp.] = Siviglia (I)
    21 BCb
Sevlijevo [Bulg.] **49** Ba
Seyðisfjörður [Isl.] **77** Eb
Sézanne [Fr.] **11** Ba
Sfântu Gheorghe [Rom.] **51** Bb
's Gravenhage / Den Haag
    [P.B.] = L'Aia (I) **7** Ca
Shannon **3** Bb
Sheerness [RU] **5** Db
Sheffield [RU] **5** Cb
Sheppey **5** Db
's Hertogenbosch / Den Bosch
    [P.B.] **7** Ca
Shetland, Isole– (I) = Shetland
    Islands (Zetland) **1** ins.a
Shetland Islands [RU] =
    Shetland, Isole– (I) **1** ins.a
Shkodra [Alb.] = Scutari (I)
    41 Cb
Shkodrës, Liqen i– = Scutari,
    Lago di– (I) **41** Cb
Shrewsbury [RU] **5** Cb
Šiauliai / Šjaiuljaj [Lit.] **57** Cb
Šibenik [Cro.] **41** Bb
Sibillini, Monti– **29** Ca
Sibiu [Rom.] **51** Bb
Sicilia **25** Bb
Sicilia, Canale di– **25** Ab
Sicilia, Canale di– (I) = Tūnis,
    Canal de– **25** Ab
Sicilia, Mar di– **25** Bb
Šid [Iug.] **41** Cab
Siders / Sierre [Svizz.] **31** Aa
Sídheros, Ákra– **45** Bc
Sidhirókastron [Grecia] **43** Bb
Sidmouth [RU] **5** Bc
Siedlce [Pol.] **37** Cb
Siegburg [D] **7** Db
Siegen [D] **35** Bbc
Siemiatycze [Pol.] **37** Cb
Siena [It.] **31** Bb
Sieppijärvi [Finl.] **67** BCb

Sieradz [Pol.] **37** Bb
Sierpc [Pol.] **37** Bb
Sierre / Siders [Svizz.] **31** Aa
Sífnos **45** Bb
Sig [Alg.] **23** Bc
Sighetu Marmaţiei [Rom.]
    39 CDab
Sighişoara [Rom.] **51** Bb
Siglufjörður [Isl.] **77** Cab
Sigmaringen [D] **33** Bab
Sigtuna [Svezia] **59** Ab
Sigüenza [Sp.] **17** Bb
Sigués [Sp.] **17** Ba
Sigulda [Lett.] **57** Dab
Siilinjärvi [Finl.] **65** Ebc
Sikéa [Grecia] **43** BCb
Síkinos **45** Bb
Sila, La– **25** Ca
Şile [Tur.] **47** Cb
Silistra [Bulg.] **49** Ca
Silivri [Tur.] **47** Cb
Siljan **73** Da
Silkeborg [Dan.] **75** Bb
Sillé–le–Guillaume [Fr.] **9** BCa
Šilutė / Šilutė [Lit.] **57** Cb
Šilutė / Šilute [Lit.] **57** Cb
Silvretta **33** Bb
Simav [Tur.] **47** Cbc
Sími [Grecia] **45** Cb
Sími [Grecia] **45** Cb
Şimleu Silvaniei [Rom.] **39** Cb
Simo [Finl.] **65** Db
Simojoki **65** Db
Simplon Pass **31** Aa
Simrishamn [Svezia] **75** Cb
Sinaia [Rom.] **51** Bb
Sındırgı [Tur.] **47** Cb
Sines [Port.] **21** ABb
Sinettä [Finl.] **67** Cb
Singen (Hohentwiel) [D] **33** Ab
Siniscola [It.] **29** Cb
Sinite Kamâni **49** Ba
Sinj [Cro.] **41** Bb
Sinjuža **51** Ba
Sinnicolau Mare [Rom.] **41** Ca
Sint Niklaas / Saint–Nicolas
    [Bel.] **7** Ca
Sintra [Port.] **21** Aab
Sint–Truiden / Saint–Trond
    [Bel.] **7** Ca
Siófok [Ung.] **39** ABb
Sion / Sitten [Svizz.] **11** Cb
Šipčenski prohod **49** Ba
Siracusa [It.] **25** Cb
Siret [Eur.] **51** Cb
Siret [Rom.] **51** Bab
Sirína **45** Bb
Sirkka [Finl.] **67** Ca
Sirmione [It.] **31** Ba
Síros **45** Bb
Širvintos [Lit.] **57** Db
Sisak [Cro.] **41** Ba
Šiščicy [R.B.] **53** Ba
Sisteron [Fr.] **13** BCb
Sistranda [Norv.] **71** Ba
Sithonía = Sitonia (I) **43** BCb
Sitía [Grecia] **45** Bc
Sitonia (I) = Sithonía **43** BCb
Sittard [P.B.] **7** CDab
Sitten / Sion [Svizz.] **11** Cb
Siverski [Russia] **61** ABb
Siviglia (I) = Sevilla [Sp.]
    21 BCb
Sjælland = Sjelland (I) **75** Bb
Sjamozero, ozero– **61** Ca
Sjasstroj [Russia] **61** Bab
Šjauljaj / Siauliai [Lit.] **57** Cb
Sjelland (I) = Sjælland **75** Bb
Sjenica [Iug.] **41** Cb
Skadarsko jezero = Scutari,
    Lago di– (I) **41** Cb
Skadovsk [Ucr.] **51** Db
Skælskør [Dan.] **75** Bb

Skærbæk [Dan.] **75** Ab
Skaftafell [Isl.] **77** Db
Skaftafell [Isl.] **77** Db
Skagafjörður **77** Cab
Skagaströnd [Isl.] **77** Cb
Skagen [Dan.] **75** Ba
Skagerrak **75** ABa
Skála Oropoú [Grecia] **45** Ab
Skanderborg [Dan.] **75** Bb
Skåne = Scania (I) **75** Cb
Skånevik [Norv.] **73** ABb
Skara [Svezia] **75** Ca
Skara Brae **1** Ca
Skarberget [Norv.] **69** Bb
Skarnes [Norv.] **73** Ca
Skarżysko–Kamienna [Pol.]
    37 BCbc
Skaudvilé / Skaudvile [Lit.]
    57 Cb
Skaudvile / Skaudvilé [Lit.]
    57 Cb
Skegness [RU] **5** Db
Skellefteå [Svezia] **71** EFb
Skellefteälven **65** BCb
Skhíza **45** Ab
Ski [Norv.] **73** Cb
Skíathos [Grecia] **43** Bb
Skíathos [Grecia] **43** Bb
Skibbereen / An Sciobairín
    [Eire] **3** Ab
Skibotn [Norv.] **69** Ca
Skidel [R.B.] **37** Db
Skien [Norv.] **73** Cb
Skierniewice [Pol.] **37** Bb
Skipton [RU] **5** Cab
Skíros [Grecia] **45** Bab
Skíros [Grecia] **45** Bab
Skive [Dan.] **75** ABb
Skjálfandafljót **77** Dab
Skjálfandi **77** Dab
Skjern [Dan.] **75** Ab
Skogar [Isl.] **77** Cb
Skole [Ucr.] **39** Ca
Skópelos [Grecia] **43** Bbc
Skópelos [Grecia] **43** Bab
Skopje [Maced.] **43** Bab
Skorovatn [Norv.] **71** Cb
Skövde [Svezia] **75** Ca
Skrunda [Lett.] **57** Cb
Skudeneshavn [Norv.] **73** Ab
Skuleskogen **71** Ebc
Skuodas [Lit.] **57** Cb
Skurup [Svezia] **75** Cb
Skutvik [Norv.] **69** Bb
Skvira [Ucr.] **53** Bb
Skwierzyna [Pol.] **37** Ab
Skye, Island of– **1** BCa
Slagelse [Dan.] **75** Bb
Slagnäs [Svezia] **71** DEb
Slánčev brjag [Bulg.] **49** Ca
Slancy [Russia] **61** Ab
Slánic Moldova [Rom.] **51** Bb
Slano [Cro.] **41** BCb
Slaný [Rep.Ceca] **33** Ca
Slavgorod [R.B.] **53** Ca
Slatina [Rom.] **49** Ba
Slavkovu Brna [Rep.Ceca]
    39 Aa
Slavonia (I) = Slavonija **41** BCa
Slavonija = Slavonia (I) **41** BCa
Slavonska Požega [Cro.] **41** Ba
Slavonski Brod [Cro.] **41** BCa
Sławno [Pol.] **37** Aa
Slesia (I) = Śląsk **37** Abc
Sligeach / Sligo [Eire] **3** Ba
Sligo / Sligeach [Eire] **3** Ba
Slite [Svezia] **57** Ba
Sliven [Bulg.] **49** Ca
Slobozia [Rom.] **49** Ca
Slonim [R.B.] **53** Aa
Slovacchia (I) = Slovensko
    39 Ba

Slovenjgradec [Slo.] **33** CDb
Slovenska Bistrica [Slo.] **33** Db
Slovensko = Slovacchia (I)
    39 Ba
Slovenský Ray **39** Ba
Słowiński **37** Aa
Słubice [Pol.] **35** Db
Sluč [R.B.] **53** Bb
Sluč [Ucr.] **53** Ba
Sluck [R.B.] **53** Ba
Slunj [Cro.] **41** Bab
Stupsk [Pol.] **37** Aa
Smålandsstenar [Svezia]
    75 Cab
Smalininkaj / Smalininkaj [Lit.]
    57 Cb
Smalininkaj / Smalininkaj [Lit.]
    57 Cb
Smederevo [Iug.] **41** CDb
Smela [Ucr.] **53** Cb
Smiltene [Lett.] **57** Da
Smøla **71** Ab
Smolensk [Russia] **55** Cb
Smólikas Óros **43** ABb
Smoljan [Bulg.] **47** Bb
Smorgon [R.B.] **57** Db
Smyga [Ucr.] **53** Ab
Snæfell **77** Db
Snåsa [Norv.] **71** Cb
Sneek [P.B.] **7** Ca
Śniardwy, Jezioro– **57** Cc
Śnieżka **37** Ac
Snigirevka [Ucr.] **51** Db
Snillfjord [Norv.] **71** Bb
Snina [Slovac.] **39** Ca
Snjatyn [Ucr.] **51** Ba
Snowdon **5** Bb
Snowdonia **5** Bb
Sochaczew [Pol.] **37** Bb
Sodankylä [Finl.] **67** Cb
Söderhamn [Svezia] **59** Aa
Södertälje [Svezia] **59** Ab
Soest [D] **35** Bb
Sofia (I) = Sofija [Bulg.] **49** Aa
Sofija [Bulg.] = Sofia (I) **49** Aa
Sogndalsfjøra [Norv.] **73** Ba
Sognefjorden **73** Aa
Soignies / Zinnik [Bel.] **7** Ca
Soissons [Fr.] **11** Ba
Söke [Tur.] **45** Cb
Soko Banja [Iug.] **41** Db
Sokol [Russia] **61** Eb
Sokółka [Pol.] **37** Cb
Sokolov [Rep.Ceca] **33** Ca
Sokołów Podlaski [Pol.] **37** Cb
Šokša [Russia] **61** Ca
Sol, Costa del– **21** Cb
Solberg [Svezia] **71** Db
Solcy [Russia] **61** Bb
Sölden [Aus.] **33** Bb
Solenzara [Fr.] **13** Dc
Soligorsk [R.B.] **53** Ba
Solin [Cro.] **41** Bb
Solingen [D] **7** Db
Sollefteå [Svezia] **71** Dbc
Sóller [Sp.] **23** Ca
Solnečnogorsk [Russia] **55** Eb
Solothurn [Svizz.] **33** Ab
Solovjevka [Russia] **61** Ba
Solsona [Sp.] **17** Cab
Šolta **41** Bb
Soltau [D] **35** Cb
Soma [Tur.] **47** Cbc
Šomba [Russia] **63** BCb
Sombor [Iug.] **41** Ca
Somero [Finl.] **59** Ca
Someş **39** Cb
Somino [Russia] **61** Cb
Somme **5** Dc
Somosierra, Puerto de– **19** Cb
Somport, Puerto de– **17** Ba
Sønderborg [Dan.] **35** Ca

Sondrio [It.] **31** Ba
Sonneberg [D] **35** Cc
Soomenlaht = Finlandia, Golfo
di– (I) **59** DEab
Sopoćani, Manastir– **41** Cb
Sopot [Pol.] **57** Bb
Sopron [Ung.] **39** Ab
Sora [It.] **29** Cb
Sorbas [Sp.] **23** Bb
Soria [Sp.] **17** Bb
Soroca [Mold.] **51** Cab
Sørøya **69** Da
Sørreisa [Norv.] **69** BCab
Sorrento [It.] **29** Cc
Sorsele [Svezia] **71** Db
Sort [Sp.] **17** Ca
Sortavala [Russia] **61** Ba
Sortland [Norv.] **69** Bab
Sørvær [Norv.] **69** Da
Sørvågen [Norv.] **69** Ab
Sosnovy Bor [Russia] **61** Ab
Sosnowiec [Pol.] **39** Ba
Sospel [Fr.] **31** Ab
Šostka [Ucr.] **53** Da
Sotkamo [Finl.] **65** Eb
Soúdha [Grecia] **45** ABc
Souflíon [Grecia] **47** Bb
Souíllac [Fr.] **15** Cab
Souk el Arba du Rharb [Mar.]
21 BCc
Soulac-sur-Mer [Fr.] **15** Ba
Soúnion [Grecia] **45** ABb
Soúnion [Grecia] **45** ABb
Southampton [RU] **5** Cbc
Southend–on–Sea [RU] **5** Db
Southport [RU] **5** BCb
South Ronaldsay **1** CDa
South Shields [RU] **3** Da
South Uist **1** Ba
Sovata [Rom.] **51** Bb
Soverato [It.] **25** Cb
Sovetsk [Russia] **57** Cb
Sož **53** Ca
Sozopol [Bulg.] **49** Ca
Spa [Bel.] **7** Cb
Spada, Capo– (I) = Spátha,
Ákra– **45** Ac
Spalato (I) = Split [Cro.]
41 Bb
Spalding [RU] **5** CDb
Spartel, Cap– **21** BCc
Spárti [Grecia] **45** Ab
Spartivento, Capo– [It.] **29** Abc
Spartivento, Capo– [It.] **25** Cb
Spátha, Ákra– = Spada,
Capo– (I) **45** Ac
Spello [It.] **29** Ca
Spétsai **45** Ab
Spey **1** Ca
Speyer [D] **33** Aa
Spezzano Albanese [It.] **25** Ca
Spildağı **45** Cb
Spišská Nová Ves [Slovac.]
39 Ba
Spittal an der Drau [Aus.]
33 Cb
Split [Cro.] = Spalato (I) **41** Bb
Spoleto [It.] **29** Ca
Sporádhes, Vórioi– = Sporadi
Settentrionali (I) **43** BCb
Sporadi Meridionali (I) = Nótioi
Sporádhes **45** Bbc
Sporadi Settentrionali (I) =
Sporádhes, Vórioi– **43** BCb
Srbija = Serbia (I) **41** CDb
Srbobran [Iug.] **41** Cab
Srebnoje [Ucr.] **53** CDb
Sredni Kujto, ozero– **63** Bb
Sredni Verecki, pereval– **39** Ca
Srednogorie [Bulg.] **49** ABa
Šrem [Pol.] **37** Ab
Sremska Mitrovica [Iug.]
41 Cab

Środa Wielkopolska [Pol.]
37 Ab
Stabbursdalen **69** Ea
Stade [D] **35** Cb
Stafford [RU] **5** Cb
Stalowa Wola [Pol.] **37** Cc
Stamford [RU] **5** Cb
Starachowice [Pol.] **37** BCbc
Staraja Russa [Russia] **61** Bb
Stará Ľubovňa [Slovac.] **39** Ba
Stara Planina = Balcani (I)
49 ABa
Stara Zagora [Bulg.] **49** Ba
Stargard Szczeciński [Pol.]
37 Ab
Starica [Russia] **55** Db
Starigrad [Cro.] **27** Ca
Starnberg [D] **33** Bab
Starogard Gdański [Pol.]
57 Bbc
Starokonstantinov [Ucr.] **53** Bb
Staro Nagoričane, Manastir–
41 Db
Start Point **5** Bc
Staryje Dorogi [R.B.] **53** Ba
Staszów [Pol.] **37** BCc
Stavanger [Norv.] **73** Ab
St.David's [RU] **5** Bb
Stege [Dan.] **75** Db
Steiermark = Stiria (I) **33** CDb
Steinkjer [Norv.] **71** Bb
Stelvio **33** Bb
Stelvio, Passo dello– / Stilfser
Joch **33** Bb
Stenay [Fr.] **11** Ba
Stendal [D] **35** CDb
Stenungsund [Svezia] **75** Ba
Šternberk [Rep.Ceca] **39** Aa
Sterzing / Vipiteno [It.] **33** Bb
Stęszew [Pol.] **37** Ab
Stettiner Haff **35** Db
Stettino (I) = Szczecin [Pol.]
35 Db
Steyr [Aus.] **33** Cab
Stif [Alg.] **23** Db
Stigliano [It.] **27** Cb
Stilfser Joch / Stelvio, Passo
dello– **33** Bb
Stintino [It.] **29** Ab
Štip [Maced.] **43** Bb
Stíra [Grecia] **45** Bb
Stiria (I) = Steiermark **33** CDb
Stirling [RU] **1** Cb
Stjernøya **69** Da
Stjørdalshalsen [Norv.] **71** Bb
Stoccarda (I) = Stuttgart [D]
33 Ba
Stoccolma (I) = Stockholm
[Svezia] **59** ABb
Stockach [D] **33** ABab
Stockerau [Aus.] **39** Aa
Stockholm [Svezia] =
Stoccolma (I) **59** ABb
Stockport [RU] **5** Cb
Stöde [Svezia] **71** Dc
Stoj, gora– **39** Ca
Stoke–on–Trent [RU] **5** Cb
Stolin [R.B.] **53** ABa
Stöllet [Svezia] **73** Da
Ston [Cro.] **41** Bb
Stonehaven [RU] **1** Dab
Stonehenge **5** Cb
Stora Lulevatten **69** Cb
Stora Sjöfallet **69** BCb
Storavan **71** Eb
Storby [Finl.] **59** Ba
Stord **73** Aab
Store Bælt = Grande Belt (I)
75 Bb
Store Heddinge [Dan.] **75** Cb
Store Mosse **75** Ca
Støren [Norv.] **71** Bbc
Storlien [Svezia] **71** BCb

Stornoway [RU] **1** Ba
Storsjön **71** Cb
Storslett [Norv.] **69** CDa
Storuman [Svezia] **71** Db
Storuman [Svezia] **71** Db
Støvring [Dan.] **75** Bab
Strabane / An Srath Bán [RU]
3 Ba
Strakonice [Rep.Ceca] **33** Ca
Stralsund [D] **35** Da
Stranda [Norv.] **71** Ab
Strängnäs [Svezia] **59** Ab
Stranraer [RU] **3** Ca
Strasbourg [Fr.] = Strasburgo (I)
33 Aa
Strasburgo (I) = Strasbourg
[Fr.] **33** Aa
Stratford–upon–Avon [RU]
5 Cb
Straubing [D] **33** Ca
Straumnes **77** Ba
Strehaia [Rom.] **49** Aa
Stresa [It.] **31** Aa
Stříbro [Rep.Ceca] **33** Ca
Strimón **43** Bb
Stromboli **25** Cb
Stromness [RU] **1** Ca
Strømø **75** ins.a
Strömstad [Svezia] **73** Cb
Strömsund [Svezia] **71** Db
Stronsay **1** Da
Struer [Dan.] **75** Ab
Struga [Maced.] **43** Ab
Struma **43** Bb
Strumica [Maced.] **43** Bb
Stry [Ucr.] **53** Aa
Stry [Ucr.] **39** CDa
Stryn [Norv.] **73** Ba
Strzelce Opolskie [Pol.] **37** Bc
Strzelno [Pol.] **37** Bb
Stubbekøbing [Dan.] **35** CDa
Studenica, Manastir– **41** Cb
Stugun [Svezia] **71** Db
Stuttgart [D] = Stoccarda (I)
33 Ba
Stykkishólmur [Isl.] **77** Bb
Subiaco [It.] **29** Cab
Subotica [Iug.] **41** Ca
Suceava [Rom.] **51** Ba
Suceviţa, Mănăstirea– **51** Ba
Sućuraj [Cro.] **27** Ca
Suda [Russia] **61** Db
Suda [Russia] **61** Db
Suderø **75** ins.a
Sudeti (I) = Sudety **37** Ac
Sudety = Sudeti (I) **37** Ac
Suir **3** Bb
Šuja [Russia] **61** Ca
Šuja [Russia] **61** Ca
Sujstamo [Russia] **61** Ba
Sula [Norv.] **73** Aa
Sula [Ucr.] **53** Cb
Sula Sgeir **1** Ba
Sulechów [Pol.] **37** Ab
Sulina [Rom.] **51** Cbc
Sulitjelma [Norv.] **69** Bb
Sulmona [It.] **29** Cab
Sumava **33** Ca
Šumava = Selva Boema (I)
33 Ca
Sumburgh Head **1** ins.a
Sümeg [Ung.] **39** Ab
Šumen [Bulg.] **49** BCa
Šuměnsko Plato **49** BCa
Šumperk [Rep.Ceca] **39** Aa
Sumski Posad [Russia] **63** Cb
Sumy [Ucr.] **53** Db
Sunde [Norv.] **73** Aab
Sunderland [RU] **3** Da
Sundsvall [Svezia] **71** Dc
Sunnadalsøra [Norv.] **73** Ba
Sunne [Svezia] **73** Dab

Suojarvi [Russia] **61** Ba
Suolahti [Finl.] **65** Dc
Suomenlahti = Finlandia, Golfo
di– (I) **59** DEab
Suomenselkä **65** CDbc
Suomussalmi [Finl.] **63** Ab
Suonenjoki [Finl.] **65** DEc
Supetar [Cro.] **41** Bb
Suraž [R.B.] **55** Cb
Surnadalsøra [Norv.] **73** Ba
Surtsey **77** Cb
Susa [It.] **13** Cab
Süsah [Tun.] **25** Ac
Sustenpass **33** Ab
Susurluk [Tur.] **47** Cb
Sutjeska **41** Cb
Suvasvesi **65** Ec
Suvo Rudište **41** Cb
Suwałki [Pol.] **57** Cbc
Svappavaara [Svezia] **67** ABb
Svartevatn [Norv.] **73** Bb
Svealand **73** DEa
Sveg [Svezia] **73** Ca
Svelgen [Norv.] **73** Aa
Svendborg [Dan.] **75** Bb
Svenljunga [Svezia] **75** Ca
Svensby [Norv.] **69** Ca
Svenstavik [Svezia] **73** Ca
Sveti Naum **43** Ab
Sveti Stefan [Cro.] **41** Cb
Svetlovodsk [Ucr.] **53** Db
Svetozarevo [Iug.] **41** Db
Svidník [Slovac.] **39** Ca
Svilengrad [Bulg.] **47** Bb
Svir **61** Ca
Svisloč **55** Bc
Svištov [Bulg.] **49** Ba
Svitavy [Rep.Ceca] **39** Aa
Svjatozero [Russia] **61** Ca
Svoge [Bulg.] **49** Aa
Svolvær [Norv.] **69** Ab
Swansea [RU] **5** Bb
Świdnica [Pol.] **37** Abc
Świdwin [Pol.] **37** Ab
Świebodzin [Pol.] **37** Ab
Świecie [Pol.] **37** Bb
Świętokrzyskie, Góry– **37** BCbc
Swindon [RU] **5** Cb
Świnoujście [Pol.] **35** Dab
Syčevka [Russia] **55** Db
Sykkylven [Norv.] **73** Ba
Sylt **35** Ba
Syssleback [Svezia] **73** Ca
Syväjärvi [Finl.] **67** Cb
Szamos **39** Cab
Szarvas [Ung.] **39** Bb
Szczecin [Pol.] = Stettino (I)
35 Db
Szczecinek [Pol.] **37** Ab
Szczeciński, Zalew– **35** Db
Szczytno [Pol.] **57** BCc
Szeged [Ung.] = Seghedino (I)
41 Ca
Szeghalom [Ung.] **39** BCb
Székesfehérvár [Ung.] **39** Bb
Szekszárd [Ung.] **39** Bb
Szentendre [Ung.] **39** Bb
Szentes [Ung.] **39** Bb
Szigetvár [Ung.] **41** Ba
Szolnok [Ung.] **39** Bb
Szombathely [Ung.] **39** Ab
Szprotawa [Pol.] **37** Ab
Szubin [Pol.] **37** Ab

T

Taavetti [Finl.] **59** Ea
Tablas de Daimiel, Las– **21** Ca
Tábor [Rep.Ceca] **33** Ca
Tafalla [Sp.] **17** Ba
Tago (I) = Tajo **19** Bb

Tago (I) = Tejo **19** Bb
Taínaron, Ákra– = Matapán,
Capo– (I) **45** Ab
Taivalkoski [Finl.] **65** Eb
Tajo = Tago (I) **19** Bb
Talavera de la Reina [Sp.]
19 Cb
Tallinn [Est.] **59** Db
Talsi [Lett.] **57** Ca
Tamási [Ung.] **39** Bb
Tâmega **19** Bb
Tamigi (I) = Thames **5** Cb
Tamiš **41** Ca
Tammerfors / Tampere [Finl.]
59 Ca
Tammisaaren Saaristo **59** Cab
Tammisaari / Ekenäs [Finl.]
59 Cab
Tampere / Tammerfors [Finl.]
59 Ca
Tamsweg [Aus.] **33** Cb
Tanafjorden **69** Fa
Tanaro **31** Ab
Tandsjöborg [Svezia] **73** Da
Tanger [Mar.] **21** Cc
Tännäs [Svezia] **73** Ca
Tanum [Svezia] **75** Ba
Taormina [It.] **25** Cb
Tapa [Est.] **59** Db
Tara **41** Cb
Taran, mys– **57** Bb
Tarancón [Sp.] **19** CDb
Taranto [It.] **27** Cb
Tarare [Fr.] **11** Bb
Tarazona [Sp.] **17** Bab
Tarbert [RU] **1** Ba
Tarbes [Fr.] **17** BCa
Tärendö [Svezia] **67** Bb
Târgovişte [Bulg.] **49** Ba
Targuist [Mar.] **21** Cc
Tarhankut, mys– **51** Db
Tarifa [Sp.] **21** Cbc
Tarn **15** Cb
Tärnaby [Svezia] **71** Db
Tarnobrzeg [Pol.] **37** Cc
Tarnów [Pol.] **39** Ba
Tarnowskie Góry [Pol.] **37** Bc
Tarquinia [It.] **29** Ba
Tarragona [Sp.] **17** Cb
Tarrasa / Terrassa [Sp.] **17** Cb
Tartas [Fr.] **15** Ba
Tartu [Est.] **59** Db
Tarutino [Ucr.] **51** Cb
Tarvisio [It.] **33** Cb
Taso (I) = Thásos [Grecia]
47 Bb
Tatabánya [Ung.] **39** Bb
Tatarbunary [Ucr.] **51** Cb
Tatra (I) = Tatry **39** Ba
Tatry [Eur.] **39** Ba
Tatry [Eur.] = Tatra (I) **39** Ba
Tau [Norv.] **73** ABb
Tauern = Tauri (I) **33** Cb
Tauern Pass **33** Cb
Taunton [RU] **5** BCb
Taurage / Tauragé [Lit.] **57** Cb
Taurage / Tauragé [Lit.] **57** Cb
Tauri (I) = Tauern **33** Cb
Tavas [Tur.] **45** Cb
Tavastehus / Hämeenlinna
[Finl.] **59** Ca
Tavau / Davos (Svizz.] **33** Bb
Tavira [Port.] **21** Bb
Tavşanlı [Tur.] **47** Cb
Tczew [Pol.] **57** Bbc
Tecuci [Rom.] **51** Cb
Tegernsee [D] **33** Bb
Teguise [Sp.] **23** ins.a
Tejo = Tago (I) **19** Bb
Tekirdağ [Tur.] **47** Cb
Telč [Rep.Ceca] **33** Da
Telde [Sp.] **23** ins.a

Telšiai / Telšjaj [Lit.] **57** Cb
Telšjaj / Telšiai [Lit.] **57** Cb
Tembleque [Sp.] **19** Cb
Temerin [Iug.] **41** Ca
Tempio Pausania [It.] **29** ABb
Templin [D] **35** Db
Tenda, Col di– **31** Ab
Tende [Fr.] **31** Ab
Tenerife **23** ins.a
Tepelena [Alb.] **43** Ab
Teplice [Rep.Ceca] **35** Dc
Tepsa [Finl.] **67** Cb
Ter **17** Dab
Teramo [It.] **29** Ca
Terceira **21** ins.a
Terebovlja [Ucr.] **53** Ab
Terespol [Pol.] **37** Cb
Termini Imerese [It.] **25** Bb
Termoli [It.] **29** CDab
Terneuzen [P.B.] **7** Ca
Terni [It.] **29** Ca
Ternopol [Ucr.] **53** Ab
Terracina [It.] **29** Cb
Terråk [Norv.] **71** Cb
Terrassa / Tarrasa [Sp.] **17** Cb
Terschelling **7** Ca
Teruel [Sp.] **17** Bb
Tervel [Bulg.] **49** Ca
Tervola [Finl.] **65** Dab
Tessaglia (I) = Thessalía **43** Bb
Teterev **53** Bb
Teterow [D] **35** Db
Teteven [Bulg.] **49** Ba
Tétouan [Mar.] **21** Cc
Tetovo [Maced.] **43** ABab
Teulada [It.] **29** Abc
Teulada, Capo– **29** Abc
Teuva / Östermark [Finl.] **65** Cc
Tevere **29** Ca
Texel **7** Ca
Thames = Tamigi (I) **5** Cb
Thann [Fr.] **11** Cb
Thásos [Grecia] **47** Bb
Thásos [Grecia] = Taso (I) **47** Bb
The Little Minch **1** Ba
Theológos [Grecia] **47** Bb
Thermaïkós Kólpos =
    Salonicco, Golfo di– (I) **43** Bb
Thessalía = Tessaglia (I) **43** Bb
Thessaloníki [Grecia] =
    Salonicco (I) **43** Bb
Thetford [RU] **5** Db
The Trossachs **1** Cb
The Wash **5** Db
Thiers [Fr.] **13** Ba
Thingvallavatn **77** BCb
Thingvellir [Isl.] **77** Bb
Thingvellir [Isl.] **77** BCb
Thionville [Fr.] **11** BCa
Thíra [Grecia] **45** Bb
Thíra [Grecia] = Santorino (I) **45** Bb
Thirsk [RU] **3** Da
Thisted [Dan.] **75** Aab
Thívai [Grecia] **45** Ab
Thiviers [Fr.] **15** Ca
Thjórsá **77** Cb
Thonon–les–Bains [Fr.] **11** Cb
Thórisvatn **77** Cb
Thorshavn [Dan.] **75** ins.a
Thórshfn [Isl.] **77** Dab
Thouars [Fr.] **9** Bb
Thráki = Tracia (I) **47** Bb
Thrakikón Pélagos **47** Bb
Thun [Svizz.] **33** Ab
Thüringen / Mühlhausen [D]
    35 Cb
Thüringen = Turingia (I) **35** Cb
Thurso [RU] **1** Ca
Thusis / Tusaun [Svizz.] **33** Bb
Thyborøn [Dan.] **75** Ab

Ţib, Ra's aţ– = Bon, Capo– (I)
    25 Ab
Tibisco (I) = Tisa **41** Ca
Tibisco (I) = Tisza **39** Bb
Ticino **31** Bab
Tidirhine **21** Cc
Tighina [Mold.] **51** Cb
Tihert [Alg.] **23** Cc
Tihuţa, Pasul– **51** Bb
Tihvin [Russia] **61** Cb
Tilburg [P.B.] **7** Ca
Tilikkajärvi **65** Eb
Tilos **45** Cb
Timanfaya **23** ins.a
Timiş **41** Cab
Timişoara [Rom.] **41** Da
Timok **41** Db
Timrå [Svezia] **71** Dc
Tineo [Sp.] **19** Ba
Tingsryd [Svezia] **75** CDb
Tingvoll [Norv.] **73** Ba
Tínos [Grecia] **45** Bb
Tínos [Grecia] **45** Bb
Tiobraid Árann / Tipperary
    [Eire] **3** Bb
Tipperary / Tiobraid Árann
    [Eire] **3** Bb
Tirana [Alb.] **43** Ab
Tirano [It.] **31** Ba
Tiraspol [Mold.] **51** Cb
Tire [Tur.] **45** Cb
Tiree **1** Bb
Tîrgovişte [Rom.] **49** Ba
Tîrgu Frumos [Rom.] **51** BCb
Tîrgu Jiu [Rom.] **41** Dab
Tîrgu Lăpuş [Rom.] **39** CDb
Tîrgu Mureş [Rom.] **51** Bb
Tîrgu Neamţ [Rom.] **51** Bb
Tîrgu Secuiesc [Rom.] **51** Bb
Tírins = Tirinto (I) **45** Ab
Tirinto (I) = Tírins **45** Ab
Tîrnăveni [Rom.] **51** Bb
Tirol **33** Bb
Tirreno, Mar– **29** BCb
Tirso **29** Bb
Tirstrup [Dan.] **75** Bb
Tisa = Tibisco (I) **41** Ca
Tismana, Mănăstirea– **41** Dab
Tisovec [Slovac.] **39** Ba
Tissemsilt [Alg.] **23** Cc
Tisza = Tibisco (I) **39** Bb
Tiszafüred [Ung.] **39** Bb
Titova Mitrovica [Iug.] **41** CDb
Titovo Užice [Iug.] **41** Cb
Titov Veles [Maced.] **43** Bb
Titran [Norv.] **71** Ab
Tiveden **75** Ca
Tivoli [It.] **29** Cab
Tjøtta [Norv.] **71** Cb
Tobermory [RU] **1** BCb
Toblach / Dobbiaco [It.] **33** Cb
Todi [It.] **29** Cb
Töfsingdalen **73** Da
Tokaj [Ung.] **39** Cab
Toksovo [Russia] **61** Bab
Toledo [Sp.] **19** Cb
Tolga [Norv.] **73** Cab
Tolmezzo [It.] **33** Cb
Tolmin [Slo.] **31** Ca
Toločín [R.B.] **55** Bb
Tolone (I) = Toulon [Fr.]
    13 BCb
Tolosa [Sp.] **17** Ba
Tolosa (I) = Toulouse [Fr.]
    15 Cb
Tolstoje [Ucr.] **51** Ba
Tomar [Port.] **19** Bb
Tomaszów Lubelski [Pol.]
    37 Cc
Tomaszów Mazowiecki [Pol.]
    37 Bb

Tomelloso [Sp.] **21** CDa
Tomorit, Mali i– **43** Ab
Tonale, Passo del– **31** Ba
Tønder [Dan.] **35** BCa
Tongue [RU] **1** Ca
Tonnerre [Fr.] **11** Bab
Tønsberg [Norv.] **73** Cb
Tonstad [Norv.] **75** Aa
Topliţa [Rom.] **51** Bb
Topo [Port.] **21** ins.a
Topola [Iug.] **41** Cb
Topol'čany [Slovac.] **39** ABa
Topozero, ozero– **63** Bb
Torball [Tur.] **45** Cb
Tordesillas [Sp.] **19** Cb
Töre [Svezia] **65** Db
Töreboda [Svezia] **75** Ca
Torgau [D] **35** Db
Torino [It.] **31** Aab
Tornea / Tornio [Finl.] **65** CDab
Tornealven **67** Bb
Torneträsk **69** Cb
Tornio / Tornea [Finl.] **65** CDab
Tornionjoki **67** Bb
Toro [Sp.] **19** Cb
Törökszentmiklós [Ung.] **39** Bb
Torquay [RU] **5** Bc
Torrão / Baixo Alentejo [Port.]
    21 Bb
Torre de Moncorvo [Port.]
    19 Bb
Torrelaguna [Sp.] **19** Cb
Torrelavega [Sp.] **19** Ca
Torremolinos [Sp.] **21** Cb
Torrent de l'Horta / Torrente
    [Sp.] **23** Ba
Torrente / Torrent de l'Horta
    [Sp.] **23** Ba
Torres Novas [Port.] **21** Ba
Torres Vedras [Port.] **21** Aab
Torrevieja [Sp.] **23** Bb
Torrijos [Sp.] **19** Cb
Torröjen **71** Cb
Torronsuo **59** Ca
Torsby [Svezia] **73** Dab
Torsken [Norv.] **69** Ba
Tortona [It.] **31** ABab
Tortosa [Sp.] **17** Cb
Tortosa, Cabo de– **17** Cb
Toruń [Pol.] **37** Bb
Toržok [Russia] **55** Cab
Toscano, Arcipelago– **29** Ba
Tosno [Russia] **61** Bb
Tossa de Mar [Sp.] **17** CDb
Tołana [Iug.] **23** Bb
Toul [Fr.] **11** BCa
Toulon [Fr.] = Tolone (I)
    13 BCb
Toulouse [Fr.] = Tolosa (I)
    15 Cb
Tourcoing [Fr.] **7** BCb
Touríñán, Cabo– **19** Aa
Tourmalet, Col du– **17** BCa
Tournai / Doornik [Bel.] **7** Cb
Tournon–sur–Rhône [Fr.]
    13 Bab
Tournus [Fr.] **11** Bb
Tours [Fr.] **9** Cb
Tracia (I) = Thráki **47** Bb
Tracia (I) = Trakya **47** Bb
Trafalgar, Cabo– **21** BCb
Trakai [Lit.] **57** Cb
Trakya = Tracia (I) **47** Bb
Tralee / Trá Lí [Eire] **3** Ab
Trá Lí / Tralee [Eire] **3** Ab
Tranás [Svezia] **75** CDa
Trani [It.] **27** Ca
Transilvania **51** Bb
Trapani [It.] **25** Bb

Travnik [Bos.Erz.] **41** Bb
Trbovlje [Slo.] **41** ABa
Trebević [Bos.–Erz.] **41** Cb
Trebević [Bos.–Erz.] **41** Cb
Třebíč [Rep.Ceca] **39** Aa
Trebinje [Bos.Erz.] **41** Cb
Trebisacce [It.] **25** Ca
Trebišov [Slovac.] **39** Ca
Třeboň [Rep.Ceca] **33** Ca
Tréguier [Fr.] **9** Aa
Trelleborg [Svezia] **75** Cb
Tremiti, Isole– **27** Ca
Tremp [Sp.] **17** Cab
Trenčín [Slovac.] **39** Ba
Trent **5** Cb
Trento [It.] **31** Ba
Tretten [Norv.] **73** Ca
Treungen [Norv.] **73** Cb
Treviglio [It.] **31** Ba
Treviso [It.] **31** Ca
Tricarico [It.] **27** Cb
Trier [D] **11** Ca
Trieste [It.] **31** Ca
Triglav [Slo.] **33** Cb
Triglav [Slo.] **33** Cb
Trikala [Grecia] **43** Bb
Trípolis [Grecia] **45** Ab
Trnava [Slovac.] **39** Aa
Trofors [Norv.] **71** Cb
Trogir [Cro.] **41** Bb
Troia [It.] **27** Cb
Troia (I) = Truva **47** Bb
Troickoje [Ucr.] **51** Db
Trois Fourches, Cap des–
    21 CDc
Trojan [Bulg.] **49** Ba
Trollhättan [Svezia] **75** Ca
Tromsø [Norv.] **69** Ca
Trondheim [Norv.] **71** Bb
Trondheimsfjorden **71** Bb
Tropea [It.] **25** Cb
Trostberg [D] **33** Cab
Troyes [Fr.] **11** Ba
Trujillo [Sp.] **21** Ca
Trutnov [Rep.Ceca] **37** Ac
Truva = Troia (I) **47** Bb
Trzebiatów [Pol.] **37** Aab
Trzebnica [Pol.] **37** Bb
Tübingen [D] **33** ABa
Tuchola [Pol.] **37** Bb
Tudela [Sp.] **17** Bab
Tukums [Lett.] **57** Cab
Tula [Russia] **55** Eb
Tulcea [Rom.] **51** Cb
Tulčín [Ucr.] **51** Ca
Tullamore / An Tulach Mhór
    [Eire] **3** Bb
Tulle [Fr.] **15** Ca
Tullins [Fr.] **13** Ba
Tuloma **67** Cb
Tumanny [Russia] **67** Fab
Tundža **47** Bb
Tungozero [Russia] **63** Bb
Tunguda [Russia] **63** Cb
Tünis [Tun.] **25** Ab
Tünis, Canal di– = Sicilia,
    Canale di– (I) **25** Ab
Tünis, Khalíj– = Tunisi, Golfo
    di– (I) **25** Ab
Tunisi, Golfo di– (I) = Tünis,
    Khalíj– **25** Ab
Turda [Rom.] **39** Cb
Turek [Pol.] **37** Bb
Turgutlu [Tur.] **45** Cb
Turia **23** Ba
Turijsk [Ucr.] **37** Dbc
Turingia (I) = Thüringen
    35 Cc
Turja **53** Aa
Turka [Ucr.] **39** Ca
Turku / Åbo [Finl.] **59** Ca
Turnhout [Bel.] **7** Ca
Turnov [Rep.Ceca] **37** Ac

Turnu Măgurele [Rom.] **49** Ba
Turnu Roşu, Pasul– **51** Bb
Turtola [Finl.] **67** BCb
Tusaun / Thusis [Svizz.] **33** Bb
Tuscania [It.] **29** BCa
Tutajev [Russia] **61** Eb
Tutrakan [Bulg.] **49** Ba
Tuttlingen [D] **33** Aab
Tuusniemi [Finl.] **65** Ec
Tuy [Sp.] **19** Bab
Tuzla [Bos.Erz.] **41** Cb
Tvedestrand [Norv.] **75** ABa
Tver (Kalinin) [Russia] **55** DEb
Tweed **1** Cb
Tydal [Norv.] **71** Bbc
Tympákion [Grecia] **45** Bc
Tyne **3** Da
Tynemouth [RU] **3** Da
Tynset [Norv.] **73** Ca
Tysnesøy **73** Aab

U

Úbeda [Sp.] **21** Cb
Überlingen [D] **33** Bb
Ubort **53** Ba
Udaj **53** Cb
Udbina [Cro.] **41** Bb
Uddevalla [Svezia] **75** BCa
Uddjaure **71** Dab
Udine [It.] **31** Ca
Ueckermünde [D] **35** Db
Uelzen [D] **35** Cb
Ugåle [Lett.] **57** Ca
Uglič [Russia] **61** Db
Ugra **55** Db
Uherské Hradiště [Rep.Ceca]
    39 Aa
Uig [RU] **1** Ba
Újfehértó [Ung.] **39** Cb
Ukmergė / Ukmerge [Lit.]
    57 Db
Ukmerge / Ukmergė [Lit.]
    57 Db
Ulcinj [Iug.] **43** Aab
Uleåborg / Oulu [Finl.] **65** Db
Ulla [R.B.] **55** Bb
Ullapool [RU] **1** Ca
Ullared [Svezia] **75** Cab
Ullsfjorden **69** Cab
Ulm [D] **33** Ba
Ulpia Traina **41** Da
Ulricehamn [Svezia] **75** Ca
Ulsta [RU] **1** ins.a
Ulsteinvik [Norv.] **73** ABa
Ulster **3** Ba
Ulu / Uulu [Est.] **59** Db
Ulubat Gölü **47** Cb
Uludağ [Tur.] **47** Cb
Uludağ [Tur.] **47** Cb
Uman [Ucr.] **51** CDa
Umba [Russia] **67** Fb
Umbozero, ozero– **67** Fb
Umeå [Svezia] **71** Eb
Umeälven **71** Eb
Ungheni [Mold.] **51** Cb
Unna [D] **35** Bb
Unst **1** ins.a
Uppsala [Svezia] **59** Aab
Urbino [It.] **31** Cb
Urho Kekkonen **67** Cb
Urk [P.B.] **7** Ca
Urla [Tur.] **45** Bb
Urnes [Norv.] **73** Ba
Urziceni [Rom.] **49** Ba
Uşak [Tur.] **47** Cc
Ušče [Iug.] **41** Cb
Usedom **35** Dab
Üsküdar, İstanbul– [Tur.] **47** Cb
Ussel [Fr.] **15** Ca
Ustica **25** Bb

Ústí nad Labem [Rep.Ceca] **35** Dc
Ústí nad Orlicí [Rep.Ceca] **39** Aa
Ustjužna [Russia] **61** Db
Ustka [Pol.] **37** Aa
Ust-Koža [Russia] **63** Db
Ust-Pinega [Russia] **63** EFb
Ust-Reka [Russia] **61** Da
Ustrzyki Dolne [Pol.] **39** Ca
Utajärvi [Finl.] **65** Db
Utena [Lit.] **57** Db
Utiel [Sp.] **23** Ba
Utrecht [P.B.] **7** Ca
Utrera [Sp.] **21** Cb
Utsjoki [Finl.] **69** EFa
Uulu / Ulu [Est.] **59** Db
Uusikaaelepyy / Nykarleby [Finl.] **65** Cb
Uusikaupunki / Nystad [Finl.] **59** Ca
Uzerche [Fr.] **15** Ca
Užgorod [Ucr.] **39** Ca
Užokski, pereval– **39** Ca
Uzunköprü [Tur.] **47** Bb

 **V**

Vaala [Finl.] **65** DEb
Vaasa / Vasa [Finl.] **65** Cb
Vác [Ung.] **39** Bb
Vadheim [Norv.] **73** Aa
Vadsø [Norv.] **69** Fa
Vadstena [Svezia] **75** CDa
Vaduz [Liech.] **33** Bb
Vadvetjåkka **69** Cb
Vågø **75** ins.a
Váh **39** Bab
Valacchia (I) = Valahia **49** Ba
Valahia = Valacchia (I) **49** Ba
Valašské Meziříčí [Rep.Ceca] **39** ABa
Valdagno [It.] **31** Ba
Valdaj [Russia] **63** Cb
Valdaj [Russia] **61** Cb
Valdaj (I) = Valdajskaja vozvyšennost **55** CDab
Valdajskaja vozvyšennost = Valdaj (I) **55** CDab
Valdemarsvik [Svezia] **75** Da
Valdepeñas [Sp.] **21** Cb
Val d'Isère [Fr.] **13** Ca
Valea lui Mihai [Rom.] **39** Ca
Valença do Minho [Port.] **19** Bab
Valençay [Fr.] **9** Cb
Valence [Fr.] **13** Bab
Valencia / València [Sp.] **23** Ba
Valencia / València [Sp.] **23** Ba
Valencia, Golfo de– **23** Ca
Valencia de Alcántara [Sp.] **21** Ba
Valencia de Don Juan [Sp.] **19** Ca
Valenciennes [Fr.] **7** Cb
Vălenii de Munte [Rom.] **51** Bb
Valga [Est.] **59** Db
Valka [Lett.] **59** Db
Valkeakoski [Finl.] **59** CDa
Valladolid [Sp.] **19** Cb
Valldal [Norv.] **73** Ba
Valle dei Templi **25** Bb
Vallehermoso [Sp.] **23** ins.a
Valletta [Malta] **25** Bbc
Vallgrund **65** Cb
Vallo della Lucania [It.] **27** Cb
Vallo di Traiano (I) = Valul–Lui Traian **49** Ca
Vallo Settentrionale di Traiano (I) = Verhni Trajanov Val **51** Cb

Valls [Sp.] **17** Cb
Valmiera [Lett.] **57** Da
Valognes [Fr.] **9** Ba
Valøy [Norv.] **71** Bb
Valset [Norv.] **71** Bb
Valtimo [Finl.] **63** Ab
Valul–Lui Traian = Vallo di Traiano (I) **49** Ca
Valverde del Camino [Sp.] **21** Bb
Vammala [Finl.] **59** Ca
Vändra [Est.] **59** Db
Vänern **73** Bb
Vänersborg [Svezia] **75** Ca
Vanna **69** Ca
Vännäs [Svezia] **71** Eb
Vannes [Fr.] **9** Bb
Vanoise **13** Ca
Vansbro [Svezia] **73** Da
Varallo [It.] **31** Aa
Varangerbotn [Norv.] **69** Fa
Varangerfjorden **67** DEa
Varaždin [Cro.] **41** Ba
Varberg [Svezia] **75** Cab
Vardar **43** Bb
Varde [Dan.] **75** Ab
Vardø [Norv.] **67** Ea
Varese [It.] **31** Aa
Vårgårda [Svezia] **75** Ca
Varkaus [Finl.] **65** Ec
Varna [Bulg.] **49** Ca
Värnamo [Svezia] **75** Ca
Várpalota [Ung.] **39** ABb
Varsavia (I) = Warszawa [Pol.] **37** BCb
Varzuga [Russia] **63** Da
Vasa / Vasaa [Finl.] **65** Cb
Vásárosnamény [Ung.] **39** Cab
Vasilkov [Ucr.] **53** Cb
Vaslui [Rom.] **51** Cb
Västeras [Svezia] **59** Ab
Västerdalälven **73** Ca
Västervik [Svezia] **75** Da
Vasto [It.] **27** Cb
Vasvár [Ung.] **39** Ab
Vaticano, Capo– **25** Cb
Vatnajökull **77** Bb
Vatra Dornei [Rom.] **51** Bb
Vättern **75** Ca
Växjö [Svezia] **75** Cab
Vecchia Castiglia [Sp.] = Castilla la Vieja **19** Cb
Vega **71** Bb
Vegarus [Russia] **63** Bc
Vejen [Dan.] **75** ABb
Vejle [Dan.] **75** Bb
Vela Luka [Cro.] **27** Ca
Velas [Port.] **21** ins.a
Velenje [Slo.] **33** CDb
Vélez-Málaga [Sp.] **21** Cb
Vélez Rubio [Sp.] **23** Bb
Velikaja Guba [Russia] **63** Cc
Velika Morava **41** Db
Veliki Berezny [Ucr.] **39** Ca
Velikije Luki [Russia] **55** Cb
Veliko Tărnovo [Bulg.] **49** Ba
Velingrad [Bulg.] **49** ABab
Veliž [Russia] **55** Cb
Velké Meziříčí [Rep.Ceca] **39** Aa
Velletri [It.] **29** Cb
Velsen–IJmuiden [P.B.] **7** Ca
Veluwezoom **7** Cba
Vemdalen [Svezia] **73** Da
Vendas Novas [Port.] **21** Bb
Vendesund [Norv.] **71** BCb
Vendôme [Fr.] **9** Cb
Venezia [It.] **31** Ca
Venezia, Golfo di– **31** Ca
Venezia–Lido [It.] **31** Ca
Venezia–Mestre [It.] **31** Ca
Venlo [P.B.] **7** Da
Vennesla [Norv.] **75** Aa

Venosa [It.] **27** Cb
Venta **57** Ca
Ventimiglia [It.] **31** Ab
Ventotene **29** Cb
Ventspils [Lett.] **57** Ca
Vera [Sp.] **23** Bb
Verbania [It.] **31** Aa
Vercelli [It.] **31** Aa
Verdalsøra [Norv.] **71** Bb
Verde, Costa– **19** BCa
Verden [D] **35** Cb
Verdun [Fr.] **11** Ba
Verhnedvinsk [R.B.] **55** Bb
Verhnetulomski [Russia] **67** Eb
Verhnetulomskoje vodohranilišče **67** Eb
Verhni Kujto, ozero– **63** Bb
Verhni Trajanov Val = Vallo Settentrionale di Traiano (I) **51** Cb
Verneuil–sur–Avre [Fr.] **9** Ca
Vernon [Fr.] **9** Ca
Véroia [Grecia] **43** Bb
Verona [It.] **31** Ba
Versailles [Fr.] **9** Ca
Verviers [Bel.] **7** CDb
Vervins [Fr.] **11** Ba
Veselí nad Lužnici [Rep.Ceca] **33** Ca
Veselinovo [Ucr.] **51** Db
Vesjegonsk [Russia] **61** Db
Veškelica [Russia] **61** BCa
Vesoul [Fr.] **11** BCb
Vesterålen **69** ABab
Vesterøhavn [Dan.] **75** Ba
Vestfjorden **69** ABb
Vestmannaeyjar [Isl.] **77** Cb
Vestnes [Norv.] **73** Ba
Vestvågøy **69** Ab
Vesuvio [It.] **29** Cb
Vesuvio [It.] **29** Cb
Veszprém [Ung.] **39** ABb
Vetlanda [Svezia] **75** CDa
Veurne / Furnes [Bel.] **7** Bab
Vevey [Svizz.] **11** Cb
Vézelay [Fr.] **11** Bb
Viana do Castelo [Port.] **19** ABb
Vianden [Luss.] **7** Db
Viareggio [It.] **31** Bb
Víborg [Dan.] **75** Bb
Vibo Valentia [It.] **25** Cb
Vic [Sp.] **17** Cab
Vicenza [It.] **31** Ba
Vichy [Fr.] **11** Bb
Victoria / Rabat [Malta] **25** Bbc
Videle [Rom.] **49** Ba
Vidigueira [Port.] **21** Bb
Vidin [Bulg.] **49** Aa
Vidlica [Russia] **61** Ba
Vidsel [Svezia] **71** Eb
Vidzy [R.B.] **57** Db
Vielha / Viella [Sp.] **17** Ca
Viella / Vielha [Sp.] **17** Ca
Vienna (I) = Wien [Aus.] **39** Aa
Vienne [Fr.] **13** Ba
Vienne [Fr.] **9** Cb
Vierwaldstätter See = Quattro Cantoni, Lago dei– (I) **33** Ab
Vierzon [Fr.] **9** Cb
Vieste [It.] **27** Cab
Vietas [Svezia] **71** Db
Vigevano [It.] **31** ABa
Vigo [Sp.] **19** Ba
Vihanti [Finl.] **65** Db
Vihren **43** Bb
Viitasaari [Finl.] **65** Dbc
Vík [Isl.] **77** Cb
Vikajärvi [Finl.] **67** Cb
Viksersund [Norv.] **73** Cab
Vikna **71** Bb
Vikos-Aoós **43** Ab

Viksøyri [Norv.] **73** Ba
Vila do Bispo [Port.] **21** ABb
Vila do Porto [Port.] **21** ins.a
Vilafranca del Penedès [Sp.] **17** Cb
Vila Franca de Xira [Port.] **21** ABab
Vilaine **9** Bb
Vijãni [Lett.] **55** ABb
Vila Nova de Famalicão [Port.] **19** Bb
Vila Nova de Gaia [Port.] **19** Bb
Vilanova i la Geltrú [Sp.] **17** Cb
Vila Pouca de Aguiar [Port.] **19** Bb
Vila Real [Port.] **19** Bb
Vila–Real / Villarreal de los Infantes [Sp.] **23** BCa
Vila Real de Santo António [Port.] **21** Bb
Vilar Formoso [Port.] **19** Bb
Vilejka [R.B.] **57** DEb
Vilhelmina [Svezia] **71** Db
Vilija **57** Db
Viljandi [Est.] **59** Db
Vilkaviškis [Lit.] **57** Cb
Vilkija [Lit.] **57** Cb
Villablino [Sp.] **19** Ba
Villacarrillo [Sp.] **21** CDb
Villacastín [Sp.] **19** Cb
Villach [Aus.] **33** Cb
Villadiego [Sp.] **19** Ca
Villafranca del Bierzo [Sp.] **19** Ba
Villajoyosa / La Vila Joiosa [Sp.] **23** Bb
Villalba [Sp.] **19** Ba
Villalón de Campos [Sp.] **19** Ca
Villalpando [Sp.] **19** Cab
Villanueva de la Serena [Sp.] **21** Cab
Villanueva del Fresno [Sp.] **21** Bb
Villanueva de los Infantes [Sp.] **21** CDb
Villarcayo [Sp.] **19** Ca
Villarreal de los Infantes / Vila–Real [Sp.] **23** BCa
Villa San Giovanni [It.] **25** Cb
Villaviciosa [Sp.] **19** Ca
Villedieu–les–Poëles [Fr.] **9** Ba
Villefranche–de–Rouergue [Fr.] **15** Cb
Villefranche–sur–Saône [Fr.] **11** Bb
Villena [Sp.] **23** Bb
Villeneuve–sur–Lot [Fr.] **15** Cb
Villingen–Schwenningen [D] **33** Aab
Villmanstrand / Lappeenranta [Finl.] **61** Aa
Vilnius / Vilnjus [Lit.] **57** Db
Vilnjus / Vilnius [Lit.] **57** Db
Vimmerby [Svezia] **75** Da
Vimperk [Rep.Ceca] **33** Ca
Vinarós / Vinaroz [Sp.] **17** Cb
Vinaroz / Vinarós [Sp.] **17** Cb
Vindelälven **71** Eb
Vinhais [Port.] **19** Bb
Vinkovci [Iug.] **41** Ca
Vinnica [Ucr.] **53** Bb
Vinogradov [Ucr.] **39** Cab
Vinstra [Norv.] **73** Ba
Vipiteno / Sterzing [It.] **33** Bb
Virdois / Virrat [Finl.] **65** Cc
Vire [Fr.] **9** Ba
Virful, Curcubăta– **39** Cb
Viriharue **69** Bb
Virovitica [Cro.] **41** Ba
Virrat / Virdois [Finl.] **65** Cc

Virtsu [Est.] **59** Cb
Vis [Cro.] **27** Ca
Vis [Cro.] **27** Ca
Visby [Svezia] **57** Ba
Višegrad [Bos.Erz.] **41** Cb
Viseu [Port.] **19** Bb
Visoki Dečani **41** Cb
Visoko [Bos.Erz.] **41** Cb
Vistola (I) = Wisła **57** Bc
Vitebsk [R.B.] **55** Cb
Viterbo [It.] **29** BCa
Vitigudino [Sp.] **19** Bb
Vitoria / Vitoria–Gasteiz [Sp.] **17** Ba
Vitoria–Gasteiz / Vitoria [Sp.] **17** Ba
Vitoša **49** Aa
Vitré [Fr.] **9** Bab
Vitry–le–François [Fr.] **11** Ba
Vittangi [Svezia] **67** Bb
Vitteaux [Fr.] **11** Bb
Vittel [Fr.] **11** BCa
Vittoria [It.] **25** Bb
Vittorio Veneto [It.] **31** Ca
Viver [Sp.] **23** Ba
Vivero [Sp.] **19** Ba
Vizcaya, Golfo de– = Biscaglia, Golfo di– (I) **15** Bb
Vjartsilja [Russia] **63** Bc
Vjazma [Russia] **55** Db
Vjosa **43** Bb
Vladimir–Volynski [Ucr.] **37** Dc
Vlasenika [Bos.Erz.] **41** Cb
Vlissingen [P.B.] **7** Ca
Vlora [Alb.] **43** Bb
Vltava = Moldava (I) **33** Ca
Vöcklabruck [Aus.] **33** Cab
Vodice [Cro.] **41** Bb
Vodla **61** Da
Vodlozero, ozero– **63** Dc
Vodnjan [Cro.] **31** Cab
Voghera [It.] **31** ABab
Voinica [Russia] **63** ABb
Voiron [Fr.] **13** Ba
Vojens [Dan.] **75** Bb
Vojmsjön **71** Db
Vojvodina **41** Ca
Volda [Norv.] **73** ABa
Volhov [Russia] **61** Bab
Volhov [Russia] **61** Bab
Volissós [Grecia] **45** Bb
Völkermarkt [Aus.] **33** Cb
Volo (I) = Vólos [Grecia] **43** Bb
Voločisk [Ucr.] **53** Ab
Vologda [Russia] **61** Eb
Volokolamsk [Russia] **55** DEb
Vólos [Grecia] = Volo (I) **43** Bb
Volosovo [Russia] **61** Ab
Vološin [R.B.] **57** Dbc
Volterra [It.] **31** Bb
Volturno **29** Cb
Vónitsa [Grecia] **43** ABbc
Vopnafjörður [Isl.] **77** Eb
Vopnafjörður [Isl.] **77** Eb
Vordingborg [Dan.] **75** BCb
Vorma **73** Ca
Voroneţ, Mănăstirea– **51** Bb
Voronja **67** Fb
Vorožba [Ucr.] **53** Dab
Vorpommersche Boddenlandschaft **35** Da
Vörts järv **59** Db
Võru / Vyru [Est.] **59** DEb
Vosges = Vosgi (I) **11** Ca
Vosgi (I) = Vosges **11** Ca
Voss [Norv.] **73** Ba
Vossijatskoje [Ucr.] **51** Db
Voúxa, Ákra– **45** Ac
Vouziers [Fr.] **11** Ba
Vože, ozero– **61** DEa
Voznesenje [Russia] **61** Ca
Voznesensk [Ucr.] **51** Db

Vraca [Bulg.] **49** Aa
Vranje [Iug.] **41** Db
Vranov nad Topl'ou [Slovac.] **39** Ca
Vrbas [Bos.-Erz.] **41** Bb
Vrbas [Iug.] **41** Ca
Vrchlabí [Rep.Ceca] **37** Ac
Vrnjačka Banja [Iug.] **41** CDb
Vršac [Iug.] **41** Dab
Vsetín [Rep.Ceca] **39** ABa
Vukovar [Cro.] **41** Ca
Vulcăneşti [Mold.] **51** Cb
Vulcano **25** BCb
Vuollerim [Svezia] **71** Ea
Vuotso [Finl.] **67** CDb
Vyborg [Russia] **61** Aa
Vygozero, ozero– **63** Cb
Vyru / Võru [Est.] **59** DEb
Vyškov [Rep.Ceca] **39** Aa
Vyšni Voloček [Russia] **61** Da
Vytegra [Russia] **61** Da

W

Waal **7** Ca
Wąbrzeźno [Pol.] **37** Bb
Waddeneilanden / Friesische Inseln = Frisone, Isole– (I) **35** ABab
Wadowice [Pol.] **39** Ba
Wągrowiec [Pol.] **37** Ab
Waidhofen an der Thaya [Aus.] **33** Da
Waidhofen an der Ybbs [Aus.] **33** Cab
Wałbrzych [Pol.] **37** Ac
Walcheren **7** Ca
Wałcz [Pol.] **37** Ab
Wales = Galles (I) **5** Bb
Walsall [RU] **5** Cb
Wangen im Allgäu [D] **33** Bb
Warburg [D] **35** BCb
Waren [D] **35** Db
Warminster [RU] **5** Cb
Warnemünde, Rostock– [D] **35** CDab
Warrington [RU] **5** Cb
Warszawa [Pol.] = Varsavia (I) **37** BCb
Warta **37** Ab
Warwick [RU] **5** Cb
Wasserburg am Inn [D] **33** Cab
Waterford / Port Láirge [Eire] **3** Bb
Waterloo [Bel.] **7** Cb
Weert [P.B.] **7** Ca
Węgorzewo [Pol.] **57** Cb
Węgrów [Pol.] **37** Cb
Weiden in der Oberpfalz [D] **33** BCa
Weimar [D] **35** Cbc
Weingarten [D] **33** Bb

Weinheim [D] **33** Aa
Weißenburg in Bayern [D] **33** Ba
Weißenfels [D] **35** CDb
Weitra [Aus.] **33** CDa
Weiz [Aus.] **33** Db
Wejherowo [Pol.] **57** Bb
Wells [RU] **5** Cb
Wels [Aus.] **33** Cab
Wernigerode [D] **35** Cb
Werra **35** Cb
Wesel [D] **7** Da
Weser **35** Cb
Westerland [D] **35** Ba
Weston–super–Mare [RU] **5** BCb
Westport / Cathair na Mart [Eire] **3** Ab
Westray **1** CDa
Wetzlar [D] **35** Bc
Wexford / Loch Garman [Eire] **3** Bb
Weymouth and Melcombe Regis [RU] **5** Cc
Whitby [RU] **3** Da
Whitchurch [RU] **5** Cb
Whitehaven [RU] **3** Ca
Wick [RU] **1** CDa
Wicklow / Cill Mhantáin [Eire] **3** BCb
Więcbork [Pol.] **37** Ab
Wielbark [Pol.] **37** BCb
Wieliczka [Pol.] **39** Ba
Wielkopolska **37** Ab
Wieluń [Pol.] **37** Bb
Wien [Aus.] = Vienna (I) **39** Aa
Wiener Neustadt [Aus.] **39** Ab
Wieprz **37** Cb
Wiesbaden [D] **33** Aa
Wiesloch [D] **33** Aa
Wight, Isle of– = Wight, Isola di– (I) **5** Cc
Wight, Isola di– (I) = Wight, Isle of– **5** Cc
Wigry **57** Cbc
Wil [Svizz.] **33** ABb
Wildspitze **33** Bb
Wilhelmshaven [D] **35** Bb
Winchester [RU] **5** Cbc
Windermere [RU] **3** Da
Windischgarsten [Aus.] **33** Cb
Windsor [RU] **5** Cb
Winschoten [P.B.] **7** Da
Winsen (Lühe) [D] **35** Db
Winterthur [Svizz.] **33** Ab
Wisbech [RU] **5** CDb
Wisła = Vistola (I) **57** Bc
Wisłoka **39** Ca
Wismar [D] **35** Cab
Wissembourg [Fr.] **33** Aa
Wittenberge [D] **35** Db
Wittenberg Lutherstadt [D] **35** Db
Wittlich [D] **7** Db

Władysławowo [Pol.] **57** Bb
Włocławek [Pol.] **37** Bb
Włodawa [Pol.] **37** Cb
Wodzisław Śląski [Pol.] **39** Ba
Wojerecy / Hoyerswerda [D] **35** Db
Wolbrom [Pol.] **37** Bc
Wolfenbüttel [D] **35** Cb
Wolfhagen [D] **35** BCb
Wolfratshausen [D] **33** Bab
Wolfsberg [Aus.] **33** Cb
Wolfsburg [D] **35** Cb
Wolgast [D] **35** Dab
Wolin [Pol.] **35** Dab
Wolin [Pol.] **35** Dab
Wolsztyn [Pol.] **37** Ab
Wolverhampton [RU] **5** Cb
Worcester [RU] **5** Cb
Workington [RU] **3** Ca
Worms [D] **33** Aa
Worthing [RU] **5** Cbc
Wrath, Cape– **1** Ca
Wrexham [RU] **5** BCb
Wrocław [Pol.] = Breslavia (I) **37** Abc
Wronki [Pol.] **37** Ab
Września [Pol.] **37** Ab
Wschowa [Pol.] **37** Ab
Wuppertal [D] **7** Da
Würzburg [D] **33** Ba
Wurzen [D] **35** Db
Wye **5** Bb
Wyk auf Föhr [D] **35** Ba
Wyszków [Pol.] **37** Cb
Wyszogród [Pol.] **37** Bb

X

Xánthi [Grecia] **47** Bb
Xàtiva / Játiva [Sp.] **23** Bab
Xilókastron [Grecia] **45** Ab
Xixona / Jijona [Sp.] **23** Bb

Y

Yecla [Sp.] **23** Bb
Yell **1** ins.a
Yenişehir [Tur.] **47** Cb
Yeovil [RU] **5** Cbc
Yerolimín [Grecia] **45** Ab
Yeşilova [Tur.] **47** Cc
Yeste [Sp.] **23** Bb
Yeu, Ile d'– **9** Bb
Yiannitsá [Grecia] **43** Bb
Yíaros **45** Bb
Yíthion [Grecia] **45** Ab
Ylikitka **65** Eab
Yli–Ii [Finl.] **65** Db
Ylitornio [Finl.] **65** Ca
Ylivieska [Finl.] **65** Db
Yonne **9** Da

York [RU] **3** Da
York [RU] **5** Cab
Yorkshire Dales **3** Da
Youghal [Eire] **3** Bb
Ypres / Ieper [Bel.] **7** BCab
Yssingeaux [Fr.] **13** Bab
Ystad [Svezia] **75** Cb
Ytterhogdal [Svezia] **73** DEa
Yverdon [Svizz.] **11** Ca
Yvetot [Fr.] **9** Ca

Z

Zaanstad [P.B.] **7** Ca
Ząbkowice Śląskie [Pol.] **37** Ac
Žabljak [Iug.] **41** Cb
Zadar [Cro.] = Zara (I) **41** Bb
Zafra [Sp.] **21** Bb
Zagabria (I) = Zagreb [Cro.] **41** Ba
Żagań [Pol.] **37** Ab
Zaghwān [Tun.] **25** Ab
Zagreb [Cro.] = Zagabria (I) **41** Ba
Zaječar [Iug.] **41** Db
Zákinthos [Grecia] **43** ABc
Zákinthos [Grecia] = Zante (I) **43** Ac
Zakopane [Pol.] **39** Ba
Zalaegerszeg [Ung.] **39** Ab
Zălau [Rom.] **39** Ba
Zaleščiki [Ucr.] **51** Ba
Zambrah, Jazīrat– **25** Ab
Zambrów [Pol.] **37** Cb
Zamora [Sp.] **19** Cb
Zamość [Pol.] **37** Cc
Zandvoort [P.B.] **7** Ca
Zannone **29** Cb
Zante (I) = Zákinthos [Grecia] **43** Ac
Zapadnaja Dvina = Dvina Occidentale (I) **57** Eb
Zapadna Morava **41** Db
Zapoljarny [Russia] **67** Ea
Zara (I) = Zadar [Cro.] **41** Bb
Zaragoza [Sp.] = Saragozza (I) **17** Bb
Zarasai / Zarasaj [Lit.] **57** Db
Zarasaj / Zarasai [Lit.] **57** Db
Zarečensk [Russia] **67** Eb
Zărneşti [Rom.] **51** Bb
Żary [Pol.] **37** Ab
Žaškov [Ucr.] **53** BCb
Žatec [Rep.Ceca] **35** Dc
Zawiercie [Pol.] **37** Bc
Žďár nad Sázavou [Rep.Ceca] **39** Aa
Zduńska Wola [Pol.] **37** Bb
Zehdenick [D] **35** Db
Zeitz [D] **35** CDb
Zelenogorsk [Russia] **61** Aa
Zelenogradsk [Russia] **57** Bb

York [RU] **3** Da

Železná Ruda [Rep.Ceca] **33** Ca
Zell am See [Aus.] **33** Cb
Žemaitija **57** Cb
Zenica [Bos.Erz.] **41** BCb
Zerbst [D] **35** CDb
Zermatt [Svizz.] **31** Aa
Zetland → Shetland Islands **1** ins.a
Zeven [D] **35** Cb
Zêzere **19** Bb
Zgierz [Pol.] **37** Bb
Zgorzelec [Pol.] **35** DEbc
Ziama Mansouria [Alg.] **23** Db
Zielona Góra [Pol.] **37** Ab
Zierikzee [P.B.] **7** Ca
Žilina [Slovac.] **39** Ba
Zimnicea [Rom.] **49** Ba
Zinnik / Soignies [Bel.] **7** Cb
Zirc [Ung.] **39** ABb
Žitkoviči [R.B.] **53** Bab
Žitomir [Ucr.] **53** Bb
Zittau [D] **35** Dbc
Žizdra **55** Dc
Zlatar **41** Cb
Zlatni Pjasăci **49** Ca
Zlatni pjasáci [Bulg.] **49** Ca
Zlín [Rep.Ceca] **39** Aa
Žlobin [R.B.] **53** BCa
Žłocieniec [Pol.] **37** Ab
Złoczew [Pol.] **37** Bb
Zły Komorow / Senftenberg [D] **35** Db
Zlynka [Russia] **53** Ca
Žmerinka [Ucr.] **51** Ca
Znamenka [Russia] **55** Db
Znamenka [Ucr.] **51** Db
Żnin [Pol.] **37** Ab
Znojmo [Rep.Ceca] **39** Aa
Žodino [R.B.] **55** Bb
Zolotonoša [Ucr.] **53** Cb
Zorita [Sp.] **21** Ca
Žovkva [Ucr.] **39** CDa
Žovten [Ucr.] **51** Da
Zrenjanin [Iug.] **41** Ca
Zubcov [Russia] **55** Db
Zug [Svizz.] **33** Ab
Zuid Kennemerland **7** Ca
Zújar **21** Bb
Zürich [Svizz.] = Zurigo (I) **33** Ab
Zurigo (I) = Zürich [Svizz.] **33** Ab
Zutphen [P.B.] **7** Da
Zvolen [Slovac.] **39** Ba
Zvornik [Bos.Erz.] **41** Cb
Zwettl–Niederösterreich [Aus.] **33** CDa·
Zwickau [D] **35** Dc
Zwiefalten [D] **33** Ba
Zwoleń [Pol.] **37** Bb
Zwolle [P.B.] **7** CDa
Żyrardów [Pol.] **37** Bb
Żywiec [Pol.] **39** Ba